Challenges of a Changing America

Perspectives on Immigration and Multiculturalism in the United States

Second Edition

Edited by
Ernest R. Myers

Foreword by
Danny K. Davis
United States Congressman

Published by
Caddo Gap Press

Challenges of a Changing America

**Challenges of a Changing America:
Perspectives on Immigration and Multiculturalism in the United States**

Second Edition

Edited by Ernest R. Myers

Published by
Caddo Gap Press
3145 Geary Boulevard PMB 275
San Francisco, California 94118

Copyright 2001 by Ernest R. Myers

First Edition Published 1993
by Austin & Winfield Publishers
San Francisco, California

ISBN 1-880192-37-3

Price - $29.95

Library of Congress Cataloging-in-Publication Data

Challenges of a changing America : perspectives of immigration and multiculturalism in the United States / edited by Ernest R. Myers ; foreword by Danny K. Davis.-- 2nd ed.
   p. cm.
  Originally published: San Francisco : Austin & Winfield, 1993.
  Includes bibliographical references and index.
  ISBN 1-880192-37-3 (alk. paper)
   1. Immigrants--Government policy--United States. 2. United States--Emigration and immigration--Government policy. 3. Multiculturalism--United States. I. Myers, Ernest R., 1935-

JV6483 .C455 2001
305.8'00973--dc21
                                                                                2001025910

Challenges of a Changing America

*America
is not like a blanket—
one piee of unbroken cloth,
the same color,
the same texture,
the same size:
America is more
like a quilt—
many pieces,
many colors,
many sizes,
all woven
and held together
by a common thread.*

—Jesse L. Jackson, Sr.
Presidential Candidate, 1988

Other Books by Ernest R. Myers

Challenges of a Changing America:
Perspectives on Immigration and Multiculturalism
in the United States (first edition)
(editor), 1993

Race and Culture
in the Mental Health Service Delivery System
(editor), 1981

The Community Psychology Concept:
Integrating Theory and Practice in Psychology,
Social Work, and Public Administration
1977

An Urban University-Community Interface Prototype
1971

Dedication

This book is dedicated
to the heritage and parentage
of its editor and its other authors,
and to the future—
where hope abounds
for all humanity.

Special Permissions

The editor is grateful to the following sources for permission to quote from copyrighted or otherwise special works:

Rev. Jesse L. Jackson, for permission to quote from his presidential candidacy speech, "Keep Hope Alive," at the National Democratic Convention in 1988, Atlanta, Georgia.

Harold Ober Associates, Incorporated, representing the estates of Langston Hughes and Arna Bontemps, for permission to quote from "Let America Be America Again" included in *The Poetry of the Negro: 1746-1970,* edited by Langston Hughes and Arna Bontemps, Copyright, 1970.

Contents

Acknowledgements xii

Foreword xiii

Preface xv

Part One
The Impact of Immigration:
An Historical World View 1

Chapter One
Immigration:
A Changing Force and Changing Face 3
Ernest R. Myers

Chapter Two
A Fourth World View:
The South Pacific's Parallel to Colonialism in America 31
Robert Staples

Part Two
African Americans:
Contemporary Issues 39

Chapter Three
Who Are The African Americans? 41
Yosef Ford

Chapter Four
Psychology And African Americans:
New Perspectives For The 1990s 45
Courtland C. Lee

Part Three
Challenges of Cultural Diversity for Human Service Systems 53

Chapter Five
Southeast Asian Expatriates:
From Aliens To Citizens 55
Tran Minh Tung

Chapter Six
A Challenge To The Mental Health System:
Central American Refugees 71
Leland K. Hall, Sr.

Chapter Seven
Understanding the Plight of Cuba's Marielitos:
A Mental Health Perspective 81
Roberto J. Velásquez & Michaelanthony Brown-Cheatham

Chapter Eight
Ethiopia's Exodus Of Human Resources:
Adjustment And Acculturation Issues 97
Maigenet Shifferraw & Getachew Metaferia

Part Four
The Multicultural Public Education Challenge 117

Chapter Nine
Multiculturalism:
A Paradigm For Educational Reform 119
Aaron B. Stills & Constance M. Ellison

Part Five
The Community Market Place:
Intercultural Conflict 135

Chapter Ten
African Americans and Korean Americans:
Cultures In Conflict 137
Halford H. Fairchild & Denise G. Fairchild

Chapter Eleven
Korean-American Marketing in the African-American Community:
An Exploratory Study in the Nation's Capital City 143
Ernest R. Myers

Part Six
Consumer Research and Intercultural Dialogue 169

Chapter Twelve
African-American Perceptions of Asian-American Merchants:
An Exploratory Study 171
Ernest R. Myers

Chapter Thirteen
Multicultural Sensitivity in the Marketplace:
A Seminar-Workshop 181
Ernest R. Myers

Part Seven
Epilogue 187

Epilogue
Can We Get Along? 189
Ernest R. Myers

Appendix
African-American Perspectives of Asian-American Merchants 195
Ernest R. Myers

About The Editor And Contributors 203

Indexes
Author Index 207
Subject Index 210

List of Figures

1.1 The World Population 18
1.2 United States Population 19
7.1 Flow Chart of the Plight of the Marielitos 85

List of Tables

Series 1: Immigration to the U. S. & World Population
1.1 Immigration to the U. S.: 1820-1990 11
1.2 World Population - 2000 13
1.3 Immigration by Continental Areas: 1820-1880 14
1.4 Immigration by Continental Areas: 1881-1950 15
1.5 Immigration by Continental Areas: 1951-1978 16
1.6 Immigration by Continental Areas: 1979-1990 17

Series 7: Cuban Marielitos
7.1 Mental Health Research on the Marielitos: An Overview 87
7.2 Psychopathology of the Marielitos 89
7.3 Relationship Between Marielitos Stress and Psychological Prognosis:
    A Framework 89

Series 8: Ethiopian Refugees Survey Data
8.1 Respondents' Level of Formal Education by Gender 103
8.2 Respondents' Educational Background and Relation to Current Job . 107
8.3 Feeling of Integration into American Society
    by Length of Stay in the U. S. 110
8.4 Family Visitations and Support 114

Series 11: Korean Merchants Survey Data
11.1 Korean-American Merchants Years at Business Locations
     in Washington, D. C 147
11.2 Korean-American Merchants Residence
     in Greater Washington, D. C., Metropolitan Area 147
11.3 Korean-American Merchants Length of Time
     Residing in Greater Washington, D. C., Metropolitan Area 148
11.4 Korean-American Merchants Sex of Respondents 148
11.5 Korean-American Merchants Marital Status of Respondents 148
11.6 Korean-American Merchants Respondents'
     Educational Achievement Levels 149
11.7 Korean-American Merchants Respondents' Religious Affiliation 149

11.8	Korean-American Merchants Respondents' Citizenship	150
11.9	Korean-American Merchants Respondents Experiencing Language Problems with Customers	150
11.10	Korean-American Merchants Respondents' Education by Association with Black Entrepreneurs	151
11.11	Korean-American Merchants Respondents' Education and Potential Hiring of African Americans	151
11.12	Korean-American Merchants: Would Respondents Hire African Americans in the Future?	152
11.12a	Korean-American Merchants: Location of Respondents' Residence by Those Employing African Americans	153
11.13	Korean-American Merchants: Respondents' Sensitivity to African American Culture	153
11.14	Korean American Merchants' Ratings of Customer Contacts by Race of Customer	154
11.15	Korean-American Merchants: Race of Customers by Ethnicity of Business Neighborhood	155
11.16	Korean-American Merchants: Sex of Merchants by Their Ratings of Customers	155
11.17	Korean-American Merchants Respondents' Perception of Special Police Protection Needs	156
11.18	Korean-American Merchants: Categorical Reasons Merchants Perceive for Police Services	156
11.19	Korean-American Merchants: Perception of Respondents' Longevity in a Neighborhood by the Number of Problems They Experience	157
11.20	Korean-American Merchants: Types of Offenses Identified by Respondents	157
11.21	Korean-American Merchants: Volume of Offenses Respondents Identified	158
11.22	Korean-American Merchants Decision Basis for Location of Respondents' Businesses	159
11.23	Korean American Merchants Respondents' Types of Businesses	160
11.24	Korean-American Merchants Respondents' Means of Start-up Support	161

Acknowledgements

The production of this book has required the commitment, authorship, and energy of many who made its achievement possible. I am deeply grateful to all the authors who contributed their writings and thereby empowered my role as editor in the final product. Such expressions of confidence from colleagues served as continuous sources of nourishment and inspiration.

For support and technical assistance, I am thankful to my wife, Carole, for her dedication in providing editorial assistance and for typing the entire original version of the manuscript as well as this volume's updated second edition. In a word, her contributions were indispensable. She deserves a standing ovation for responsiveness to and tolerance of my obsession to complete this work. Indebtedness too is acknowledged for the splendid graphics and tables developed by my brother, Donald L. Myers, Sr., which enhanced the updated demographic information on populations of both the United States of America and the World, displayed in the first chapter, and the survey data displayed in the last chapter. My appreciation also endures for the patience and skills applied in the original word processing of the first edition of this volume by Walter A. DeLegall.

Dr. Alvis V. Adair, professor of social research at Howard University, generously guided the pre-coding of the data collection instruments and directed the computerized application of data analysis—the Statistical Package for Social Sciences (SPSS)—which was utilized in the survey reported in the last chapter. Richard Pennington, former assistant chief of Metropolitan Washington's (D.C.) police department, contributed also to the survey's conceptualization and content of the questionnaire. I acknowledge also the cooperative support of Lloyd Lee, president of the Greater Metropolitan Washington Korean-American Chamber of Commerce, who administered the mailings to the Washington, D. C., membership of the association. I thank Hyo C. Lee for his excellent work in translating the questionnaire into Korean, which I had developed in English, and for his supervising the coding of responses for the SPSS software application. I also appreciate the cooperation of the Korean merchants and their African-American customers that made the survey successful.

Last, but not least, I deeply appreciate the approval I received for my sabbatical leave from executive administrative staff at the University of the District of Columbia (UDC) that made this book project possible.

Foreword

We face the new millennium with lingering societal challenges and new issues confronting our nation. It is incumbent upon all Americans to engage in some reflection on our nationalistic evolution, the impact of past and present immigration policies, and the resourceful role of cultural diversity in our development.

This second edition of *Challenges of a Changing America* serves as an insightful contribution to promoting understanding and appreciation of our demographic metamorphosis despite the recurrence of inter-cultural adjustments which are too often impaired by persistent racial barriers and the politics of cultural pluralism.

Professor Myers, as the editor and contributing author of this comprehensive work, explores the roots and impact of slavery in America, and the ongoing role of immigration in shaping the profile of the United States as a multicultural, "super power" society. This volume's introductory chapter also highlights the historical rationale and importance of reparations in bringing closure to dialogues on injured race relations. His landmark research on Korean-American merchants in predominantly African-American communities is on the cutting edge of foresight in psycho-social research. This collection of scholarly writings is a uniquely representative witness of the trials and tribulations of many generations of African Americans, and more recent Hispanic-American, Ethiopian-American, and Asian-American immigrants. This book is a tool to be used for cultivation of awareness of the immigrant experience and multicultural dialogues. It exemplifies the importance of America's multi-ethnic composition in its complementary perspectives by culturally sensitive authors and its illuminating data.

I commend Professor Myers and his colleagues for a timely resource for students, academicians, practitioners, and legislators as well. We can all benefit from a deeper understanding of the history, crises, and opportunity presented in *Challenges of a Changing America*.

—**Danny K. Davis**
U. S. Congress, 7th District, Illinois
May 22, 2000

Challenges of a Changing America

We must remember that America
cannot lead the world
unless here at home
we weave the threads of our coat
of many colors into the fabric
of one America.
As we become ever more diverse,
we must work harder
to unite around our common values
and our common humanity.

—**President Bill Clinton**
Farewell Address
January 18, 2001

Preface

Eight years ago, a major publishing firm rejected a detailed, proposal description of this book with the rationale that despite, "... This worthy project—a number of our authors have already tackled the formidable subject of ethnicity and its impact on America..." such as "Arthur Schlesinger, Jr. ... and we cannot in good faith to them accept another manuscript on the subject." Sympathetically, the rejection letter further stated, "I wish you the best of luck in securing publication, as your project does deserve a home." Schlesinger's book, *The Disuniting of America* (1992), argues that multiculturalism will damage America's future. Hence, we see that Eurocentric publishing firms are also in denial about the inevitable, and discourage balanced views on the rainbow reality of America.

A year later, *Challenges of a Changing America* was first published by a small firm, but within two years it became "out-of-print" as a result of the publisher's relocation from the West to the East Coast of the country. In the five-year hiatus of this book's absence from the literary marketplace, the significance of this volume's research and writings has actually increased with the growing challenges it addresses. Indeed, how the United States copes with our cultural diversity and multicultural demography will be a key determinant in the longevity of the nation's capacity to continue its global leadership role, not only in this century's entry phase but for the balance of the "New Millennium" as well.

The general or central theme of this volume is reflected in the title. As immigration has been an historically dynamic force in building the national profile of the United States, change has been and continues to be an ongoing challenge to the American creed. The challenges which the nation now faces are substantially related to the multi-ethnic societal chemistry resulting from the increasing Third World presence in the American population. The change dimensions necessarily impact every institutional arrangement in our culturally diverse society.

Since the mid-1980s, one of the most popular topics of concern and controversy to emerge in the nation is cultural diversity resulting from immigrations of Third

Challenges of a Changing America

World populations to the United States. Beginning in 1965, the rolling out of the welcome mat to non-white émigrés to the nation was primarily the influence of U. S. immigration policy reforms. In 1965, the Immigration and Nationality Act of 1952 was amended to abolish the national origins (ethnic and racial) quota system which first translated into law in 1921 the admission *practices* of "favored people." However, to borrow a phrase from Mark Twain, the "death" of immigration quotas has been "greatly exaggerated." For example, since 1981, Haitians have been stopped on the high seas from gaining asylum in the United States, instructed by Presidential Order EO-12324. Earlier, however, in 1975 the immigration door opened to accommodate the Indo-Chinese refugee resettlement program, an act of redemption resulting from the Vietnam War. Two other congressional actions admitted other asylees onto U. S. shores: the Refugee Act of 1980 and the Immigration Reform and Control Act of 1986.

The increasing coloration of the population of the United States has been the feature story highlighted in numerous media forms since the late 1970s. For example, *Time* magazine's cover title included a rhetorical question (and implicit criticism): "America's Changing Colors—What Will the U. S. Be Like When Whites Are No Longer the Majority?" (*Time*, April 9, 1990). Earlier, the Hudson Institute sounded a similar alarm in its 1987 publication of *Workforce 2000,* noting that "immigrants will be a growing share of the population and the labor force" and that "non-whites, for example, will comprise 29 percent of the net additions to the workforce between 1985 and 2000" (*Workforce 2000*, pp. 89-91). The American public has seemingly been force-fed recurrent dosages of xenophobic-oriented messages: *Japan is buying America. Non-whites are on the verge of taking over the job market. Whites are headed for disadvantaged, minority group status. Unqualified minorities are the undeserving beneficiaries of "affirmative action" programs. Multiculturalism or cultural diversity is the tribalistic Balkanization that will destroy the white American culture.* This past generation of the nation's youths has been spoon-fed this diet of propagandized paranoia. Yet, multicultural, demographic changes in the nation's profile necessarily confront the American creed as never before and challenge numerous aspects of our host society's supportive, institutional resources including the labor market, the workplace environment, health and human service systems, mental health services, educational systems (particularly public), the business community, and so on.

This is the setting (stage) for this volume of scholarly readings by a range of authors representing the target populations who are under attack by the anti-immigrationists, reverse discrimination proponents, the "yellow peril" revivalists, and the multicultural education critics.

The curtain opens reflectively with a flashback of historical notes on immigration as a global phenomenon and often as a prelude to imperialistic aims. This retrospective, introductory chapter by the editor of this book proceeds in historical sequence with a focus on America's only *involuntary immigrant*—the

African slave, the prize "commodity" in this nation's first, fledgling import enterprise—the *slave industry*. This opening chapter is an attempt to establish a historical perspective and to provide insights undergirding the massive exodus of Europeans bound for the greener pastures of distant, more fertile lands between the 15th and 19th centuries. Significantly, a global pattern of migration is chronicled to explain America's past and present national immigration policies and trends. This analysis underscores the quota system as a legislative strategy to guarantee the white majority population's dominance while minimizing the admission of non-whites, especially people of African descent. *Part One* also includes the work of a prolific sociologist, Robert Staples, whose educational travels and studies in Australia and other South Pacific countries offer a new "Fourth World" concept of conquest and colonialism. Staple's perspectives complement the introductory chapter's focus on immigration and colonialism—with the particular parallel of Australia—of the majority group-scheme in populating America. Ironically, the mythical "melting pot" is a reality in many *island* nations of the Pacific world, notwithstanding Australia's history of restricting citizenship to *whites only* until a mere generation ago.

In *Part Two*, Yosef Ford reflects on the issue of cultural identity for African Americans and other people of African heritage in the United States. Ford's writing is also a global view that addresses the destructive effect of European colonialism that continues to divide African people and their sense of selfhood. Implicitly, it is a call for the revival of Pan-Africanism.

Courtland Lee's chapter is an articulation of the psychology profession's potential contribution in devising family and community-oriented interventions which promote cultural identity, ethnic solidarity and the mental health of African-Americans. These 1990's perspectives remain applicable in the 21st Century.

Part Three introduces the formidable challenge that the nation faces in absorbing a variety of Third World groups into the increasing minority classifications in America since the mid-1970s. Tran Minh Tung presents a comprehensive assessment of the difficulties experienced by Southeast Asian populations in their efforts to effectively resettle in America. Highlighted in his observation is a critique of the general administration of resettlement programs. The chapter by Leland Hall addresses the myriad challenges faced by mental health systems in effectively serving the needs of Central Americans—the most recent Hispanic refugee group to become members of United States' communities. The chapter by Roberto Velasquez is an insightful examination that compares the plight of the *Cuban refugee of African heritage* with the white Cuban refugee. In part, this juxtaposes the contrasting demographics of the "Marielitos" who entered the United States in the early 1980s with their predecessors of the 1960s.

The "brain drain" of Ethiopia's most highly educated and professionally trained human resources is the focus of the closing chapter by Maigenet Shifferraw and Getachew Metaferia in *Part Three* of this volume. Uniquely, this writing includes data from a national survey conducted by the authors and describes the numerous obstacles the Ethiopian exiles face, particularly as under-employed, new members of the African-American population. As in other writings of *Part Three*, critical views are balanced with recommendations by these authors.

Part Four consists of an exclusive chapter by Aaron Stills and Constance Ellison on the relevance of multiculturalism for public school systems. As such, this work is responsive to the challenges of public educational institutions to engage in curricular and programmatic reforms in line with the nation's contemporary, multicultural school-age populations.

Part Five addresses the integral aspects between immigrant entrepreneurs and intercultural conflicts as reflected in Korean merchant enterprises in or that overlap onto the borders of African-American communities. The writing by Denise and Halford Fairchild is an astute description of their naturalistic observations of this intercultural controversy in Los Angeles.

Part Six includes new chapters which were not in the first edition of this book—perceptions of a surveyed sample of Black customers about Asian merchants' enterprises, the survey's hard data, and a follow-up, multicultural workshop report.

Part Seven is the editor's critique in a national and world view context of human ecological, geopolitical, and inter-cultural issues germane to the focus of this volume of writings. Multiculturalism and race relations are the basic, underlying challenges addressed in the Epilogue: "Can We Get Along?"

The editor concludes this book with a complementary perspective to the Fairchilds' chapter based on two landmark surveys that he conducted in the Korean business community in the nation's capital. Recommendations are suggested as potential intervention remedies for conflict resolution applicable for both African-American and Korean merchants.

Six of this volume's 13 chapters are previous conference presentations and published works which were revised and edited for this book. The other seven chapters were written exclusively for this volume of interdisciplinary readings. Unlike many books on the topics of immigration and cultural pluralism, this volume is not restricted to a singular, discipline-specific focus such as the workforce, cross-cultural counseling, and so forth. Instead, this eclectic anthology includes the works of authors who represent a wide range of professions and disciplines including psychology, sociology, social work, anthropology, counseling, psychiatry, public administration, political science, and urban education. Significantly, historical and global perspectives are prevalent frameworks for a good number of the chapters.

Also, this volume's examination of the impact of Third World immigrants on America is unique in its highlighting of people of African descent—African Americans, Ethiopians, Afro-Cubans, and Haitians—as a traditionally provocative issue for America's historically restrictive immigration quotas.

Challenges of a Changing America

This second edition includes several new inputs. First, a chapter on "African American Perceptions of Asian Merchants" is based on data from a community survey, and a new appendix section displays the data analysis from the respondents of this community survey. Second, following this research description is a report on a multicultural seminar-workshop conducted at the University of the District of Columbia (UDC). Further, the Epilogue is revised to make note of an apparent relationship between our society's advances in multiculturalism and the seething development of Eurocentrically oriented hate groups in the U. S.

Since the publication of the first edition of this book in 1994, a number of societal events have occurred which reinforce the relevance of the topics in this volume. Immigration reforms recommended by the President's Commission on Immigration reform have decreased admissions for both legal and illegal immigrants.

Affirmative action programs have been weakened by political demagoguery, but survive with debatable potency. The *Million Man March* demonstrated a unique solidarity among African Americans for group self-assertiveness and interpersonal accountability for familial and many other conditions endangering Black communities. The presidential elections of 1996 were characterized with debate on issues concerning the impact of immigration on jobs here and abroad such as welfare and educational entitlements, and again, affirmative action. The refugee crises in war-torn African nations have escalated beyond envisioned resolution. The dis-uniting of the Soviet Union, followed by so-called ethnic cleansing invasions, threaten peace and prosperity in nations of Europe—*push* factors to further immigrations to America.

Insidiously, the notion of *Hi-tech* lynching is no longer a mere sound bite from a U. S. Senate chamber hearing. The *Intelligence Report* (Fall, 1999) notes over 500 active white supremacist hate groups in the U. S., buttressed with over 300 counterpart Internet web sites.

Finally, the nation's ineffective gun control laws imply added insult to this injurious state of affairs. Gun-toting militia and hate groups declaring white supremacy as a virtue continue to spread their forecast of a so-called inevitable "Holy Race War" in America. Moreover, these pronouncements have contaminated the Internet nationally and internationally. In this 21st Century our greatest challenge is to nurture our multicultural family of humanity.

It is expected that various readers will find this book a useful resource in undergraduate, graduate, and continuing education studies in the fields of history, psychology, mental health studies, social work, sociology, counseling, political science, education, public administration, ethnic studies (African, Asian, and Hispanic), intergroup relations, and even marketing research. While in some measure we are all affected by the issues touched on in this text, it is also my hope that it contributes to the work of educators, human resource development personnel, legislators, and providers of human services.

Challenges of a Changing America

As editor of this work, I accept responsibility for its design, contents, and imperfections. I am hopeful that the contents will overshadow its limitations.

—**Ernest R. Myers**
University of the District of Columbia
Washington, D. C.

Part One

The Impact of Immigration: An Historical World View

From Slavery through the present, this nation has never opened its doors sufficiently to give black Americans a chance to become full citizens.
—Andrew Hacker,
Two Nations, Black and White, Separate, Hostile, Unequal
(New York: Charles Scribner's Sons, 1992)

And HE has made from *one* blood every nation of men to dwell on *all* the face of the earth.
—Acts 17:26

The slave trade was one of the major means of bringing immigrants to the New World in general and the United States in particular.
—Roger Daniels,
Coming to America
(New York: Harper Collins, 1990

Chapter One

Immigration:
A Changing Force and Changing Face

Ernest R. Myers

It is in the contexts of territorial expansion, large-scale civil wars, race, and inter-ethnic based aggressions, geared to acquire economic and political control over adjacent or foreign lands and populations, that the historically global relevance of immigration and national immigration policies and practices is revealed.

The Colonizers' Cloak: Global Immigration

History reveals the ethnocentric tendencies of man which have often resulted in aggression and the subjugation of others. In modern times, for example, Japan invaded China, Korea, Southeast Asia, and the Philippine Islands; Germany invaded England, the Soviet Union, Romania, Belgium, France and Luxembourg. Numerous other nations have similar histories of imperialistic, hostile migrations. While in modern times Japan has been the most frequent aggressor against other Asian nations (Burstein, 1990; Blustein, 1991), Anglo-Saxons and Germans have led the record of Europeans waging war against other whites and colonizing the Third World nations. Overall, however, as a continental ethnic group, Europeans have held the record for worldwide emigration designed to conquer unsuspecting nations comprised of peoples of color, particularly the continents of Africa, Australia, and the Americas, and the island nations from the Atlantic to the Pacific. (Taft, 1955; *Encyclopedia Americana*, 1986).

On the other hand, civil wars have been the greatest manifestations of extreme displays of internal, nationalistic antipathies. Between the American Revolution and America's civil war, dictatorships and revolutions abounded in Europe—France, Greece, Germany, Belgium, Italy and Spain—concurrently during periods of disastrous floods and famines (Boorstin, 1987).

The Colonial Movement

Cheikh Anta Diop (1981) further observed that most of the modern world, which encompasses three-quarters of the earth's land, was founded on the general rule of genocide. He further concluded:

> The European group has thus confiscated the quasi-totality of the habitable land of this planet, in only four centuries, and it categorically refuses the reintroduction of ethnic heterogeneity in all countries in which it physically destroyed the former *native* inhabitants. (p. 133)

It is this writer's view that Europe's recurrent crop failures and famines, associated with its ecological and epidemiological conditions and congested populations, were combined pivotal forces influencing Europe's massive trans-oceanic explorations during the 15th and 16th centuries.

After a quarter of Europe's population was devastated by the spread of the so-called *black death* epidemic (Bubonic plague), and in view of the relatively primitive state of the continent's agricultural technology (*Encyclopedia Americana*, 1986), it was time to seek "greener pastures" and perhaps healthier and wealthier environments in distant lands. The continent of Europe was experiencing starvation. Boorstin (1987) noted that European nations also doubled their populations during the 18th and 19th centuries. The news spread throughout Europe that "... with an empty continent to be filled, the United States was more than ever different from the crowded nations of Europe" (p. 94).

Indeed, the successful adventures of Portuguese and Spanish navigators and cartographers, especially Prince Henry and Christopher Columbus in the 15th century, ignited a movement to search the world for resources, including human labor, to enrich their native lands and, of course, themselves. This was the age of the Renaissance in Europe. An entire continent was experiencing the labor pains of a determined rebirth by whatever means necessary and at whoseever's expense.

During this period the rape of the New World and the African continent began. Eventually this ravishing by colonialists included nearly every major nation in Europe. Portugal and Spain led these early invasions as if this surge of imperialism was a mission of Christianity—a corroborated point verified by the diary notes of Columbus. Columbus returned from several voyages with an abundance of *loot*—gold, exotic spices, and 550 captured natives from *Hispaniola* (the Dominican Republic and Haiti) to serve as slaves for Spain's monarchy (Gelman, 1991; Gates, 1991). This importation of human cargo ushered in the trans-Atlantic slave trade industry. The governments of Europe were consequently convinced to invest in this new international trade. Unlimited human and natural resources simply awaited their exploitive initiatives. Their division of the *loot* often resulted in in-fighting for the prizes. For instance, the wars among the Dutch, Germans and English in South Africa were promoted by such greed over imperialistic entitlement notions. These conflicts were equivalent to and explain the postures taken by the British and the French forces in the American Revolution.

Europeans controlled only nine percent of the world when Columbus first set foot in the New World. Within 300 years they had colonized a third of the globe's humanity. By 1880, they ruled over two-thirds. And by 1935, Europe was in political control of not only 85 percent of the land on the Earth, but 70 percent of the world's population (Toffler, 1980).

European explorers' imports were evidence that Europe's level of agriculture, natural resources, and land fertility were inferior to Africa's and the resources of other tropical lands of the world. Armed with missionary piety, desire to escape congested and impoverished communities, biblical distortions, and lethal weapons, Europe began its journey to establish the *New World Order* of that time. Shortly thereafter, emigrations of Europeans for resettlements were launched.

Toffler (1980) concluded that Europe faced "... a single hard reality. It desperately needed the raw materials (natural resources) found outside its borders. But primarily its agenda called for "... a single integrated world market through which to siphon the hidden subsidy of cheap resources from the outside ... made possible by imperialism ...". With this mission then, a small group of European nations systematically rotated in exploiting the majority populations of the world (pp. 102-3, 113). Toffler further admonished that Europe was a blood-sucking leech attached to the bosoms of Africa, India, Latin America, and so on, to drain the natural wealth (raw materials) of these lands. It was, in fact, a system of global thievery.

In time Europeans were successful in selective genocidal and colonization efforts in the North and South American continents as well as Africa. Significantly, history does not record any era where peoples of color initiated international and trans-oceanic invasions to colonize predominantly white populations.

The American and Australian Experiences

During the past two centuries the United States Congress has established numerous key public laws that have determined the racial and ethnic populations of the United States. These U. S. immigration policies, beginning in 1783, have categorically been the pivotal factors determining whether the world's oppressed, impoverished, and persecuted peoples of *all* nationalities and races achieve refuge in the United States. In effect, however, because of the restrictive immigration policies targeted to curb or restrict non-European entrants, the most telling interpretation of these laws for populating this nation can be referred to as a legislative strategy that is reflective of the "White Australian Policy."

Challenges of a Changing America

Australia's nation-building has some parallels in the development of the United States' population. The British began its migrations to this ocean-surrounded continent by using it as a resettlement site for convicts in 1788; but soon after, free settlers were drawn to this sparsely populated paradise. These newcomers decimated much of the Aboriginal population. Australia then instituted immigration restrictions "against all coloured persons" (up to the mid-1970s) (*Australian Encyclopedia*, 1988; Taft & Robbins, 1955).

Similarly, there is the gruesome story of European outcasts and impoverished exiles who in large part left conditions of famine in Europe to better their lot by colonizing in North America at the expense of the Native Americans and involuntarily imported Black people. Some émigrés were escaping oppressive governmental conditions in Europe. Yet, it has been largely motives of economic survival and the pursuit of prosperity that influenced nearly 50 million whites to leave their native lands during the 1800s through the early l900s—like sailors leaving sinking ships of despair in search of seashores of hope. Daniels (1990) asserted that the popularized view that persecution was the grounds for the English Puritans' immigrations to America is "a self-serving myth." Most who came were actively "recruited" and often sponsored by promoters and later industrialists whose promises for a better life were irresistible (p. 43).

England's exiled convicts were Australia's counterparts to the slaves in America. Britain's free settlers went to Australia influenced by this cheap convict labor, which was arranged earlier by the Australian government. This government recruited and paid the English to immigrate and resettle in Australia.

The *parallel* of *Australia's* development and that of the *United States* is remarkable in that both included:

1. Some forced migrations; from Europe these were ostracized populations including convicts, poor underclasses, prostitutes, the mentally ill, and so on, although other settlers voluntarily sought economic betterment and freedom of worship.

2. Massive, governmentally institutionalized arrangements to exploit fellow human beings for cheap labor sources. However, Europe's convicts were compensated and perceived as human in contrast to victims of the slave industry in America.

3. Out of fear about their minority population status, both *Australia and the American colonies* sponsored/paid for the massive immigration of other whites, especially Anglos, as a perceived defensive investment strategy to outnumber their oppressed victims.

4. The discovery of gold deposits in both of these "new worlds" in the mid-1800s promoted even further emigrations from Europe to their shores.

5. The importation of Chinese "coolie" laborers for project-oriented tasks—railroad building in western America, and gold mining in Australia.

6. Legislation that excluded "all Orientals" as both nations perceived of a "yellow peril." Australia's occurred in 1866 and was again re-enacted when it gained commonwealth status in 1901. The U. S. Exclusion Act of 1882 banned immigration of Chinese (repealed in 1943). In 1917, the U. S. Congress established the *Asiatic Barred Zone* which banned the admissions of Pacific Islanders and natives of India, Burma, Siam, the Malay States, the East Indies and parts of China, Persia, and Afghanistan. Japanese *exclusion* was particularly included in the Act of 1924 when immigration quotas based on national origins were first instituted. These anti-Asian acts in the U. S. were repealed in 1952 by the McCarran-Walter Act, but the national origins quota systems favoring whites were kept intact.

7. Traditionally, both Australia and the United States have instituted immigration policies to insure that a *majority* of their populations are of northern European stock.

In addition to the above points, Taft and Robbins (1955) noted that: "Extreme care is exercised to keep above 90 percent the proportion of Australia's stock of British origin" (pp. 346-77; pp. 422-23). Ironically, *Japanese* leadership has recently voiced an identical justification for their achievements—a homogenous society—as has been *Australia's* historical view that the presence of "Orientals would be sociologically unsound in that race friction would be created and that building a great welfare state in the Commonwealth scheme of things requires cultural homogeneity" (p. 347).

Parenthetically, Brazil has been called the true "melting pot" of the world as "the ethnic and cultural heir to three continents—America, Europe, and Africa," and to a lesser degree, Asia, particularly Japan. Further, the Brazilian population census, according to Taft and Robbins, revealed an underrated African heritage of at least 40 percent of its 50 million citizenry, in a census of three generations ago (p. 354). Today, Brazil's population of African descent is estimated to be over 50 percent. Significantly, it has about one-half the population of the entire South American continent (*World Almanac and Book of Facts*, 1990). However, the United States was a role-model for Brazil's racist, nationality immigration quota system, established in the 1924 policy instituted first in the United States. The key agenda of immigration quotas has been to maintain non-whites as America's *minorities*.

Involuntary Immigration: The Slave Trade

One of the most comprehensive books on the topic of immigration, *Interna-*

tional Migrations, maintained that the study of the institution of slavery has global relevance for the study of migration (Taft and Robbins, 1955). The impact of historical and contemporary immigration in the United States can only be fully understood within a chronological context of immigration policies and their demographic effects on America's human resources and inter-group relations.

Historians have typically neglected to note the pervasive fears of the white colonialists concerning their population size in contrast to first, the Native Americans, then to the ever-growing population of imported Black slaves. This constant threat particularly surfaced in the Virginia Tidewater region. In 1790, the U. S. census counted nearly four million residents in the land including less than 20 percent slaves. Yet, by the 1820 census, the population of this Virginia region was nearly 50 percent Black (Smith & Brown, 1982; Wood, 1974; Zinn, 1980; Steiner, 1976). By 1830, Blacks (slaves) were in the majority in the Virginia Tidewater area. These population statistics terrified whites (Boorstin, 1987).

Furthermore, historians have almost invariably failed to include the Black slave in their writings on immigration to America. The slaves' arrival in America as *involuntary immigrants* required trans-Atlantic travel under the most inhumane conditions in the world's recorded history. Yet, before the 1960s, immigration historians uniformly harbored no loss of scholarship or intellectual integrity in their neglectful literary treatment of the topic (America, 1990; Zinn, 1980; Daniels, 1990). It was as if the African in America was non-existent. Indeed, Ralph Ellison's "invisible man" has haunted white America for nearly 400 years. The white psyche and slavocracy could not recognize "human property" as human peers. But what was the excuse of historians for the century after the abolishment of slavery in theUnited States? Why did they not articulate the reality of massive, involuntary migrations or importation of the African to America as an indelible statistic in the study of migration?

In effect, the importation of slaves was America's *premiere* system of world trade since at this juncture in world affairs, neither Europe nor the "New World" colonies could fill their own consumable needs or produce anything in demand inside their borders. *The Wealth of Races*, by Richard America (1990), argues that as an economic system, slavery was an indispensable factor in the very growth of England, the United States, and Western Europe. The enterprise of slavery had profits linking four continents, all of which included slaves as property plus the Africans' uncompensated labor, for over 400 years. Thus, in the Thirteen (original) Colonies and later in the United States alone the capital endowment to whites, as produced by the Black labor force who were denied equitable distribution of resources by the government, has cost African Americans an estimated *Three Trillion Dollars* of expected lifetime earnings. Analyses by a number of economists conclude that "the United States' emergence as an industrial (super power) nation was possible only because of the massive input provided by slave labor" (p. 202). This legacy of loss due to slavery finds a growing number of advocates concluding that native African-Americans, descendants of America's *only involuntary immigrants*, are due reparations (Swinton, 1991; Robinson, 2000).

This observation, however, is illustrative of the rationale currently so popular in multicultural, academic debates in support of promoting Afrocentric curricula. Could it be that white historians and academicians simply knew (or were advised) that their writings would be rejected by publishers if they recognized Blacks in America as a significant part of the immigrant humanity—a publish or perish imperative? Were they in collusion with politicians who were bent on manipulating the U. S. census count to influence a skewed distribution of federal revenues? Whatever the rationale for this gap, fault by omission is the vulnerable element in the criticism of Euro-centric curricula today.

Single Missions—Double Standards

The current population problems in the United States today in part originated with the institutionalization of the Black slave industry. Although involuntary but with the highest priority, slaves were indeed the first massive migrant group to come to *colonial* America. They were foreigners brought to the American colonies to build the cotton industry, energize the economy, and provide trade skills, all at no cost to the oppressed political and economic refugees from Europe. Raped psychologically, physically and economically, denied their family and cultural identities, selfhood and human rights, the slaves' only documentation were the superimposed "for sale" descriptions and cattle-like brandings with the names of "benevolent" European immigrants who were all too eager to supervise the slaves' resettlement as unpaid laborers in the plantation society of that day. It is estimated that untold millions of the approximate 50 million human beings who were taken from African villages to ships bound for North and South America and the Caribbean nations were lost at sea in the vast and numerous ocean crossings of the slave trade (Bennett, 1982; Davidson; 1989; Daniels, 1990; Zinn, 1980). This holocaust and human tragedy of commercial slavery drastically changed the racial and cultural demography of entire American nations. In fact, of the original 13 American colonies, the Black population comprised from 35 to 50 percent of four of the colonies, such as Virginia, South Carolina, North Carolina, and Maryland (Faulkner, 1957; Smith, Levy, & Brown, 1982). Faulkner (1957) further noted that the U. S. census of 1790 reported a total population of six of the 13 colonies to be 1,902,078, of which 64 percent were white and 36 percent Black (p. 350). By 1860, the U.S. census showed that in 11 slave states there were 8,099,760 whites versus 3,953,580 slaves, or 67 percent versus 33 percent (p. 353). The other three-quarters of U.S. territories included free Blacks, which meant that the actual size of the Black population in the United States then was likely a threatening magnitude of nearly 40 percent. There was nothing more disturbing for America's colonizers. Nearly half of the population in five of the

Challenges of a Changing America

original 13 colonies (Georgia, North and South Carolina, Maryland and Virginia) were composed of enslaved Blacks. For whites then, especially slave owners, their exploitation of the *American Dream* was cause for *nightmares* of retribution. Further, in the early 1800s, over 30 percent of the population in the United States were Blacks. However, following the dethroning of "King Cotton" and the outlawing of slavery, massive solicitations of Europeans to migrate to the United States were conducted by America's governmental and industrial leadership. Advertisements promising free land ownership and sponsored transportation were sent throughout Europe. Apparently, it was felt that slaves would indeed wage war and eventually seek revenge if America's white population did not outnumber them to a significant degree (Bennett, 1982; Daniels, 1990; Faulkner, 1957; Smith, et. al., 1982).

There were at least 200 insurrections or revolts by Africans during the era of slavery in the United States. The fear instilled in whites lasted for years after a thousand slaves revolted in Richmond, Virginia in 1800 (Davis, 1969). Also, the American colonists had surely become aware of the 1791 revolution led by Haiti's liberator, Toussaint L'Ouverture. By 1804, Haiti's army of slaves had conquered the French forces and established Haiti as the second independent republic in the Western Hemisphere (Adams, 1987). The United States, the first such republic of the region, was still adjusting to its mere generation of independence. The imperialistic world was now put on notice by the success of this liberated Black republic. Consequently, it was not for moral redemption that a constitutional prohibition was made in 1808 to stop and forbid any further importation of Africans into the United States. In effect, this was the nation's *first* bar against an entire group of people based on race or nationality.

Since 1981, the United States government has threatened to deport Ethiopians, Haitians, and new arrivals from Hispanic societies and the Caribbean. According to official government records only 261,739 African immigrants were admitted into the United States between 1820 and 1987. In fact, 72 percent of the total admitted from the African continent in United States' history occurred only since 1961; that is an average of 1,558 per year since official immigration records have been maintained - since 1820. During this 167-year period the record shows that while only a total of 261,739 Africans were admitted to the United States, 5,140,954 Asians (nearly 20 times the level or quota of Africans immigrants), and 299,595 unspecified nationalities were admitted. Also during this period only a total 3,994,821 admissions to the United States have been from Latin America and the Caribbean countries (Myers, 1989).

Conversely, immigrants of European origins—admitted between 1820 and 1987—numbered 41,047,633, nearly 77 percent of the total immigrants ever to gain permanent residency (Vialet, 1980) in the United States during this period. Thus, America's immigration policies of massive private and public, commercial solicitation of European immigrants into the United States can be interpreted as a deliberate *movement* to increase a defense force (reinforcements) for the insecure white population to effectively resist any Black liberation efforts. Understandably, slaves had persistently continued their periodic insurrections and revolts throughout the 1800s while nearly 20 million (19,095,221) Europeans were migrating to the United States. Up to 1860, about five million had come to the U. S. compared with the over 14 million (14,041,192) or 74 percent of the immigrants that the U. S. had welcomed between 1860 and 1899. In a mere 24-year period, 16 million more European immigrants came between 1900 and 1924 (*1987 Statistical Yearbook of the Immigration and Naturalization Service* [Table I, Immigration to the U. S.: Fiscal Years 1820-1987]).

By the time the French sculptor, Frederic Auguste Bartholdi, announced his completion of France's gift to America—the Statue of Liberty—in 1883, 9 million European immigrants had *already* resettled in the United States (U. S. Immigration and Naturalization Service, 1988). The statistical yearbook of the INS also records that between 1820 and 1880 the United States welcomed approximately 10,189,429 European immigrants to its shores; that is 97.7 percent of the 9 million "refugees" who journeyed to the "Promised Land" during this period. By contrast, only 230, 689 Asians (2.2 percent) and a mere 1, 006 Africans (0.89 percent) gained admission as immigrants during this same period—a total of 3.9 percent of all immigrants accepted in the U. S. over this 60-year period. From 1821 until 1920 an average of 290,000 immigrants entered the United States each year (U. S. Immigration and Naturalization Service, 1988).

By 1921, the Statue of Liberty's light, already dimming, became a flicker. The U. S. Congress had imposed an immigration quota system restricting newcomers

Table 1.1
Immigrantion to the U. S.: 1820-1990

Europe	35,984,122
Asia	6,030,031
Canada and Newfoundland	4,246,725
Mexico	2,815,731
West Indies	2,586,323
So. America	1,190,352
Central America	627,217
Africa	300,367
Australia/New Zealand	145,009
Other America	109,483
Pacific Islands	50,672
Unspecified	182,497

Source: U. S. Department of Justice, Immigration and Naturalization Service, Statistical Division, 1992

based on the number of people of each race or "national origin" *already* representative of America's population in 1920. Consequently, northwestern Europeans were officially awarded a quota of 82 percent; southeastern Europe, 16 percent—leaving two (2) percent for the rest of the world. In effect, this national origin policy simply *legally* institutionalized an ethnic and racial quota which had already been the practice of the U. S. immigration system since America gained independence from its European monarchy (Lurie, 1965). The philosophy undergirding U. S. immigration laws implies that the national origin of an immigrant is sound criterion for determining one's capacity for effective resettlement and citizenship. Significantly, the Ku Klux Klan, at its peak of influence in American government in the 1920s, pushed a letter-writing campaign in support of Congressman Albert Johnson's "anti-polyglotism" legislation for restrictive immigration policies. The Klan, then, represented the "moral majority" of that time. Their *National Kourier* reminded the nation of immigrants that "every signer of the Declaration of Independence was white" (Chalmers, 1965, pp. 283-84).

Unfortunately, the Klan did not consider it relevant that the first martyr of the U. S. Colonial (American) Revolution, Crispus Attucks, was a Black man, killed fighting the British in Boston in 1770, and that Black Minutemen fought in nearly every battle of the Colonial Revolution (Smith & Brown, 1982).

In 1924, U. S. Secretary of Labor James J. Davis (1925) declared, "... we can do much toward keeping blood of the nation unpolluted by inferior strains" (p. 6). Popular ethnocentrism had already influenced the Emergency Quota Act of 1921, restricting certain undesirable European nationalities from U. S. shores, and the Johnson-Reed Act of 1924 established the National Origins Quota System, designed to freeze the prevalent, preferred white and ethnic profile of the U. S. population. According to Bernard (1965), our immigration policy, as re-stipulated in the Immigration and Nationality Act of 1952, was America's basic law up to 1968 although this 1952 act included some reforms. For example, it reversed the 1888 ban and the 1907 restriction against entry of Asians. However, it included 13 new grounds for their deportation and retroactive grounds for de-naturalization. The *Torch* of "Lady Liberty" was burning low. The annual quota was set at 150,000 immigrants, to be proportional to the makeup of groups already in the United States in 1920 (Faulkner, 1957; Handlin, 1959). This quota specifically excluded "descendants of slave immigrants." This racist legislation, biased against Southern and Eastern Europeans and non-whites of Asia and Africa, was the basic official U. S. immigration statute from 1924 through 1965, with periodic amendments which only expanded the quota for Europeans. Although only about 125,000 émigrés had entered the U. S. between the Revolutionary War and 1819 (Daniels, 1990), the great movement to America followed, as shown in Tables 1.3 through 1.6.

Large influxes of immigrants are frequently referred to as "waves." There have been four major waves of immigrants building this nation's majority population profile (Dudley, 1990):

Immigration

1st Wave 1820-1880	Over 10 million - Basically North and West (rural) Europeans
2nd Wave 1880-1920	Over 23.5 million - Basically South and East Europeans, many recruited for U. S. factory work (steel mills, etc.)
3rd Wave 1920-1950	5.5 million - Basically from Europe
4th Wave 1950-1990	Nearly 10 million - Basically from Europe

Note: According to the national capital city-based Urban Institute, other émigrés—undocumented aliens (essentially Spanish-speaking populations)—amounted to an influx of 10.6 million more between 1960 through 1990. Thus, total immigration waves were apparently 60.6 million people—82.5 percent from Europe (*The Washington Post*, Dec. 31, 1990). Ironically, the white population of the U. S. maintains a 75 percent majority (Bureau of the Census, 2000), according to the most current controversial count.

While immigration restrictions in all nations also serve to regulate their markets, immigration policies are the most potent forces used to establish, make,

Table 1.2
World Population - 2000
(in Millions)

Continents	Population	% of World	Area (Sq. Miles)	% of Area
North America	480,000	7.8	9,400,000	16.2
South and Central America	384,000	6.2	6,900,000	11.9
Europe	708,000	11.4	3,800,000	6.6
Asia	3,730,600	60.1	17,400,000	30.1
Africa	825,100	14.0	11,700,000	20.2
Oceania/Australia	32,300	0.5	3,300,000	5.7
Antarctica	0	0.0	5,400,000	9.3
Totals	6,145,000	100%		100%

Source: *World Book Encyclopedia 2000,* World Book, Inc., Chicago, Illinois

Notes
1. The North American continent includes the United States, which has a population of approximately 281.4 million and nearly 5 percent of the world's population; and Canada, with approximately 207 million population according to the U. S. Census Bureau in 1999.
2. Australia's population is approximately 18 million in a land area nearly the size of the United States. It is the world's most spacious area available for population increases.
3. Japan, the 2nd wealthiest nation in the world (included in the Asian continent count), has also the 7th largest population—123.6 million, or 2.4 percent of the world's population, yet it has only 0.3 percent of the world's square mile area.
4. The Asian continent data includes India's and Indo-China's lands populations and together contain over 60 percent.

or maintain a country's ethnic, cultural, and racial profiles. As discussed earlier, Australia has been *open* about the traditional intent of its laws of exclusive immigration—referred to as the "White Australia Policy." Designed to give immigration and refugee preference to people of the British Isles and other northern Europeans, this policy prevailed throughout Australia's history up to the mid-1970s. Since then, Australia has professed an equal opportunity for aspiring immigrants, regardless of race, color, nationality, creed, politics, or sex (*Australian Encyclopedia*, 1988). This continent's *homogeneous nation-building* now thwarts its efforts

Table 1.3
Immigration by Continental Areas, 1820-1880

Countries	1820	1821-1830	1831-1840	1841-1850	1851-1860	1861-1870	1871-1880
All	8,385	143,439	599,125	1,713,251	2,598,214	2,314,824	2,812,191
Europe	7,690	98,797	495,681	1,597,442	2,452,577	2,065,141	2,271,925
Asia	6	30	55	141	41,538	64,759	124,160
China							
India							
Japan							
Turkey							
Other Asia							
America	387	11,564	33,424	62,469	74,720	166,607	404,044
Canada & Newfoundland							
Mexico							
West Indies							
Central America							
South America							
Africa	1	16	54	55	210	312	358
Australia & New Zealand						36	9,886
Pacific Islands (U.S. adm.)							1,028
Not Spec.	301	33,032	69,911	53,144	29,169	17,969	790

Notes for Tables 1.3 & 1.4:
1. From 1820-1867, figures represent alien *passengers arrived* at seaports, including 1868-1891. From 1890 and 1892-94 refer to aliens *admitted*. Data for years prior to 1906 relates to country from when alien came; thereafter, to country of last permanent residence. Because of changes in boundaries and changes in lists of countries, data for certain countries are not comparable throughout. Also, from 1892-1903, aliens entering the United States by sea and who traveled cabin class were not counted as immigrants, and land arrivals were not completely enumerated until 1908.
2. The Immigration and Naturalization Service's (INS) statistical categories of grand totals for Asia also include Hong Kong, Korea, Vietnam, Iran, Israel, and the Philippines.
3. See 1881 through 1990 immigration on next three pages.

Source: United States Department of Justice Immigration and Naturalization Service. *Statistical Yearbook of INS-1991*, p. 28.

Immigration

to balance labor demands with available human resources. There is a message here for America's opponents of *unbiased* (open) immigration.

The racial preference policy intent of the United States' laws is discernible in the "Chronology of U. S. Immigration Policy," displayed after the "Immigration" charts at the end of this chapter. The key exposing cue for this conclusion was the steadfast reiteration of the quota system which restricted immigration of peoples based on the U. S.' "national character" or "national origins" from 1921 to 1965. In simple English these terms (codes) guaranteed the priority admission of whites to the U. S. *by law* although this preferential population campaign had actually been

Table 1.4
Immigration by Continental Areas, 1881-1950

Countries	1881-1920	1891-1900	1901-1910	1911-1920	1921-1930	1931-1940	1941-1950
All	5,256,613	3,687,564	8,795,386	5,735,811	4,107,209	528,431	1,035,039
Europe	4,735,484	3,555,352	8,056,040	4,321,887	2,463,194	347,552	621,124
Asia	69,942	74,862	323,543	247,236	112,059	16,081	32,360
China							
India							
Japan							
Turkey							
Other Asia							
America	426,967	38,972	361,888	1,143,671	1,516,716	160,037	354,804
Canada & Newfoundland							
Mexico							
West Indies							
Central America							
South America							
Other America							
Africa	875	350	7,368	8,443	6,286	1,750	7,367
Australia & New Zealand	7,017	2,740	11,975	12,348	88,299	2,231	13,805
Pacific Islands (U.S. adm.)	5,557	1,225	1,049	1,079	427	780	5,437
Not Specified	789	14,063	33,523	1,147	228		142

Source: United States Department of Justice Immigration and Naturalization Service. *Statistical Yearbook of INS-1991*, pp. 28-29.

Challenges of a Changing America

the practice since the 1808 constitutional maneuver to stop the importation of Africans into this country. In 1988, legislation was even prepared to establish a preferential, exceptional immigration category to accept 30,000 émigrés a year from the Soviet Union. This was slated to be done by taking *authorized* Indo-Chinese slots from their quota (*Washington Post*, 1988). In 1965, U. S. immigration policy finally abolished the racist national origin quota which had been in effect for 44 years, and provided for selective entry of refugee immigrants. The Immigra-

Table 1.5
Immigration by Continental Areas, 1951-1978

Countries	1951-1960	1961-1970	1971-1975	1976	To 1976*	1977	1978
All	2,515,479	3,321,677	1,936,281	398,613	103,676	462,315	601,442
Europe[1]	1,325,640	1,123,363	422,194	73,035	18,641	74,048	76,156
Asia[2]	150,106	427,771	590,223	146,725	37,725	150,842	243,395
China[5]							
India							
Japan							
Turkey							
Other Asia							
America	996,944	1,716,374	378,027	169,150	44,272	223,174	266,470
Canada & Newfoundland							
Mexico							
West Indies							
Central America							
South America							
Other America[3]							
Africa	14,092	28,954	27,948	5,723	1,967	9,612	10,336
Australia & New Zealand	11,506	19,562	11,155	2,133	606	2,544	2,665
Pacific Islands (U.S. adm.)[2]	4,698	1,769	935	195	60	195	137
Not Specified[4]	12,493	3,384	5,799	1,622	405	1,900	2,082

Notes:
* This column is a transition quarter covering July-September, 1976.
1. Since 1964, *Asian USSR* has been included in Europe's total *USSR* count.
2. Beginning in 1952, *Asia* includes the Philippines. From 1934-1951, the Philippines are recorded in separate tables as insular travel.
3. Included with countries "not specified" up to 1925.
4. The figure 33,523 in column *1901-1910* includes persons returning in 1906 to their homes in the U. S.
5. Beginning in 1957, China includes Taiwan.

Source: United States Department of Justice Immigration and Naturalization Service. *Statistical Yearbook of INS-1991*, pp. 29-30.

Immigration

tion and Nationality Act of 1952 was amended again in 1975, 1976, and 1978 to increase the quotas for admissions and to establish a categorical system for *preferred* immigrants such as those with technical occupational skills. The most dramatic changes of this legislation which affects the Third World, however, were: (1) provisions to provide extended refuge to Indo-Chinese, mostly Vietnamese, which began in 1975, and (2) the pro-active Refugee Act of 1980 which expanded eligibility potential for applicants, established annual quotas, and expanded a definition of "refugee" consistent with United Nations policy embracing asylum and resettlement principles. This was a breakthrough. However, the largest benefactors were European refugees of the 1980s who were fleeing the political threats of communism (Leibowitz, 1983).

A victory for the Hispanic Diaspora was achieved with the passage of the Immigration Reform and Control Act of 1986 (IRCA). Nearly two million Mexicans and Central Americans qualified under the IRCA's amnesty for illegal immigrants living in the U. S. prior to 1982 (Passel & Woodrow, 1989).

More significantly, since the mid-1970s, the U. S. has far exceeded its past

Table 1.6
Immigration by Continental Areas, Two-Year Periods, 1979-1990

Countries	1979-80	1981-82	1983-84	1985-86	1987-88	1989-90
All countries	1,200,475	1,392,298	1,356,851	1,415,307	1,554,028	1,504,767
Europe	132,966	135,869	122,943	125,555	125,971	170,729
Asia	425,390	577,634	533,974	532,939	522,149	584,185
China						
India						
Japan						
Turkey						
Other Asia						
America	606,895	628,660	605,000	710,285	827,218	695,716
Canada & Newfoundland						
Mexico						
West Indies						
Central America						
South America						
Other America						
Africa	26,819	29,343	30,624	34,580	36,606	37,974
Australia	2,880	2,648	2,581	2,716	3,862	3,100
& New Zealand	1,328	1,308	1,201	1,289	1,259	1,429
Pacific Islands						
(U.S. adm.)	4,197	6,836	3,528	3,943	3,963	3,634
Not Specified	0	10	57	4	33	8

Source: United States Department of Justice Immigration and Naturalization Service. *Statistical Yearbook of INS-1991*, p. 30.

records in accepting immigrants and refugees from Asia, Latin America, and Africa. Although the admission of only about 60,000 Ethiopians during this period represents nearly 20 percent of all African émigrés ever to be admitted to the U. S. between 1820 and 1990. According to official records, only 300,367 Africans were permitted to *voluntarily* immigrate to the U. S. between 1820 and 1990; other Third World immigrations to the U. S during this same period are shown in Table 1.1.

That table reveals a grand total of 54.2 million immigrants admitted to this nation between 1820 and 1990. Only 22 percent of this total population came from Third World countries. These figures represent official estimates of *total* immigration to the U. S. from 1820-1990 (INS Statistical Division, 1992).

The Ethiopian Community Development Council (ECDC) noted that their population in the United States ranges between 50 to 75 thousand, including Ethiopian offspring born here, and that over 70 percent of their total population came during the 1970 decade. The Council further reported that the "quota ceilings set for African refugees have ranged from a low of 1,500 in 1980 to a high of 3,500 in 1987. It was further concluded that both funds and numbers set aside (quota allocation) for African refugees were *reallocated* to refugees from other parts of the world" (ECDC Report, September, 1990, p. 20).

The more compassionate influencers of legislation are often not participants in the on-site, hands-on implementation of U. S. immigration policies. INS officials at

Figure 1.1
The World Population

World Population, estimate of 6.1 billion*

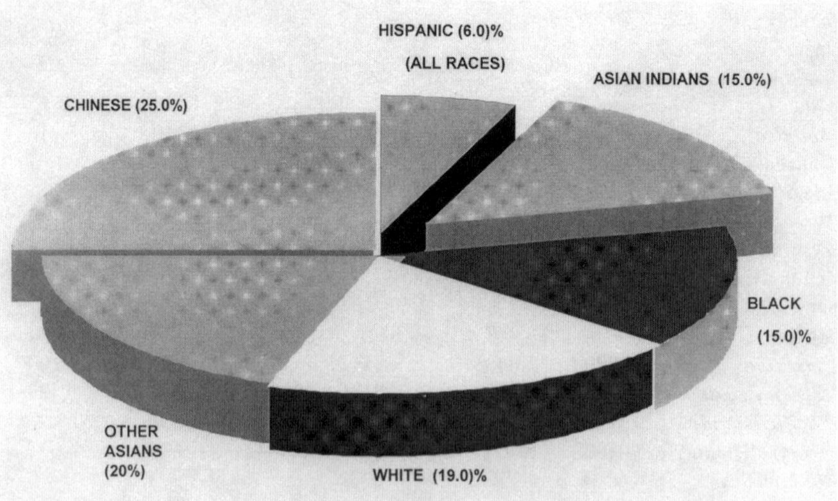

- HISPANIC (6.0)% (ALL RACES)
- ASIAN INDIANS (15.0%)
- CHINESE (25.0%)
- BLACK (15.0)%
- OTHER ASIANS (20%)
- WHITE (19.0)%

Source: *World Book Encyclopedia 2000*, World Book, Inc., 2000. Race and ethnic estimates were calculated by the author based on this data.

Immigration

entry points and the U. S. Coast Guard are the front-line obstacles for asylum seekers. Like the poetic, unconditional welcome statement inscribed on the Statue of Liberty, the United Nation's Declaration of Human Rights remains more of a proclamation of philosophical rhetoric than a commitment to universal human rights—Everyone has the *right* to freedom of movement and *determination* of residence.

Incarcerated Sanctuary: The Haitian and Cuban Refugee

The history of Anglo-American immigration policies reveals much institutionalized, insidious bias and contradictory proclamations exemplified by the U. S.' response to the world's refugee crises. Since colonial times, it has been acceptable for Anglo-Americans or immigrants of European descent to seek economic betterment toward improving their quality of life under the guise of being refugees from persecution by resettling in the United States, while such freedom of mobility and

Figure 1.2
United States Population, 1999

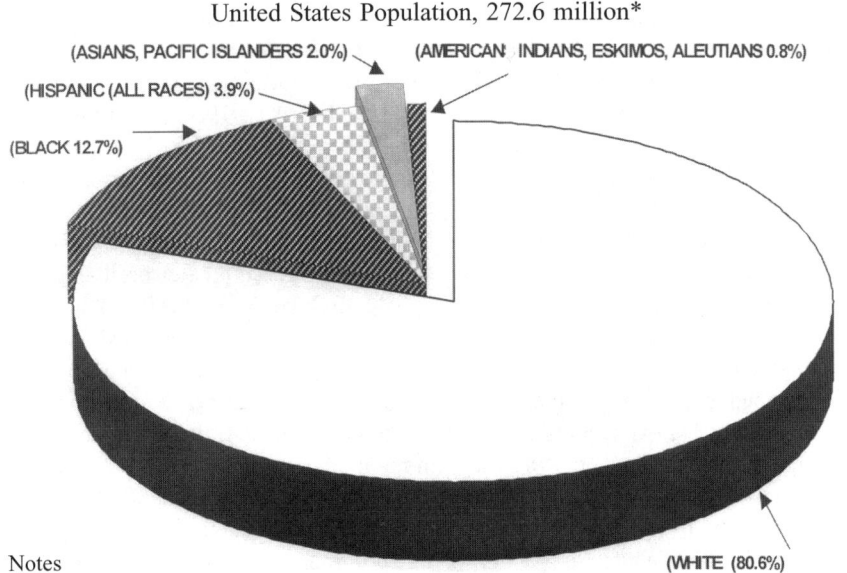

United States Population, 272.6 million*

(ASIANS, PACIFIC ISLANDERS 2.0%)
(AMERICAN INDIANS, ESKIMOS, ALEUTIANS 0.8%)
(HISPANIC (ALL RACES) 3.9%)
(BLACK 12.7%)
(WHITE (80.6%)

Notes
The legacy of slavery in America and Eurocentric racism influences the self-choice of racial classifications in the U.S.
The U.S. Census Bureau recorded a total U.S. population of 281,421,906 in 2000, the first time that people were allowed to identify themselves beyond one racial group. This count showed the following U.S. population percentages: Whites, 75.1%; Blacks, 12.3%; Hispanic, 12.5%; Asian or Pacific Islanders, 3.6%; multiracial, 2.4%; and others, 5.5%.
*Source: U. S. Department of Commerce, Bureau of the Census, 1999.

the same right to a better life has been denied to non-Europeans and peoples of color the world over who seek both political and economic sanctuary. Since the late 1970s, newspapers flash *news almost weekly* reporting the denial of asylum in the U. S. for Haitians, *allegedly* because they seek economic betterment only.

In 1981, the Reagan Administration began a so-called 90-day experimental program of interdiction to stop and search vessels on the high seas transporting Haitians to the U.S. Significantly, this unprecedented maneuver applied to *no other group of people* seeking asylum in the United States. It was initiated uniquely by Reagan by an executive order, EO-12324, and supported by an agreement with Haiti's former despotic President Duvalier (Masanz, 1982). Duvalier was thereafter rewarded with asylum in France, a likely "gentlemen's" agreement, as a trade-off for his role in preventing Haitians from fleeing to freedom to the shores of Florida.

Accused of being economic rather than political refugees, over 2,100 Haitians were detained or imprisoned in the Krome Detention Center outside Miami, Florida in 1988. A great many more have drowned enroute or have been denied entry into the U. S. and sent back to Haiti. Between 1980 and 1989, the U. S. Coast Guard intercepted and returned 13,060 refugees to Haiti. Still, 550 Haitians were locked up in the U. S. detention center, and over 10,000 more awaited deportation from the U. S. military base in Cuba (Guantanamo) as we celebrated Black History Month (February, 1992) in America (Marquis, 1989; *Washington Post*, April 30, 1991).

The U. S. Coast Guard has doubled its efforts, reportedly, to intercept the ever persistent Haitian asylum seekers, and in one month (March, 1989) the Coast Guard returned 2,359 Haitians to Port-au-Prince. Approximately 34,525 Haitians had stopped at sea since the so-called 1981 "experimental" interdiction program, as of February, 1992 (*Washington Post*, 1989, 1992). Haitians are increasingly experiencing economic despair since U. S. foreign aid was terminated in late 1987. Refugees from communist countries continue to be given greater preference for political asylum in the United States despite the Refugee Act of 1980. On the other hand, Haitians were a *mere nine percent* of applications for asylum in 1981, yet only *one percent* of their applications (5 out of 503) were approved. The treatment of them is designed to discourage all applicants from the Caribbean and Central America. Significantly, Haitians represent less than two percent of the entire illegal entry into the United States (Zucker, 1983). It is immoral, discriminatory and intellectually dishonest to deny the economic ramifications of political persecution, and vice versa. Klarreich (1992) of Global Exchange, a U. S.-based, support organization for Haiti, notes that the intent of the interdiction program was malicious. Refugees are only allowed to appeal judgments on their applications for political asylum *within* the geographical boundaries of the U. S. Consequently, interdiction of Haitians on the high seas prevents so-called "boat people" from full asylum proceedings. More than *24,000* Haitian refugees were intercepted (from dilapidated boats) between September, 1981, and June, 1991, while only *28* were approved for asylum in the United States (p. 5). Obviously, the U. S. government has determined that Europe has a monopoly on the vice of *Political Persecution*- the key category for refugee status. Refugee classifications of European émigrés have certainly been a strategic element of a geo-political cold war that has served to reinforce America's quota system.

After touring the Krome Detention Center, which warehoused Haitians for the past decade, the Reverend Jackson admonished, "There is a standard for Whites coming from Europe and another for people of African descent. There is a Statue of Liberty for Whites and a statute of limitation for Blacks" (*Jet*, January 28, 1982, p. 55). U. S. immigration quotas are experienced particularly by descendants of African heritage, including Latin American and Caribbean peoples.

Concentration camps, referred to as "resettlement" centers, were the new communities in the United States for thousands of Cubans and Haitians in the 1980s. Their new living quarters have also included federal prisons and a hospital for the mentally ill. Some 50 Cubans were maintained for years in St. Elizabeth's Hospital in Washington, D. C. (Anders, 1989).

The Krome Center had a shameful counterpart in the early 1980s—the Ft. Chaffee Readjustment Center for Cubans. This facility processed 10,000 "Cubanos Refugiados" at this military base. It was described by Cruces (1982) as a "concentration camp" where the Cubans acted out the prison inmate role in frequent violence, theft, drug abuse, drug trafficking, and rape. Cruces reported awareness of these offenses as a result of the intensive six months he worked there as a mental health counselor. He noted that rape was recurrent. Several homicides and one suicide also occurred during his tenure.

Many of the Cuban refugees were ex-prisoners and admitted drug abusers as well as former clients of in-patient mental health institutions in Cuba. The Ft. Chaffee Center operated for a mere 14 months yet Cruces and staff were able to place many of the refugees with U. S. sponsors. Over 2,000 were transferred to the Atlanta Federal Prison and other penal facilities where many have remained for the past 10 years. Others became members of the unemployed, homeless population and began existing on city streets after Fort Chaffee closed in January, 1982 (pp. 2-15).

A Human Ecological Equation

Throughout the history of U. S. immigration policies and practices, Lady Liberty's golden gate has more often than not been a hypocritical barrier to seekers of asylum or self-determination of domicile for non-European peoples. In a world order that faces reality, the new perspective for immigration laws and practices will consider the following world issues.

1. Three-fourths of the earth's 6.1 billion human population are people of color who maintain fertility rates far surpassing the population rates of whites worldwide.

2. Western society's family planning efforts in Third World countries have not been able to control their fertility rates, or the so-called population explosion. Essentially, this is based on a difference in cultural values concerned with the value of human life. In the Cameroon, for example, a female demonstrates her womanhood by giving birth to *seven* children, according to a presentation by Robinson (1982), an American anthropologist who administered family planning efforts in Africa in the mid-1970s.

3. International politics and foreign policy are inextricably bound in immigration decisions and policies. Thus, we see that for the U. S. Justice Department which oversees the implementation of America's immigration policies in collaboration with the Department of State, provides the geo-, legal, and political checks and balances. In 1982, for example, the State Department negotiated the possibility of resettling Haitians in Belize, Central America. Although the Haitians were not consulted about this proposal, its feasibility was pursued, in cooperation with the Geneva-based Intergovernmental Committee for Migration. Most Belizians are of African or Hispanic descent, and Belize (formerly colonized British Honduras up to 1981) has been under the threat of Guatemala's claim to it as its territorial entitlement (*Washington Post*, April 3, 1982). Ten years later, the U. S. made arrangements to apprehend and deport Haitian "boat people" bound for Florida and reroute many of them to other Latin countries.

4. There is an imbalance of resources (natural and human), economic sufficiency, and habitable land among the nations of the world. Even "superpower" nations cannot manufacture the land required for congested populations.

Yet, relocation or immigration from one nation to another is increasingly becoming a necessity to establish balance in the world's ecological and human resources. Today the world's population is about 6.1 billion, and over 60 percent are Asians. By the year 2015, a population of 8.2 billion is projected. Currently, China has 1.7 billion; India, about one billion; Africa, about 825 million; and South and Central America, about 384.5 million. It is noteworthy that nations inhabited mostly by whites have the smallest populations. Europe has about 685.4 million; the United States, about 273 million; Canada, about 207 million; Australia, about 18 million with two-thirds of its land uninhabited by its citizens (*World Book Encyclopedia 2000*). In contrast, Japan experiences a human ecological nightmare. Only a quarter of this island nation's volcanic terrain is habitable. Japan's 1990 population census was over 123 million, nearly half the size of the population of the U. S. although it is second only to the U. S. in wealth and its per capita gross national product (Reid, 1990).

Immigration

The table and figures presented in this chapter of the world's population and the size of each continent indicate not only population/land density but by implication point out the availability and restrictions for habitation and world migration. Human ecological equilibrium is the beckoning consideration for the future.

Conclusion

Significantly, immigration policies in the former colonies of today's "new world," such as the United States, Australia, New Zealand, and Argentina, to name a few, have served to maintain their predominantly white population profiles, namely, majority *white* countries with subcultures comprised of peoples of color or so-called *minority* groups. Immigration scholars, historians, economists, and others have long concluded that racism has been the greatest influence determining immigration laws in predominantly white societies (America, 1990; Fallows, 1990; Mazrui, 1986; Simon, 1990; Taft, 1955; Woodson, 1918; Nichols, 1969; Kennedy, 1964; Toffler, 1980). Robert Staples (1983) makes the point of parallelism in this regard by comparing Australia's former "white only" immigration policy (coupled with the decimation of Aboriginal [Black] Australians) with America's genocidal agenda against native Americans (pp.5-7). For instance, a letter has been preserved exposing that "General George Washington ordered his men to clear the New England area of the Indian population by exterminating them" (*Washington Post*, April 13, 1991, p. A 17). Also, through this colonial process and immigration policies based on race and ethnicity, Australia was re-established as a continental nation of Pacific whites. During the same period and for the past two centuries the United States has similarly restricted its immigration admissions to conform to a preferential ethnic and racial group *quota* system favoring Europeans. This has been the official *WASP* (White, Anglo-Saxon Protestant) priority program which has been in practice for centuries.

The first anti-immigrant movement in America began in the mid-1880s and resulted in the Immigration Act of 1924. A revival of this nativist attitude has resurfaced today while the media fuel the fires of public fears that America's cultural diversity spells doom for the prosperity and dominance of whites. What has fueled these fears of white America today? The following appear to be answers: the massive publicizing of so-called "reverse" discriminating effects of "affirmative action" programs, the economic recession of the 1980s and increasing unemployment, the popularity of *Work Force 2000* and its projections of minorities dominating America's workplace in less than a decade, the growing institutional challenges such as public schools being pressured to adopt multicultural educational curricula to accommodate a wide range of new Americans from Third World countries, and the proliferation of incessant reports critical of Japan's domination of the automobile and computer parts manufacturing industries and their investments in United States' real estate.

Finally, the numerous hyperbolic forecasts that *whites* are destined to be America's *minority* group in less than a century seem also to be echoed in the upsurge of vigilante, violent acts by European, neo-Nazi youth gangs against Africans, Asians, Arabs, and people of Caribbean ancestry. In the past few years, while the mass media periodically remind us that the majority Third World population is growing by leaps and bounds, young, white male hate groups have been sprouting up in major cities in Europe and the United States (Marable, 1990).

A common thread in this chain of racial and ethnic aversions is the link of economics. A sense of security, like beauty, may be in the mind of the beholder, yet, manifested notions of insecurity and perceived threats to survival must be addressed. Restructuring of the labor market must attack *un*employment. Positive regard for cultural diversity must be supported by government funds for multicultural education. The mass media system must *consciously* contribute to improved intergroup understanding.

The search for economic security has been a compelling force prompting migrations throughout human existence. It has promoted the cross-fertilization of cultures and peoples. It has figured in the imperialistic exploits of many people on Earth. It has been the avenue for the redistribution of an ever-growing human population occupying limited, habitable land. Jordan and Rowntree (1982) view migration as a key aspect of cultural geography and cultural ecology. This relationship between the physical environment and life styles is a product of environmental adjustment for survival and cultural adaptation that provide for the improvement of the quality of life. Therein lie our challenges *today* and *tomorrow*, for we are all immigrants of sorts.

As Langston Hughes wrote in **Let America Be America Again** (1938),

> O, I'm the man who sailed those early seas
> In search of what I meant to be my home—
> For I'm the one who left dark Ireland's shore,
> And Poland's plain, and England's grassy lea,
> And torn from Black Africa's strand I came
> To build a "homeland of the Free."

(Hughes & Bontemps, 1970, p. 194)

Appendix

Chronology of U. S. Immigration Policy, 1783-1990

1783   George Washington, U. S. President, proclaims that the "bosom of America is open to receive not only the opulent and respectable stranger, but the oppressed and persecuted of all nations and religions, whom we shall welcome to a participation of all our rights and privileges...."

1808   U. S. Constitution outlawed any further importation of Africans into the

Immigration

	U. S. This was the *first* U. S. government act to ban an entire group of people from entering the United States, but the slave trade continued illegally for generations.
1819	U. S. government conducts first count of immigrants in the nation.
1864	U. S. Congress legalizes the importation of contract laborers. First federal immigration restriction prohibits entry of prostitutes and convicts.
1882	The *Chinese* Exclusion Act bars all Chinese from immigrating to the U. S.—the first U. S. law to deny immigration applications based on race or nationality, an effect of the "Yellow Peril". Also excludes convicts, lunatics, idiots, those likely to require public aid, and requires a tax payment per immigrant.
1885	Legislation prohibits admission of contract laborers.
1891	Ellis Island, site of the Statue of Liberty, opened as immigration processing center for the nation.
1903	Excluded immigrants expands to include polygamists and political radicals.
1906	U. S. Naturalization Act makes the English language a requirement for citizenship.
1907	Head tax on each immigrant is increased. <u>Excluded</u> immigrants expands to those with physical or mental defects, and persons with tuberculosis. Restrictions against children unaccompanied by their parents. *Japanese* immigration outlawed, based on a "gentlemen's agreement."
1917	All immigration from Asia is banned.
1921	*U. S. Congress establishes quotas which limit the number of immigrants of each nationality to three (3) percent of the number of foreign-born persons of that nationality living in the United States in 1910.*
1921	U. S. Congress' National Origins Law (Johnson-Reed Act) sets annual quota at two (2) percent of each nationality's U. S. population in 1890. Non-Western Hemisphere countries limited to 150,000 immigrants per year.
1929	Quotas of 1924 permanently set by Congress, but altered to be determined by the 1920 census.
1942	Bilateral agreement with Mexico, British Honduras, Barbados and Jamaica for entry of temporary laborers—the Bracero Program.
1943	U. S. Congress repeals Chinese Exclusion Laws (in effect since 1882).

Challenges of a Changing America

1946   U. S. Congress passes the War Bride Act so U. S. military personnel could bring foreign-born wives to the United States.

1948   *U. S. Congress passes Displaced Persons Act so that 400,000 European refugees could enter the United States.*

1950   Internal Security Act increases grounds for immigrant exclusion and for their deportation.

1952   Immigration and Nationality Act (McCarran-Walter Act) passed by Congress.

- *Reaffirms the 1924 National Origins Quota System of immigration.*
- Limits Eastern Hemisphere nationalities.
- Reaffirms no restrictions from Western Hemisphere.
- Sets preferences for skilled immigrants and relatives of U. S. citizens.
- Increases security, procedures and screening of immigration centers.

1953   Refugee Relief Act of 1953 admits 200,000 refugees outside the quota.

1957   Refugee-Escape Act defines a refugee as an alien fleeing from a communist country or from the Middle East because of persecution or fear of persecution on account of race, religion or political opinion.

1958   Hungarian Refugee Act provided special admissions for permanent residency of Hungarians escaping from the Hungarian revolution.

1960   Cuban refugee program established in reaction to Cuba's revolution.

1964   The Bracero Program is terminated (See 1942, above.) U. S. Congress amends the Immigration and Nationality Act of 1952.

- Abolished the racist national origin quota system which began in 1921.
- Increased Eastern Hemisphere ceiling from 150,000 to 170,000, and set a 120,000 ceiling for Western Hemisphere.

1975   Indo-Chinese (Vietnamese, Laotians, Cambodians) Refugee Resettlement Program began.

1976
- U. S. Congress amends the Immigration and Nationality Act.
- Limits Western Hemisphere immigration to 20,000 per country, emphasizing a seven-category preference system (criteria for admissions)—occupational skills, and so forth.

1978   Worldwide total for immigration to the U. S. set at 290,000 based on the preference system (See 1976, above). U. S. Congress establishes the Select Commission on Immigration and Refugee Policy.

Immigration

1980 The Refugee Act of 1980 establishes criteria and procedures for admission of refugees. Lowers yearly immigration limit to 270,000.

1981 The Reagan Administration issues an Executive Order (EO 12324) to begin an "experimental" program of interdiction on the high seas to stop *Haitians,* seeking asylum, from entering the U. S.

1986 Congress passes the Immigration Reform and Control Act (IRCA). The act offers amnesty to illegal immigrants living in the U.S. prior to 1982, establishes criminal sanctions against the hiring of illegal immigrants, and approves of farm workers in temporary guest programs.

1990
- ◆ Created separate admission categories for family-sponsored, employment-based and "diversity" immigrants.
- ◆ Increased immigration cap to 675,000, effective fiscal year 1995, and to 700,000 during the fiscal years 1992-1994.
- ◆ Established new non-immigration admissions categories.
- ◆ Repealed or revised grounds for exclusion.
- ◆ Authorized the Attorney General to grant temporary protection status to undocumented, alien nationals subject to armed conflict or natural disasters.
- ◆ Made revisions of enforcement activities and authority, and requirements for naturalization.

1996 Illegal Immigration Reform and Responsibility Act: Bars undocumented émigrés from re-entering the U. S. for up to 10 years after their deportation.

Sources:
A Century of Negro Migration. Washington, D.C: The Association for the Study of Negro Life and History, 1918. *Washington Post,* Feb. 2, 1983, p. 3.

Commissioner's Fact Book, Summary of Recent Immigration Data, U. S. Department of Justice, Immigration and Naturalization Service, Statistics Division, July, 1991.

Immigration: Opposing Viewpoints, William Dudley (ed.), Greenhaven Press, 1990.

Report of the Select Commission on Immigration and Refugee Policy, U. S. Congress Committees on Judiciary and U. S. Senate, *U. S. Immigration Policy and the National Interest,* 97th Congress, 1st Session, August, 1981, pp. 88-89.

References

Adams, J. (Ed.). (1987, April). *Background notes—Haiti.* Washington, DC: U.S. Department Of State, Bureau of Public Affairs.

America, R. F. (Ed.). (1990). *The wealth of races: The present value of benefits from past injustices.* Westport, CT: Greenwood Press.

Anders, A. (1989). [Unpublished interview with director of Hispanic services, St. Elizabeth's Hospital, Washington, DC].

Australian Encyclopedia. (1988). Canberra, Australia, pp. 1608-1614.

Bennett, L., Jr. (1982). *Before the Mayflower*. New York: Penguin Books.
Blustein P. (1991, May 3). Japan issues apology for war actions. *Washington Post,* p. A18.
Boorstin, D. J. (1987). *The landmark history of the American people*. New York: Random House.
Chalmers, D. (1965). *Hooded Americanism: The history of the Ku Klux Klan*. Chicago, IL: Quadrangle Paperbacks.
Cruces, M. (1982). *Exiles in search of refuge*. Unpublished report on Cuban refugees at Fort Chaffee, AR.
Daniels, R. (1990). *Coming to America: A history of immigration and ethnicity in American life*. New York: Harper Collins.
Davidson, B. (1989). *The African slave trade*. New York: Little Brown.
Davis, J. J. (1925). *Selective immigration*. St. Paul, MN: Scott Mitchell.
Davis, J. P. (Ed.). (1969). *The American Negro reference book*. Englewood Cliffs, NJ: Prentice-Hall.
Diop, C. A. (1981). *Civilization or barbarism*. New York: Lawrence Hill Books.
Dudley, W. (Ed.). (1990). *Immigration: Opposing viewpoints*. San Diego, CA: Greenhaven Press.
Encyclopedia Americana. (1986). Danbury, CT: Grolier.
Ethiopian Community Development Council, Inc. (1990, September). *Development needs of Ethiopian refugees in the U. S.* Part I: Analysis. (Contract Rep. 233-88-0057). Arlington, VA: Ethiopian Community Development Council.
Fallows, J. (1990). Immigrants do not threaten American culture. In William Dudley (Ed.), *Immigration: Opposing viewpoints*. San Diego, CA: Greenhaven Press.
Faulkner, H. U. (1957). *American political and social history*. New York: Appleton-Century-Crofts.
Gates, D. (1991, Fall-Winter). Who was Columbus? *Newsweek,* pp. 30-31.
Gelman, D. (1991, Fall-Winter). Columbus and his four fateful voyages: When worlds collide. *Newsweek*, pp. 45-46.
Giago, T. (1991, April 13). Dancing with myths. *Washington Post*, pl. A17.
Haitians seem resigned to repatriation (1992, February 3). *Washington Post*, p. A15.
Handlin, 0. (1959). *Immigration as a factor in American history*. Englewood Cliffs, NJ: Prentice-Hall.
Hughes, L. (1970). Let America be America again. In L. Hughes and A. Bontemps (Eds.), *The poetry of the Negro: 1746-1970*. Garden City, NY: Doubleday.
Jet. (1982, February 14). Chicago, IL: Johnson Publishing, p. 55.
Jordan, T., & Rowntree, L. (1983). *Human mosaic*. New York: Harper Collins.
Kamen, A. (1992, February 1). Supreme court clears way for forced return of Haitian boat people. *Washington Post*, p. A3.
Kennedy, J. F. (1964). *A nation of immigrants*. New York: Harper Collins.
Klarreich, K. (1992). Haiti: Reclaiming democracy. *Global Exchange*, p. 5 (San Francisco, CA).
Leibowitz, A. H. (1983, May). The refugee act of 1980: Problems and congressional concerns. In G. D. Loescher and J. A. Scanlan (Eds.), *The global refugee problem: U. S. and world response. The Annals of the American Academy of Political and Social Science, 467.* 164-171.
Marable, M. (1990, November 10). New racism international. *Washington Afro-American*.
Mazrui. A. A. (1986). *The Africans: A triple heritage*. Boston, MA: Little-Brown.

Immigration

Myers, E. R. (1989, June 27). The refugee crisis in the United States. Paper presented at the 22nd Inter-American Congress of Psychology, Buenos Aires, Argentina.

Nichols, T. L. (1990). America should welcome immigration. In William Dudley (Ed.), *Immigration: Opposing viewpoints.* San Diego, CA: Greenhaven Press.

Parker, L. (1991, April 30). Disparate U. S. receptions off Florida: Haitian refugees returned, Cubans are welcomed. *Washington Post*, p. A4.

Passel, J. S., & Woodson, K. A. (1989). Immigration in the United States. Washington, DC: U. S. Bureau of the Census.

Preston, J. (1989, March 30). Haitian refugee stream grows. *Washington Post*, p. A30.

Revive the immigration bill. (1983, January 28). [Editorial]. *Washington Post*, p. A18.

Robinson, L. (1982, March 31). Paper presented at Howard University School of Social Work alumni meeting, Washington, DC.

Settling Haitians in Belize proposed, U. S. official says. (1982, April 3). *Washington Post.*

Smith, R., Levy, E., and Brown, M. (1982). *Faces of America: A history of the United States.* New York: Harper & Row.

Staples, R. (1983). Race and racism in the South Pacific: An exploration of the fourth world. In *The Western Journal of Black Studies, 7(1)*, 2-9.

Steiner, S. (1976). *The vanishing white man.* New York: Harper & Row.

Swinton, D. H. (1991). The economic status of African Americans: "Permanent" poverty and inequality. Unnumbered chapter in *The State of Black America 1991.* New York: National Urban League.

Taft, D. R., & Robbins, R. (1955). *International migrations.* New York: Ronald Press.

Taylor, R. (1989, April 13). Did you know? *The Washington New Observer*, p. 18 (Washington, DC).

Toffler, A. (1980). *The third wave.* New York: William Morrow.

U. S. Congress Committees on Judiciary and U. S. Senate. (1981, August). *Immigration policy and the national interest,* 97th Congress, 1st Session.

U. S. Central Intelligence Agency. (1988). *World fact book.* McLean, VA: U. S. Central Intelligence Agency.

U. S. Department of Justice. (1987). *1987 Statistical yearbook* (Table 1, fiscal years 1820-1987). Washington, DC: Immigration and Naturalization Service, Statistical Division.

U. S. Department of Justice. (1988). *1988 Statistical yearbook* (1820-1988 tables). Washington, DC: Immigration and Naturalization Service, Statistical Division.

U. S. Department of Justice. (1990). *Immigration by country* (1820-1990 tables). Washington, DC: Immigration and Naturalization Service, Statistical Division.

U. S. Department of Justice. (1992). *1992 Statistical data report* (1820-1992 tables). Washington, DC: Immigration and Naturalization Service, Statistical Division.

Urban Institute Report. (1990, December 31). *Washington Post.*

Vialet, J. (1980, December 22). *A brief history of U. S. immigration policy* (Report No. 80-223 EPW). Washington, DC: U. S. Library of Congress, Congressional Research Service, CRS 31-33.

Washington Post. (1982, March 31). Revive the immigration bill. [Editorial], p. A18.

Washington Post. (1982, April 3). Settling Haitians in Belize proposed, U. S. official says.

Washington Post. (1992, February 3). Haitians seem resigned to repatriation, p. A15.

Wood, L., Gabriel, R. H., & Biller, E. L. (1985). *America: Its people and values.* New York: Harcourt-Brace-Jovanovich.

Wood, P. H. (1974). *Black majority*. New York: W. W. Norton.
World Book Encyclopedia 2000 (2000). Chicago, IL: World Book, Inc.
Wright, R., & McManus, D. (1991, December 29). History tomorrow. *Washington Post*, p. C3.
Zinn, H. (1980). *A Peoples history of the United States*. New York: Harper Perennial.
Zucker, N. F. (1983, May). The Haitians versus the United States: The courts as last resort. In G. D. Loescher & J. A. Scanlan (Eds.), *The global refugee problem: U. S. and world response. The Annals of the American Academy of Political and Social Science, 467*. 151-162.

Bibliography

Bell, D. (1991). The elusive quest for racial justice: The chronicle of the constitutional contradiction. Unnumbered chapter in *The state of Black America 1991*. New York: National Urban League.
Burstein, D. (1990). *YEN: Japan's financial empire and its threat to America*. New York: Fawcett Columbine.
Copeland, R. (1983, May). The Cuban boatlift of 1980: Strategies in federal crisis management. In G. D. Loescher and J. A. Scanlan (Eds.), *The global refugee problem: U. S. and world response. The Annals of the American Academy of Political and Social Science, 467*. 138-150.
Ehrlich, P. R. (1978). *The population bomb*. New York: Ballantine.
Henry, W. A. (1990, April 9). Beyond the melting pot. *Time*, p. 30.
Jackson, J. L. (1991, April 9). Presentation at the National Press Club, Washington, DC.
James, G. G. M. (1976). *Stolen legacy*. San Francisco, CA: Julian Richardson.
Johnston, W. B., and Packer, A. E. (1987). *Workforce 2000*. Indianapolis, IN: Hudson Institute.
Kitano, H. L., & Daniels, R. (1988). *Asian Americans: Emerging minorities*. Englewood Cliffs, NJ: Prentice-Hall.
Koslow, D. R., & Salett, E. P. (1989). Crossing cultures in mental health. Washington, D C: SIETAR International.
Lester, J. (1968). *To be a slave*. New York: Scholastic.
Loden, M., & Rosener, J. B. (1991) *Workforce America*. Homewood, IL: Business One Irwin.
McHenry, D. F. (1991). A changing world order: Implications for Black America. Unnumbered chapter in *The state of Black America 1991*. New York: National Urban League.
Myers, E. R. (1977). *The community psychology concept*. Washington, DC: University Press of America.
Myers, E. R. (1981). *Race and culture in the mental health service delivery system*. Washington, DC: University Press of America.
Rowan, C. T., & Mazie, D. (1983, January). Our immigration nightmare. *Readers' Digest*, pp. 87-93.
Sowell, T. (1981). *Ethnic America: A history*. New York: Basic Books.
Velàsquez, R. J. (1982). Predicting psychological adaptation for recent Cuban refugees. [Unpublished research report].
Welsing, F. C. (1991). *The Isis papers*. Chicago, IL: Third World Press.
Weyr, T. (1988). *Hispanic U. S .A.: Breaking the melting pot*. New York: Harper & Row.

Chapter Two

A Fourth World View:
The South Pacific's Parallel to Colonialism in America

Robert Staples

When Black Americans go on vacations or scholarly expeditions, they generally choose Europe, Africa, and the Caribbean. In recent years more of them are going to Latin American and Asian countries. A neglected area of the world has been the South Pacific. With the exception of Hawaii, an American state, few Blacks have a desire to go to or know about the South Pacific region. This area of the world contains a number of Blacks and Polynesians who hold Black Americans in high esteem and who wish greater inter-cultural contacts.

The South Pacific is an arc of islands located on the fringe of Asia. Some anthropologists and archaeologists believe the origin of Homo sapiens was in Africa and that they eventually dispersed into Europe, Asia, the South Pacific, and ultimately the American continents. Due to the necessity to adapt to their physical environment, they lost some of their African characteristics but retained their pigmentation in other tropical or temperate climates. In the South Pacific there was a tripartite racial division: (1) Melanesians, prototypically Black people; (2) Micronesians, island people composed of a racial hybrid of Black and Asian peoples; and (3) Polynesians, a group assumed to be Black in origin but amalgamated with Asian Mongoloids and white Europeans (Mitchell, 1982). As is true of other Blacks throughout the world who would be classified as Black by the American criteria of racial membership, many of the groups have taken on a racial identity that fuses their African heritage.

Whatever their racial origins and contemporary labels, these groups now have an American Black strain in their genetic makeup. Around the middle of the nineteenth century, Black Americans came to the South Pacific as whalers from ports in Rhode Island and Massachusetts. These Black sailors were welcomed by the Pacific Islanders who valued them for their knowledge of Western customs and their skills with munitions. Many of these Black Americans mated with the native women

---

This chapter is a reprinted version of Race and Racism in the South Pacific: An Exploration of the Fourth World by Robert Staples, *The Western Journal of Black Studies* (Pullman, WA: Washington State University Press, Vol. 7, No. 1, 1983). Reprinted with permission of the author and the publisher.

and produced offspring who were assimilated into the Pacific Island community. Unlike the rigid American system of racial classification, the Pacific Islanders accept multiple racial identities without any invidious evaluation. Consequently, those who are partly Black American are no different from Melanesians and Polynesians in physical appearance, dress, manners, language, or self-identification. Hence, they are absorbed and accepted into the South Pacific Island society (McFerson, June 1982).

Probably the greatest influx of Black Americans in the Pacific Islands occurred during World War II. Many were stationed in those islands and mingled without discrimination among the native islanders. As in the nineteenth century, similar behavior resulted. Some met and mated with native women, and the children of such unions were often absorbed into the Pacific Island community. Others, where possible, married and brought the women to the United States. In the white settler nations, Australia and New Zealand, they were not as welcome. During World War II, planes carrying Black soldiers were not permitted to land in Australia. Later, this policy was changed to allow Black soldiers into some northern Australian territories that were war-affected or war-likely areas. However, Black soldiers were confined to the more squalid areas and forbidden to venture into other parts of town. Folklore has it that when Black soldiers attempted to venture beyond their designated areas, white American soldiers lined them up and killed them (B. Sykes, personal correspondence, October 1982).

Among those countries in the South Pacific with a substantial or interesting Black/Polynesian population are Australia, New Zealand, Tahiti, Papua-New Guinea, the Solomons, New Caledonia, Samoa, and the Fiji Islands. Many of these groups identify with the minority status of Black Americans but do not regard themselves as members of the African Diaspora. While they would be defined as Black by American standards, their racial identity is often based on their geographical location, language, hair texture, and religion. Africans, and even some Black Americans, came to that part of the world years ago.

The most prominent country in the area is Australia, a nation of 14 million European immigrants and about 500,000 Blacks who are indigenous to the country. Having just returned from living there six months, this writer can speak from a personal perspective of its value to Black Americans. First, one must deal with this country's image as a racist nation. That image is based on the white Australian immigration policy that existed until 1972. That policy, which forbade citizenship for non-whites, was originally aimed at Asians but was just as strongly applied to Blacks. Since Australia is surrounded by 2.5 billion Asians, they were trying to prevent their smaller numbers from being overwhelmed by the Asian horde. Although few Blacks applied for citizenship, they too were not welcome as citizens, or visitors. Since 1972, the policy has been dropped, and about a third of the immigrants to Australia in the past three years have been Asians.

Because the racist image lingers, the only substantial number of American Blacks who visit the country are soldiers, athletes, entertainers, and a few scholars.

A Fourth World View

As for Australia's racism, presently it is probably no more racist than the United States. Most of Australia's states have laws prohibiting racial discrimination, and there is no official racial segregation and discrimination allowed. However, in certain "redneck" states, such as Queensland and the Northern territory, discrimination or poor treatment may be blatant. Most of their harsh racial practices are reserved for the domestic Blacks known popularly as Aboriginals and Torres Strait Islanders (Department of Aboriginal Affairs, 1981).

Australia is about 8,000 miles from the western coast of the United States. It looks physically very similar to the United States. Although Australia has only about a tenth of this country's population, its land mass is almost as large, with most of its citizenry residing in five large cities. English is the official language.

Generally, American Blacks are treated in a cordial manner by white Australians. In some cases they will be exceedingly friendly. Since there are very few Black Americans who visit this country, they are regarded as an exotic group to be feted with all the hospitality Australia can muster. If one is interested in what is happening with the domestic Black population, one would want to make contact with the Aboriginals. Depending on where one goes in the country, the Aboriginals are not difficult to find. The majority live in the countryside, some on what are called missions or reserves, that is, reservations. Many of them are living in substandard housing, and a few do not have English as their primary language. Still, American Blacks are greeted like long-lost cousins, and they will share whatever they have. This is a culture that is many centuries old. Their music, art, dance, and craft making are renowned for exquisite beauty.

In the cities Aboriginals are not visible although there are certain districts in which large numbers can be found. Many of the government agencies have Aboriginal units, and there are a number of Aboriginal organizations.

The Aboriginals in cities are often more educated, speak English, and represent a variety of physical types. Most will relate to some aspect of Aboriginal culture and will welcome other Blacks into their community. In addition to their political and educational activities, there are a number of social activities given to benefit Aboriginal causes.

Across the Tasmanian Sea from Australia is the island nation of New Zealand. Similar to Australia in many ways, it is a smaller country of 3 million people, most of them British immigrants. The country was originally occupied by a Polynesian group known as Maori (pronounced "marry"). There has been sufficient miscegenation in New Zealand to make racial categories meaningless. However, Maori is officially defined as any person who has 50 percent or more of Maori blood. Maoris consider any person Maori who identifies as one. By the latest unofficial count, there are approximately 300,000 Maoris, about 10 percent of the population. Unlike the Aboriginals, they are an urban, working-class group, more acculturated, have a higher level of education and income, speak English, and are more integrated into New Zealand society (Walsh, 1971).

Even fewer Black Americans visit New Zealand although it has much to offer. There is a growing population of Polynesians in Auckland, Wellington, and Christchurch—mostly Samoans, Cook Islanders, and Fijians. The southern part of the country is breathtakingly beautiful. Auckland, the largest city, is hilly and located between two harbors. Agriculture is the largest source of revenue, and meat and dairy products are plentiful and comparatively inexpensive. Although both Australia and New Zealand were colonized by the British, the British influence is more pronounced in New Zealand. Australians are more friendly, but Maoris have a much better position in New Zealand society than do the Aboriginals in Australia.

The Maoris were not as totally conquered by the white settlers as were the Aboriginals. Maoris are a more aggressive group and were still fighting the British colonialists as late as the mid-nineteenth century. Consequently, they retained more of their land, culture, and language. In the past decade New Zealand has used urbanization as a major agent of assimilation. Rural Maori land has been underdeveloped, and Maoris were enticed into urban areas where housing and other facilities are available (Wood, 1978).

Despite their war-like nature, Maoris are a hospitable people. A "Marae" visit is necessary to understand Maori culture. The "Marae" is the focal point of Maori culture. It is usually a grassed area with community buildings of which the meeting house is the most important in a Maori settlement. All important gatherings are held on the Marae; there one hears Maori spoken, and Maori social forms are followed. The Maori women are beautiful, the food delicious, and the arts and cultural life enhancing.

Other predominantly Black countries exist in the South Pacific. The Fiji Islands, Samoa, and Tahiti are small islands that are developing their tourist trade. Only in American Samoa is English extensively spoken. Papua-New Guinea is a predominantly Black country that is larger than the others (roughly 3 million inhabitants). Formerly a colony of Australia, it is a country of many tribes and more than 700 languages. Once outside the larger cities, travel can be rough because of limited roads, but plane travel is plentiful and convenient. Little English is spoken. Its customs are so unique that it has been a favorite haunt of anthropologists.

On the way to these South Pacific countries, the favorite stopover is Hawaii. Although Hawaii attained American statehood in 1959, it still retains much of its Polynesian culture. The native Polynesians are presently a numerical minority although increasing attention is being paid to preservation of their culture. As a result of the white invasion and the importation of other Asians to work in the pineapple and cane fields, their numbers have been reduced to 17.6 percent of the population today. Most of the fertile land was taken from them, and they were forced into rental housing provided by white plantation owners. Moreover, they were disproportionately represented at the bottom of the socio-economic strata, constituting 40 percent of the welfare recipients and scoring the lowest on the statewide educational tests (Curtis, 1982).

A Fourth World View

Although tourists do not realize it, there is a contingent of mainland Blacks living in Hawaii. Mainly, they are military personnel, government workers, and professionals such as physicians, lawyers, professors, and social workers. There is no Black working class. While they represent less than one percent of Hawaii's population, there are Black organizations such as the National Association for the Advancement of Colored People, and in the early 1980s, the superintendent of schools for the state was a Black woman. Hawaii is one of the few American states that has an excess of Black men vis-a-vis Black women.

Although known as an exotic land with a tropical climate and beautiful beaches, Hawaii is a classic case of white settlement and dominance. The native population has witnessed the subordination of its people to a servant class, its numbers decimated by the Euro-American's venereal diseases, liquor, and firearms. As a result of the partial destruction of native Polynesian culture, they have become a minority in their own land (like the native Americans on the mainland). What cultural styles remain have been put on display for the hordes of tourists that have corrupted and polluted this beautiful land. Most wealth of any significance is controlled by whites while the Japanese dominate the government, and the Chinese are the small businessmen.

Other native peoples in the South Pacific suffered similar or worse consequences as a result of their contact with people of European ancestry. Probably the poorest victims of European contact were the Aboriginals of Australia. These Black people had existed on the Australian continent for many centuries before Britain decided to use this beautiful land as a dumping ground for its criminal class. The Europeans brought with them diseases, liquor, and firearms which effectively decimated the Aboriginal population—as was the case in Hawaii. Aboriginals were removed from their hunting grounds and placed on reservations (like the natives in America); the women were raped or turned into concubines of Europeans; children were taken from their families and placed in foster homes; many in the group were shot at like wild animals. After the total subjugation of the Aboriginal population almost two centuries ago, Australia enjoyed the highest standard of living in the world after the United States, Canada, and New Zealand (Brumby, 1982).

While the Anglo-Saxons progressed from penal colony inmates to the most affluent residents of the South Pacific in less than 200 years, the Aboriginals were reduced to less than one percent of Australia's population and one of the most downtrodden minority groups in the world. They have a life expectancy of less than 50 years compared with more than 70 years for whites; a higher infant mortality rate; and a higher incidence of diseases, particularly eye infections and alcoholism. Few progress beyond the sixth grade in the public schools; less than 200 graduate from college each year. A recent report reveals that only six Aboriginals are lawyers, and they have no doctors or dentists. Many families live in shacks on river banks. Their unemployment rate is six times (37 percent) that in the general work force and ranges as high as 90 percent in some towns. They are 13 times more likely to be in prison than whites (World Council of Churches, 1981).

As a group, aboriginals are a racial anomaly. There is a great deal of uncertainty about their racial origins and even their current identity. Some anthropologists have classified them separately as Australoids. Others have defined them as archaic Caucasoids, and some as Mongoloids. They may be the only group regarded as belonging to all three major racial groups. Conventional scholarship in Australia views them as descendants of the Southeast Asia region. Whatever the case, they physically have Negroid traits, except for curly hair; and white Australians regard them as Blacks, with all the disadvantages and social deprivations attached thereto. Until 1972, for administrative and divide-and-conquer purposes, Aboriginals were classified by their quotient of European ancestry: full-bloods, half-caste, one-fourth caste. In some states anyone other than a full-blooded Aboriginal was classified as white. Only if an Aboriginal was fair enough to pass as European and willing to forsake his kinsmen, was the legal definition as white meaningful. Today any person who identifies as an Aboriginal is accepted in that community (Stevens, 1978).

A Personal Odyssey in the Fourth World

These observations are based on a half-year, sociological expedition in the South Pacific where the author, as a Visiting Fellow in the Institute of Family Studies in Australia, engaged in extensive travel in Australia and New Zealand and mingled with the Aboriginals and the Maori people. A compelling conclusion from this experience was how similar the struggles of American Blacks, Maoris, and Aboriginals had become, partly because the Australian and New Zealand governments, following the lead of the United States, had responded to our cultural awakening and political protests in similar fashions: handing out the carrot while carrying a big stick.

The critical issue in this analysis is the experience of non-whites in white settler societies. The concept of the Fourth World is not new. Earlier, George Manuel (1974) had written a book by the same name, referring only to indigenous people living in First World nations under Third World conditions. The writer's concept is similar except that it includes Black Americans and possibly other non-white groups not indigenous to the South Pacific. Using the Fourth World concept in this way contravenes the conventional wisdom in oppressed minority communities. Black Americans, for instance, have generally identified and aligned themselves with Africa and the Third World. The writer's feeling is that they have more in common with Aboriginals and Maoris in terms of the future issues they must confront. However oppressed and economically dependent, Third World nations have become more autonomous than non-white minorities in First World nations. Moreover, contemporary rhetoric notwithstanding, there is the critical question of how non-white minorities are to obtain full self-determination in societies where whites hold all the political and economic power. This question is particularly critical when even the whites in those societies are governed by a ruling, capitalistic elite.

A Fourth World View

This conception of the Fourth World is based on an analysis of the current world situation. It appears that the fate of non-white minorities will be determined by what happens in their host countries, not their ancestral homelands. A certain amount of progress in race relations in the United States was made because of this country's concern with its image in Third World countries. However, it seems to have reached a point of diminishing returns. Future progress may depend on the active struggles of Third World groups' domestic political strategies and concerns and the internal economic situation. Although it is contrary to some of the contemporary rhetoric of Third World groups, there has to be some kind of alliance between non-white minorities and segments of the white majority in order to obtain any significant gains past a certain point. Hence, the writer's conception of the Fourth World is based on these fundamental facts.

Without considering the case of South Africa, which contains the possibility of autonomy for the Black majority, the Fourth World is similar in many ways. All of their inhabitants are victims of a system of internal colonialism, which means that: (1) they are not in the social system voluntarily, but have it imposed on them; (2) their native culture is modified or destroyed; (3) control is in the hands of people outside their community; and (4) racism prevails, that is, a group seen as different or inferior in terms of alleged biological traits is exploited, controlled, and oppressed socially and psychologically by a group that defines itself as superior (Manuel 1974; Whitaker 1972).

Internal colonialism manifests itself in the unequal life chances of non-white minorities. Compared with class privileges, whites maintain racial privileges in racially stratified societies. Black Americans, Aboriginals, and Maoris are similar in the unequal status they hold based on the sociodynamics of racism. All three groups have lower levels of education, higher rates of unemployment, and lower incomes than the white majorities. Even when class is considered, they are more likely to be arrested and imprisoned than whites. More important are the consequences of internal colonialism for the internal functioning of the minority communities. Higher rates of homicide and lower life expectancy rates due to poorer health conditions tend to decimate the able-bodied young men in these groups. As a result, women have a much stronger position in the Fourth World. One natural consequence of the castration of men has been the destruction or unavailability of monogamous families for the women and an unequal share of the group's burden.

The salient issues that face Fourth World groups are internal divisions within their own communities. A divide-and-conquer strategy of the ruling elites exploits differences within Fourth World groups. It is instructive to note the division between grassroots and the bourgeoisie among all three groups. Among Aboriginals the division is even extended to tribal Aboriginals and those of mixed ancestry. Another variation of the above strategy is to pit them against other minorities. In the United States it is Blacks versus other minority groups. Australia will eventually pit Aboriginals against the new Asian migrants, and New Zealand already has exacerbated the conflict between Maoris and other Pacific Islanders.

Meanwhile, as Aboriginals and Maoris will belatedly find out, economic recessions tend to bring out racial tensions that remain latent in more prosperous times. Already there is the manifestation of a new kind of racism in Australia and New Zealand, a racism which has reached its apex in the United States. Increasingly, whites speak out against the special treatment and benefits accorded non-white minorities under the guise of a color-blind meritocracy. Such a philosophy is a thinly veiled attempt to stabilize present racial inequalities and roll back the meager gains of the 1970s. Minorities who seek self-determination and group solidarity are subject to charges of racial separatism and reverse racism.

Probably the greatest danger to the Fourth World groups is the issue of assimilation. This issue is particularly crucial for groups small in number such as the Maoris and Aboriginals. A pertinent issue that must be addressed is how much of an oppressed minority's culture can be maintained in the face of strong pressure to take on Anglo-Saxon lifestyles, values, and culture. However, this pressure or invitation to assimilate is generally applied to only a minority within a minority. Can these pressures be resisted when the consequences are continued isolation and the denial of the benefits of an affluent society?

Whatever the answer, these questions are at hand. In pursuit of strategies and goals of liberation, that old Biblical saying, "For the last shall be first, the first last," should be remembered.

References

Australian Council of Churches. (1981). *Justice for Aboriginal Australians*. (Report of the World Council of Churches). Sydney, Australia: Australian Council of Churches.

Brumby, J. (1982, June 14). *Wealth is passing Australia by*. Sydney, Australia: The Age.

Curtis, E. (1982, November 18). *Another view*. San Francisco, CA: The Sun Reporter.

Department of Aboriginal Affairs. (1981). *Aboriginals in Australia today*. Canberra, Australia: Australian Government Publishing Service.

Manuel G. (1974). *The fourth world*. New York: McMillan.

Mcferson, H. M. (1982, June). Part-Black Americans in the South Pacific. Atlanta University: *Phylon*, 177-180.

Mitchell, L. K. (1982, Autumn). Lost Black queens. San Francisco: *Black Male/Female Relationships*, 4-46.

Stevens, F. (1978). *Racism: The Australian experience*. Sydney, Australia: Australia and New Zealand Book Company.

Walsh, A. C. (1971). *More and more Maoris: An illustrated statistical survey of the Maori today*. New Zealand: Whitcombe and Tombs, Ltd.

Whitaker, B. (1972). *The fourth world: Victims of group oppression*. London, UK: Sidgwick & Jackson.

Wood, G. A. (1978). Race and politics in New Zealand. In Stephen Levine (Ed.), *Politics in New Zealand*. New Zealand: Allen & Unwin.

Part Two

African Americans: Contemporary Issues

I have no protection at home, or resting place abroad . . . .
I am an outcast from the society of my childhood, and an
outlaw in the land of my birth.
I am a stranger with thee, and a sojourner as all my fathers were.
—Frederick Douglass

America was built by a nation of strangers. From a hundred different places they have poured forth into an empty land, joining and blending in one mighty and irresistible tide. The land flourished because it was fed from so many sources—because it was nourished by so many cultures and traditions and people.

Lyndon B. Johnson, October 3, 1965
—Gov. Richard D. Lamm,
The Immigration Time Bomb
(New York: E. P. Dutton, 1985)

Chapter Three

Who Are the African Americans?

Yosef Ford

No group of people is less understood in a world of cultural ambiguities than the descendants of the African slave trade. Variously called *Negro*, *Colored*, *Afro-American*, and so on, none of these labels has been a comprehensive force for self-esteem or an identity badge of empowerment. Instead, these designations have served to stigmatize and isolate, making them unfavorable parts of other labels. Indeed, the most illusive fact is that these identities have served to quarantine Black people in America as though they were a contaminated group, to be avoided at almost all costs. Even more pernicious is the effort to discourage communication between Black people in America and Black people in Africa. In spite of their common heritage, each is told that time, distance, and culture—as the circumstances of history would have it—have forced them apart, that is, each belongs to different worlds. At critical stages of their respective histories, each identifies the other, perversely, based on all those identifications and roles which are polarizing or divisive. Nowhere is this identity assassination perpetuated more effectively than through the mass media. Thus, each, the African and the African American, is forced to relate to the other only in terms of the negative stereotypes each has of the other.

Better than any previous measuring index, the Jesse Jackson presidential campaigns revealed the presence of a self-identified, political entity—not one of a "Black" constituency, but one based on the affirmation of the prerogatives of a transcendental African-American agenda. It was not merely the often quoted "blind allegiance" of Blacks to the Democratic Party, but a vote of confidence for the empowerment of a self-defined constituency to implement its own agenda, not have it done for them—working with others, not working for others.

Identities and labels are not synonymous terms. A *label* is something that is superimposed from the outside, independent of a person's definition of self. One's *identity* is an assured sense of inner continuity and social sameness which will

---

This chapter is reprinted with permission from *AFRICA-USA*, (Hyattsville, MD), Vol. 1, No. 5, May, 1989.

bridge the gap between what one has experienced in a given socio-cultural and political context and what one is becoming. Identity reconciles one's perception of one's self with his or her community identity. It goes beyond a recognition of individual achievement. The final identity, then, as fixed at the end of a common experience, is superior to any single identification with individuals of the past and present—a Martin Luther King; a Marcus Garvey; a famous actor, lawyer, or doctor; as well as the disenfranchised single mother in the inner city, the young victim of drought in Africa, the detained children in South Africa, or the unemployed black male on the street corner. Thus, all significant identifications are integrated to make a unique and reasonably coherent whole. African Americans are more than just Black. They are in fact Ashanti, Ga, Mandinka, Yoruba, Mende, Talensi, and hundreds more (all from Africa), merged into a unique whole, gained through a painfully unique experience and history. Indeed, African Americans have equal and unique roles in the territorial and cultural boundaries in which they find themselves today.

In addition to fear, ignorance, and bigotry, part of the problem that makes all of this and the African-American classification an identity difficult to understand lies in the prevailing perception of society in terms of the "cookie cutter concept of culture." This concept continues to view *minorities* as an isolated, autonomous whole in a pluralistic society. Far more critical, however, is the assumption that pluralism implies equal distribution of decision-making power between the majority and the minority groups, or for that matter, among the minority groups themselves. Even in this instance, the use of the term *minority*, though valid for demographic purposes, tends to reduce groups to *pariah* status.

Unfortunately, it is precisely these labels that form the foundation upon which America's domestic social policies are made with respect to all peoples of diverse ethnic groups and cultural orientations. The defining of *minority* groups rationalizes the design of strategies for inclusion with regard to access to resources. The ambiguities contained in these definitions, however, send mixed signals, both in terms of the group name and/or the political and economic position a group occupies relative to other groups. Thus, when policies for social change are called for to satisfy a specific group's needs, the agenda is at the same time designed not to alter the existing power relationships between groups. This is most evident when groups are designated in *racial* rather than *ethnic* terms, both of which are amorphous and imprecise categories, useful only to the initiators of the agenda. The tendency is to identify these groups by name or place, as if they were closed systems, operating in a vacuum, with others having to impact them, or vice versa. In this setting, change, if it occurs, is cosmetic, providing the illusion that there is an actual shift in the power relationships. An illustration of this is the setting up of "independent tribal homelands" found under the system of apartheid in South Africa.

Therefore, the African-American designation is a positive identity that challenges the pronouncements of Western social and political sciences. By unilaterally defining the societal structure, these "sciences" determine the bases upon which the designs of social policies play major roles in the making or unmaking of identities and the nature of inter-group relations. As a discipline, Western social science emerged not to study social differences, but social deviations. Asking the question why certain peoples are so insistent upon maintaining their discrete sense of self with symbolic forms of cultural differences, is rarely, but rightly, raised.

The mission behind the Crusades, according to the ethno-historian Jennings (1975), was not to save the Holy Lands for Christianity. Jennings noted that the Christians were not only holy, but also civilized, while the dark pigmented people were "heathens, idolatrous and savage." This rationalization assured that the absolutes of predator and prey were preserved in order to justify the invasion and massacre of people of color. The papal bull *Intera Caetera* of 1493 used the Christian continuum as a unifying force among the feuding rulers of Europe, thus granting them all the world not already conquered by Christian states. The abandoned *heathens* could then be converted to the Catholic Faith. Religious beliefs, therefore, served the pragmatic purposes of the colonialists who enslaved Africans and who scourged the indigenous peoples—identified as "Indians" or "Red Skins"—as satanic agents without human virtue (p. 5).

The Reverend Jesse Jackson's reasoning that "African American" contains a cultural integrity and historical accuracy is not a refutation of the term *black*, but an attempt to place into proper context the particular cultural history of a particular people in a specific part of the world and in a particular nation-state. The discovery of black identity is to equate the African American with himself; the definition of *black* equates him with all men. Thus, African Americans are *black* in the universal sense, and *African American* in a clearly identifiable political sense. The term *black* distinguishes the African in a global, socio-political sense; and while it includes the difference between a Nigerian and an Englishman, a Haitian and a Frenchman, an Italian and an Ethiopian, it does not distinguish a Nigerian from a Kenyan, nor an African American from an African Brazilian or an African Jamaican. Today, a Nigerian, an Ethiopian, a Ghanaian, and an African American are *all Black people*, but with identities bound by particular national contexts and guided by politico-cultural agenda.

The legitimacy of the black identity emerges out of the common global experiences of suffering in the form of colonialism and servitude—ranging from chattel slavery on plantations of the Americas to its modern form in the mines of South Africa. At its peak in the late 1960s and early 1970s, the cry for *Black Power* was heard not only in the United States but around the globe. The cry came from such diverse and far-flung groups as the Aboriginal population in Australia; the Maoris of New Zealand; native peoples from the slums of Bahia in Brazil, with the largest group of African descendants in the Western Hemisphere; and North African migrant laborers in Europe, just to name a few. Even Palestinians and native Hawaiians had *Black Power* movements.

It is not at all by coincidence that in celebration of Black History Month the

Reverend Jackson should find himself fulfilling Carter G. Woodson's admonitions—to know one's *self*, one must know how and by what and by whom the world is shaped. It is worthy to note that Carter G. Woodson, who is responsible for the celebration of Black History Month, used the term *black* to include African history as well as the history of the American Negro. Even as he used the word *Negro*, his was a dedication toward the search for a more comprehensive definition. In his classic text *Mis-education of the Negro*, published in 1933, this was the legacy he bequeathed to those who were to come after him (Woodson, 1933). Caught in such a world, for generations of people of African descent, identity has been a contradiction, as noted by W. E. B. DuBois, of being in two worlds, and being in two worlds requires two *selves* in an effort to affirm oneself (Wilson, 1976). Paradoxically, the denial of either *self* results in an incomplete identity. One *self*, seeking acceptance or wanting to belong to the dominant world, undergoes cosmetic surgery, skin bleaching, pigmented contact lens, hair straightening, and so on. The other *self* belongs to an African-American world which is degraded and humiliated. Here again, to find positive identity, there is Africa to which one must go back and rediscover the *African selfhood*—not in a desperate search for lost "roots," like those which Hollywood finds marketable, but in an attempt to discover living traditions and values. The solution to this dissonance for people of African descent is universal identity with the motherland—AFRICA, the *land of origin* for all mankind, as the scientific world of anthropologists and genetic analysts have concluded (Rensberger, June, 1987). The true identity of the African American is therefore a reality of the global African Diaspora.

References

Jennings, F. (1975). *The invasion of America: Indians, colonialism and the cant of conquest.* Chapel Hill, NC: University of North Carolina Press.

Rensberger, B. (1987, June). All family trees lead to Eve, an African, scientists conclude. *Washington Post.*

Wilson, W. (Ed.). (1970). *The selected writings of W. E. B. DuBois.* New York: New American Library.

Woodson, C. G. (1933). *The mis-education of the Negro.* Washington, DC: Associated Publishers.

Chapter Four
Psychology and African Americans

Courtland C. Lee

The last several decades have seen African Americans make considerable social and economic advances. Indeed, gains made by African Americans have initiated movements for social justice and equality by groups as diverse as women, the elderly, and the physically disabled. Despite advances, however, the traditions of oppression and racism that have characterized much of the African American experience still exert profound negative pressure on the lives of many Black people. Recent demographic data (American Council on Education, 1988; Children's Defense Fund, 1988; Cordes, 1984, 1985; U.S. Bureau of the Census, 1986; U.S. Department of Labor, 1986) suggest a serious stifling of human potential in many Black communities and underscore the fact that there are serious challenges to African-American development. This brings into question how pervasive these recent social gains for African Americans have actually been.

The challenges which confront African Americans are linked in an inextricable fashion. There is no doubt that continued economic disadvantage and social discrimination are the ultimate sources of the psychosocial challenges facing African Americans. On the threshold of a new century, many African Americans still find themselves in the backwaters of career, educational, and social progress.

The contemporary psychologist, therefore, is faced with important challenges in attempting to successfully intervene in the lives of African Americans. This article offers new perspectives on African-American psychology. In addition, the article provides direction on how psychologists can be a part of the resolution of the challenges facing African Americans in the 21st Century.

This chapter is reprinted by permission of the author and publisher. This article first appeared in *The Journal of Training & Practice in Professional Psychology*, Vol. 4, No. 1, Spring, 1990.

Psychosocial Perspective on Major Contemporary Issues Impacting African-American Mental Health

Psychological well-being has been problematic for African Americans due to social forces such as racism and chronic economic disadvantage that have impacted negatively their personal and social development (Comer, 1969; Gary & Jones, 1978; King, 1980; Willie, Kramer, & Brown, 1973). African Americans, by and large, have experienced considerable frustration in their person-environment transactions with American society. The historic difficulties inherent in the restricted and often extreme conditions facing large segments of the African-American population have undermined self-esteem disrupted social relationships, caused frustration, and contributed to high levels of stress. Such difficulties have generally led to the development of maladaptive and self-destructive behavior patterns.

In recent years such behavior patterns have become increasingly evident in substance abuse among large segments of the African-American population (Clifford & Rene, 1986; Watts & Wright, 1988); in violence committed by Black males upon Black males (Cordes, 1985); and in ever-increasing rates of pregnancy among Black adolescents (Children's Defense Fund, 1988). Such phenomena have reached crisis proportions in many African-American communities. The psychological effects of such maladaptive behaviors are devastating, many times leading to a sense of intra- and interpersonal inadequacy among African Americans.

The Role of Psychologists in African-American Problem Resolution

For many years a call has gone forth to psychologists to promote personal and social development among African Americans (Gary & Jones, 1978; King, 1980; Pierce, 1980; Thomas & Comer, 1973). The main thrust of this call has been the idea that promoting personal and social development rests on the ability of African Americans to use resources to effectively combat the debilitating effects of negative environmental forces (Myers, 1973). Within this context the goal of psychologists involves helping African-American clients develop functional environmental coping behaviors that lead to personal adjustment and optimal mental health. The operational therapeutic objective should be to assist African-American clients achieve personal empowerment for environmental mastery and competence.

Psychological service delivery to African Americans, therefore, requires not only an understanding of the theoretical and practical traditions of psychology, but an appreciation of the dynamics of African-American culture. For within African-American culture lie indigenous models of helping and mental health.

African-American Culture: The Key to Black Mental Health

Any discipline that would seek to understand the dynamics of African-American behavior must take into account the experiences which shape its development. Psychotherapeutic intervention for African Americans, therefore, must be predicated on an understanding of African-American culture and its crucial role in fostering optimal mental health. African-American psychologists, attempting to establish theoretical notions of a Black psychology, have concluded that there are aspects of the African-American cultural experience that have evolved out of African tradition which have a significant relationship with Black mental health (Cross, 1974; Guthrie, 1980; Nobles, 1980; Pasteur & Toldson, 1982; White, 1970). The conclusions have led to the development of a conceptual framework for understanding African-American psychology.

An examination of core African-American culture (that is, those attitudes, values and behaviors which have developed in relatively homogeneous Black communities where rudimentary Afrocentric ways of life have been preserved in relatively large measure) will reveal that Americans of African descent have developed a world view that is grounded in an experience that has evolved out of African-oriented, philosophical assumptions. These assumptions constitute a cultural tradition that places a high premium on harmony among people and their internal and external environments, fosters self and group development through behavioral expressiveness, and recognizes the need for holistic development (Nobles, 1972).

Given this, psychologists need to find ways to incorporate African-American cultural dimensions into the therapeutic process. Culture-specific approaches to psychological intervention transform basic aspects of African-American life, generally ignored or perceived as negative in a European-American psychological framework, into positive developmental experiences.

Psychotherapeutic Approaches for African Americans

The Pitfalls of a Monolithic Perspective

Before examining notions of psychological intervention for African-American clients, it is necessary to consider a critical issue that must be understood if effective therapeutic intervention is to take place. In discussing the whole concept of African-

American psychology, there is a danger of assuming that all Black people are the same and that one methodological approach is universally applicable in any therapeutic intervention with them. Indeed, if one reviews much of the psychological literature related to African-American issues, one might be left with the impression that there is an all-encompassing Black reality and that all Americans of African descent act, feel, and think in a homogeneous fashion. Such an impression invariably leads to a monolithic perspective on the Black experience in America as well as stereotypic thinking in which African Americans are considered indistinguishable from one another in terms of attitudes, behaviors and values. Psychologists possessing such a perspective run the risk of approaching African-American clients not as distinctive human beings with individual experiences, but rather merely as stereotypes.

African Americans differ from one another in terms of experiences, as do all people. Each Black person is a unique individual who is the sum total of his or her common human experiences, specific cultural experiences, and personal life experiences. Indeed, it has been asserted that attempting to identify common experiences among African Americans is a precarious enterprise because they are not a homogeneous group (Dillard, 1983). Blackwell (1975) suggests that the African-American community is a complex entity whose strength emanates from its diverse nature. Psychotherapeutic approaches with Black individuals, therefore, must incorporate the notion that there is a high degree of intra-group variability among African Americans and that interventions must be client- and situation-specific.

Significantly, within the body of theoretical knowledge on Black psychology and mental health can be found important ideas which suggest that there is significant intra-group variability among African Americans. This knowledge base focuses on the concept of Black identity formation and the possibility that Blacks go through a series of stages in their efforts to establish stable personalities within American society (Cross, 1971).

This notion of stages in Black identity formation has led to the emergence of a body of empirical evidence which suggests that variation in Black attitudes toward racial identity may have an effect on therapeutic process and outcome (Helms, 1986; Parham & Helms, 1981; Pomales, Claiborn, & LaFromboise, 1986). If such variation has been suggested, then it is incumbent upon psychologists to approach intervention with Black clients in an individualistic as opposed to a monolithic manner.

Psychotherapeutic Direction

African-American psychologists in recent years have suggested that the discipline take new directions in its efforts to help Black clients empower themselves. These new directions include modalities that incorporate elements of the immediate environment, raise consciousness, and focus on group solidarity to promote active change (Gordon & Jones, 1978; Pierce, 1980). Modalities such as these should focus on enhancing positive African-American lifestyles and behaviors.

When psychologists seek to incorporate elements of the immediate environment into the Black empowerment process, they must facilitate the development of family and community therapeutic resources. Importantly, Nobles (1972) has stressed the importance of the African philosophical notion of kinship or collective unity as being an important foundation for African-American psychology and mental health intervention. Undoubtedly, the Black family is the most important resource that psychologists can tap into to promote psychotherapeutic effectiveness. In spite of all the challenges to its integrity, the family is the bedrock of African-American psychosocial well-being (Billingsley, 1968; Hill, 1971). Family intervention therefore should be considered as a major therapeutic modality for fostering personal empowerment.

Programmed family intervention must provide for the inclusion of significant others and the inherent strength of kinship social support processes, where appropriate, as an integral part of psychotherapeutic intervention. In helping Black clients become proactive, as opposed to reactive, in their environmental interactions, therapeutic interventions should be conducted whenever appropriate within the context of the family unit. Whenever possible, psychological services should be offered in a supportive family group format where members can draw on each others' strengths for problem resolution. Psychologists can use the strengths of Black families as a powerful force in modifying maladaptive and self-destructive behavior patterns.

In addition to the family, the Black community offers other institutions that provide a network of social support that can be incorporated into the psychotherapeutic process. The church, for example, has long been a bastion of group solidarity and an institution devoted to raising not only levels of Black spirituality, but also African-American consciousness. The Black church has been the traditional source looked to for psychological well-being by many African Americans (Gordon & Jones, 1978). As appropriate and effective, psychotherapeutic approaches should incorporate aspects of the multifaceted African-American religious experience in remediating the effects of negative environmental press as well as preventing maladaptive behavior patterns from forming.

Likewise, other social support entities within the Black community can be called into psychological service. Psychologists should find ways to coordinate paraprofessional development efforts to involve selected community members in counseling service delivery. This is of particular importance when psychologists do not share the world view or cultural reality of African-American clients. These paraprofessionals should be sensitive caring individuals who share the cultural perspective of clients. Such individuals can form a constructive part of the social network in the Black community and can be vital to the psychotherapeutic process.

Psychological practice for promoting optimal mental health among Black people must draw its strength from the collective unity of African-American communities. Psychologists working to promote environmental mastery skills and discourage self-destructive behavior among Black clients must cultivate the supportive social network and indigenous helping modalities inherent in the Black family and community. Psychotherapeutic interventions aimed at advancing personal adjustment and optimal mental health can be effective if psychological practice is conceptualized as a collective African-American enterprise.

Conclusion

As the African-American experience moves into the 21st Century and continues to be confronted with profound issues that impact mental health and well-being, a new perspective on psychology and psychological intervention with Black people is needed. Psychological services must be delivered with the knowledge that African-American culture fosters attitudes, behaviors, and values that are psychologically healthy and that within this culture are the resources for addressing mental health challenges and problems. Psychotherapeutic interventions therefore must be undertaken from the African-American cultural perspective that focuses on promoting optimal mental health and well-being. Psychologists must facilitate the development of Black environmental mastery skills that promote African/African-American notions of kinship, behavioral and emotional expressiveness, and holistic development. Such skills can serve as preventive measures against the development of maladaptive and self-destructive behavior patterns observed in ever-increasing segments of African-American communities.

The new decade must see the rise of a new psychology professional, one who is armed with a solid African-American knowledge base to meet the mental health challenges of Black people. The continued survival and development of African Americans demand no less.

References

American Council on Education. (1988). *Minorities in higher education*. Washington, DC: American Council on Education.
Billingsley, A. (1968). *Black families in White America*. Englewood Cliffs, NJ: Prentice Hall.
Blackwell, J. E. (1975). *The Black community: Diversity and unity*. New York: Dodd, Mead.
Children's Defense Fund. (1988). *The health of America's Black children*. Washington, DC: The Children's Defense Fund.
Clifford, P. R., & Rene, A. A.(1986). Substance abuse among Blacks: An epidemiological perspective. *Urban League Review, 9*, 52-58.
Comer, J. P. (1969). White racism: Its root, form and function. *American Journal of Psychiatry, 126*, 802-806.

Cordes, C. (1984, August). The rise of one parent Black families. *APA Monitor*, pp. 16-18.
Cordes, C. (1985, January). Black males face high odds in a hostile society. *APA Monitor*, pp. 9-11, 27.
Cross, A. (1974). The Black experience: Its importance in the treatment of Black clients. *Child Welfare, 52*, 158-166.
Cross, W. E. (1971). The Negro-to-Black conversion experience. *Black World, 20*, 12-27.
Dillard, (1983). *Multicultural counseling: Toward ethnic and cultural relevance in human encounters*. Chicago, IL: Nelson-Hall.
Gary, L. E., & Jones, D. J. (1978). Mental health: A conceptual overview. In L. E. Gary (Ed.), *Mental health: A challenge to the Black community*. Philadelphia, PA: Dorrance & Co.
Gordon, T. A., & Jones, N. L. (1978). Function of the social network in the Black community. In L. E. Gary (Ed.), *Mental health: A challenge to the Black community*. Philadelphia, PA: Dorrance & Co.
Guthrie, R. V. (1980). The psychology of Black Americans: An historical perspective. In R. L. Jones (Ed.), *Black psychology (Second Edition)*. New York: Harper & Row.
Helms, J. E. (1986). Expanding racial identity theory to cover counseling process. *Journal of Counseling Psychology, 33*, 62-64.
Hill, R. (1971). *The strengths of Black families*. New York: Emerson Hall.
King, L. M. (1980). Models of meaning in mental health: Model eight: The transformation of the oppressed. *Fanon Center Journal, 1*, 29-50.
Myers, E. R. (1973). Implications of the emerging discipline of community psychology for Black social workers. In *Nation building time: Proceedings of the 5th annual conference of NABSW*.
Nobles, W. (1972). African philosophy: Foundation for a Black psychology.
R. L. Jones (Ed.), *Black psychology*. New York: Harper & Row.
Parham, T. A., & Helms, J. E. (1981). The influence of Black students' racial identity attitudes on preferences for counselor's race. *Journal of Counseling Psychology, 28*, 250-257.
Pasteur, A. B., & Toldson, I. L. (1982). *Roots of soul: The psychology of Black expressiveness*. Garden City, NY: Anchor Press/Doubleday.
Pierce, W. D. (1980). The comprehensive community mental health programs and the Black community. In R. L. Jones (Ed.), *Black psychology (Second edition)*. New York: Harper & Row.
Pomales, J., Claiborn, C. D., & LaFromboise, T. D. (1986). Effects of Black students' racial identity on perceptions of White counselors varying in cultural sensitivity. *Journal of Counseling Psychology, 33*, 57-61.
Thomas, C. S., & Comer, J. P. (1973). Racism and mental health services. In C. Willie, B. Kramer, & B. Brown (Eds.). *Racism and mental health*. Pittsburgh, PA: University of Pittsburgh Press.
U. S. Bureau of the Census. (1986). *Money income of households, families, and persons in the U. S.: 1984* (Series P-60, No. 151). Washington, DC: U. S. Government Printing Office.
U. S. Department of Labor. (1986). *Geographic profile of employment and unemployment, 1985,* Table 12. Washington, DC: Bureau of Labor Statistics.
Watts, T. D., & Wright, R. (1988). Black alcoholism. *Journal of Alcohol and Drug Education, 33.* 76-80.
White, J.L. (1970). Toward a Black psychology. *Ebony, pp. 25,* 44-45, 48-50, 52.
Willie, C., Kramer, B., & Brown, B. (Eds.). (1973). *Racism and mental health*. Pittsburgh, PA: University of Pittsburgh Press.

Part Three

Challenges of Cultural Diversity for Human Service Systems

Give me your tired, your poor, your huddled masses yearning to breathe free.
The wretched refuse of your teeming shore.
Send these, the homeless, tempest-tost to me.
I lift my lamp beside the golden door...

—Emma Lazarus,
Inscription on the plaque of the Statue of Liberty, 1903

Chapter Five

Southeast Asian Expatriates:
From Aliens to Citizens

Tran Minh Tung

During the 1980s more immigrants, including refugees, from Asia and the Pacific Islands came to this country than from any other region of the world. Nearly half of the immigration from Asia and the Pacific Islands was a result of the influx of Southeast Asians (Vietnamese, Cambodians, and Laotians) to the United States after the Vietnam War (U.S. Department of Commerce, 1991). A great majority of this population is composed of refugees fleeing from the communist regimes which took over their homelands in 1975. However, their flow was strongest between 1975 and the mid-eighties. According to the preliminary report on the 1990 U.S. census, the current population of Southeast Asians or Indochinese residing in this nation is as follows: Vietnamese, 614,547; Cambodians, 147,411; H'mong, 90,082; and Laotians, 149,014 (U.S. Government Accounting Office, 1990, March, pp. 14-16). This flow dwindled somewhat during the late 1980s, but tens of thousands still flee or wait to do so yearly in spite of the immense difficulties and dangers inherent in such attempts.

In almost all cases the newcomers received effective and humane assistance from the U.S. government, voluntary agencies, and innumerable individual Americans who gave the best of themselves in trying to ease the pain of expatriation and the hardships of resettlement. Most refugee programs and services tended to focus on the immigrants' material needs, emphasizing the problems of relocation, employment, financial support, and other practical issues related to survival and immediate subsistence. Much less attention was given and consequently not many resources have gone into long-range programs and projects concerned with the task of adjusting and getting integrated into the new culture.

This writer's contention is that this was a mistake. Indeed, both the refugees and the American community would have been better served had the problem of cultural differences and cultural adjustment been tackled more decisively at the very beginning. After all, one should certainly worry about what may happen to one million persons who must engage themselves into a new society, reputedly tolerant but still basically different. And it certainly pays to help these new Americans to achieve the necessary assimilation with the least trauma to themselves and the greatest possible benefits to the host community.

This paper is an attempt to analyze the processes of change and adaptation as they have been experienced and viewed by Southeast Asian refugees, describing their struggles and their efforts to cope with the challenges of a new life in a new environment as well as the resources they have drawn upon for their support.

The lessons to be learned derive essentially from the naturalistic observations of the social and psychological factors which were called into play by the forces of events. More practically, some benefits should be gained from assessing the results of the different interventions and manipulations by which individuals and organizations have sought to direct or influence the resettlement process.

As always in human sciences, it is certain that this assessment will raise more questions than it may offer answers. However, the hope is that the necessary questions will be raised so that one can better delineate the relevant issues and render them more amenable to a systematic and rational approach for future resolution.

The Problem at Hand: The Material Environment

It is generally recognized that people will change or are forced to change when transplanted into a new environment. What is less readily appreciated is the degree to which such transformation is pervasive and extensive as well as intricate and delicate.

If one thinks only of the concrete material characteristics of the new milieu (climate, food, technological features, occupational patterns, and so on), the task of adaptation is already complex and entails much more than simply an accommodation to different or unusual environmental conditions.

The different *climate* of the continental U.S., for example, has always been a major subject of preoccupation and complaint for most refugees who are wary of the cold weather they had never experienced in their homeland. Yet nobody could have predicted the vehemence and bitterness with which many have reacted to the unfamiliar weather (especially winter) and blamed it for all kinds of troubles. In fact, climate is the single most often evoked reason given by the hundreds of thousands of refugees who migrated to the South and West in the U. S., towards sunnier Texas and California after they had been resettled elsewhere (North, 1979). Atmospheric elements do not however tell the whole story of this subsequent exodus since many important refugee communities continue to prosper under the not-so-clement skies of Illinois, Minnesota, and Pennsylvania, to mention a few exceptions to the rule. Most of those who migrated are quite frank in admitting that they have not been searching solely for a warmer climate. Rather, they have looked for a place "more like home" or at least with weather which is not so glaringly different that it keeps reminding them of their exile. Texas, California, and Louisiana, for example, have become the points of attraction for Southeast Asians because these states have the sun and the warmth of the homeland they remember so well. Also, the presence of a great number of compatriots makes for an irresistible appeal by promising that they are not alone in this "foreign" country.

Food is another element which requires a great adaptive effort, far more strenuous than most Americans can likely comprehend. One would have thought that for newcomers struggling for survival, it would be enough just to have food or some assurance that they would not go hungry. However, when people are poor, not just any "food" will do. Refugees who never knew themselves to be purist or gourmet before have gone to extremes, such as abstaining from eating if it has to be American style even when it is free. It is well known that many Southeast Asians working in American hotels forego a free lunch or dinner at their workplace, preferring to pack their own lunch or waiting till the end of their shift to go home and eat. For the same reason, many will think nothing of making frequent, long (2-3 hours) trips to the nearest Oriental grocery store to procure their special kind of food. What is at stake, it seems, is not only a matter of taste or culinary refinement, but a deeper, subtler, but definite need to maintain some consistency in one's existence. Sharing food, especially a familiar kind of food, is by far the most preferred pretext for the uprooted to get together for a few hours and enjoy a sense of oneness.

On the other hand, if there is any problem for the newcomers in getting acquainted with the new *technological environment*, this often proves to be the least complicated and most rapid of all the tasks of adaptation. After all, the world is no longer so wide that any of its corners has been spared the invasion of transistor radios, Coca Cola and other products of a consumer society. The H'Mong tribesman and his brothers, the peasant from Cambodia or from Vietnam, learned to operate the latest war equipment made in the U. S. or the USSR; they should therefore not find it more difficult to use the more prosaic tools of modern-day living available in Middletown, USA. One often finds, however, that technological learning does not necessarily imply much change in the immigrants' views of the world. They may like the convenience of the new gadgets, but many have yet to be convinced of the latter's superiority over the old ways. Hence, nostalgia is sometimes expressed about the "old time," and there is the occasional reversal to traditional routines or recipes whenever there seems to be a need for a more "authentic" indigenous Indochinese product.

Language and Social Behavior

Language proficiency is clearly recognized by everybody concerned, particularly the refugees, as critical for a good adjustment to this new land. There is almost no need to convince anyone among the newcomers that they should make an earnest effort to speak and understand English, to avoid being, in the words of one of them, "deaf, mute, and dumb though they have tongue, ears, and brains..." English is also the key to social promotion, a must for whoever wants to get out of the menial jobs—the lot of most new migrants—and ascend to better paying, more socially rewarding occupations.

What is less often remembered is that indirectly but surely English proficiency conditions the assimilation process by determining the feasibility and ultimately the desirability of such a venture. Poor proficiency in English rarely engenders a great desire to mingle with the host community. Immigrants, new and old, tend to isolate themselves and shy away from most contacts with American neighbors and co-workers, in part because they cannot communicate or think that they cannot communicate properly and in part because they do not want to present themselves in an unfavorable light since their broken or laborious English does not do justice to their real competence and experiences.

Language learning may be desirable for most newcomers, but it is not always an easy or simple enterprise. In 1980, five years after the resettlement of the first wave of refugees, a special report to the health, education and welfare secretary stated, "Most refugees cannot communicate in English, only one-third of all the refugees interviewed can be understood by the survey teams. Almost half of the old wave refugees have difficulty communicating and 25 percent could not communicate without an interpreter" (U. S. Department of Health & Human Services [U. S. DHHS], 1980).

There are many reasons for this sorry state of affairs. First, not all refugees have access to English teaching programs "...much of which is haphazard, when they are available at all" (U. S. DHHS, 1980). Things have improved greatly in recent years because in most places English training has been made compulsory for all refugees who are on welfare assistance, and English classes for refugees have become much better organized. Most programs, however, still assume too much about the newcomers' abilities to solve practical problems such as securing transportation to and from school, and especially finding time to attend classes when they typically have to work for a living. Also, most immigrants live in clusters with their own people and as a consequence have little or no contact with English-speaking persons and precious few opportunities to practice their English.

Another element often overlooked is the mind-set with which the refugees approach the task of learning English. They all start in earnest, with high hopes and the idea that a few months of hard study will be sufficient to teach them what they need to know. Most programs, however, are often taught in a traditional and perfunctory manner and are rarely intensive enough to produce rapid results. The students are assailed by the myriad problems which are the staple of all newcomers, and they have yet to feel secure enough to properly concentrate on their studies. Fear and regret, worry about their present status, sadness about losses and separations dominate so much of their existence at this point that there is rarely much peace of mind left for purely academic pursuits. Finally, the task of learning English is itself laden with anxiety coming from the perceived need—constantly emphasized from all quarters—to make good in a domain deemed essential for survival. In most cases, progress is agonizingly slow or imperceptible and rarely on par with the students' expectations and tolerance levels.

All the above often result in impatience and frustration and lead many to conclude that learning English is an impossible task. The question becomes: Should they entertain any more hope of being part of a society in which they cannot communicate? This question is especially relevant to the middle-aged emigres who, besides the real or perceived handicap of age, are usually negatively inspired to change and adjust and who are even quicker to abandon the struggle to learn the new language.

In the areas of *external appearance and social behavior*, the necessity for accommodation and assimilation is also obvious to most refugees. They all closely observe the accoutrements, manners, and postures of their American hosts and as much as possible try to conform themselves to the new milieu. How much alacrity and thoroughness will go into compliance and assimilation will depend on many factors, mainly the refugees' ages and the extent of their contacts with mainstream American society. The first to be converted, the most prone and most apt to pick up and copy what they see down to the lingo and mannerisms of their new peer groups are—not surprisingly—children and adolescents who have no qualms about enjoying the experience of immersion into a most open and permissive society.

On the other hand, elderly refugees are usually removed from close contact with the outer world because they do not have to work and are sheltered by the protective circle of their children and grand-children. They remain detached and indifferent, seemingly unaffected until the echoes of change reverberate in their own families, indirectly but unmistakably through the unwitting offices of their youngest members whose personalities and manners undergo incredibly rapid and radical transformations.

Directly involved in the struggle, the adults are often distraught and unhappy but nevertheless try hard to adjust as they must live and work daily in face-to-face contact with this strange, new world. They are witnesses to customs, behaviors, and attitudes which make them smile or sigh or wince, and leave them confused, perplexed, or upset. They cannot quite figure out the why's and how's of what they see, yet it is imperative that they act, react, or interact properly on the basis of these imperfect cues in order to be accepted or at least tolerated in the new milieu.

New Relationships: The Sponsors

The first indication of such problems comes very early in the refugees' relationships with their American sponsors. In this uniquely American institution of sponsorship, certain persons or groups of persons volunteer to serve as mentors and protectors of the new immigrants when they first arrive, helping to secure food, jobs, shelter, and generally guiding the latter's first steps in this society (Taft, North, & Ford, 1979). The assistance so provided has often been invaluable and sometimes uniquely precious. More than anything else the warmth of humane concern is the most precious among the many gifts the refugees receive during these difficult moments.

The relationships, however, are not always smooth and easy, for various reasons which are not always obvious since they stem from subtle differences in cultural references (Tung, 1979). For example, the refugees have no model for such intercourse in their culture in which similar solicitude is generated only by very personal obligations of kinship and friendship or, if this comes from strangers, by the special dedication of a few highly "virtuous" or religious individuals. None of these reasons for generosity seems to be in evidence in the present instance. Hence, the refugees are perplexed, anxious and even doubtful and suspicious about their helpers' motives.

This is also a situation of dependency which, in a culture where "face" and propriety are major concerns, calls for a finely nuanced code of conduct from both parties. The proteges (refugees) must show appreciation and gratitude but avoid being servile, while the benefactors (sponsors) should be generous but also tactful and discreet in order not to inflict further humiliation on those whom they oblige. Thus, extreme sensitivity must be used towards the refugees who are most prone to react emotionally to any minute indication or suggestion of familiarity, condescension, self-interest or simply mental reservation from their sponsors. Refugees have been known to walk out on their sponsors because of seemingly innocuous questions or comments, for example, about the amount of rice that they have consumed or about some food missing from the refrigerator. In other cases, indignation has arisen when the refugees were asked to contribute to their upkeep as soon as they have received their first paycheck; the suspicion was that a noble sentiment was being degraded and turned into a commercial transaction. Sometimes the problem was a lack of finesse. Usually, a basic discordance in the perception of culturally prescribed social roles and behavior was at stake.

Recently many Indochinese, former refugees themselves, have offered to sponsor the late-comers (second wave migrants), generally their own relatives and friends. Here the ties are personal, and the relationships are well defined and more secure with fewer problems of cultural ambiguity. The question, however, should be raised about the role and effectiveness of such sponsors as agents and facilitators of the acculturation process, sponsors who are newly or incompletely acculturated, burdened with problems similar to those they were supposed to help, and subject to biases which they may reinforce instead of clarifying for their proteges. Few sponsors, American or Indochinese, are clear about the nature or the extent of such problems. What is certain is that all sponsors definitely need more preparation and could use more support and effective back-up from the public and voluntary agencies before they can truly fulfill their functions and responsibilities.

Relating to Voluntary and Government Agencies

The same malaise and confusion mentioned above also trouble the refugees' relationships with the voluntary agencies (Volags) which administer most resettlement programs and see to the needs of the newly arrived migrants.

Again, the Indochinese have had no experience with and no model of large-scaled organized charities such as American Volags. Dealing with the complex, often impersonal bureaucracy is a problem. Another problem is believing the altruistic motives of a machine which takes a business-like approach to what, for the Indochinese, is a "matter of heart." A few suspect that Volags are making money at their expense. Many simply wonder about the motives and intentions of the organizations and more practically whether they are getting their fair share of what the government is spending for them. Much of the good will which should have been generated by the Volags' efforts never quite materialized as their services are often clouded by misunderstanding and mistrust from the refugees, and frustration, defensiveness and anger from providers.

For similar reasons, government agencies, especially social welfare services, are also the subject of much confusion. In the refugees' home countries government is less a matter of citizens' rights and participation than the manifestation of the self-vested authority and leadership of one or a few persons who are traditionally set into the role of all-providing, all-caring "parents to the people." However, human nature being what it is, one cannot assume that all leaders or administrators are necessarily the dedicated, unselfish, and exclusively public-minded persons that they are supposed to be. Most Asian citizens, therefore, tend to approach public institutions and civil servants with a high level of ambivalence that is a mixture of submission and expectation about being taken care of, combined with skepticism and fear that they may be oppressed and exploited.

As refugees, Indochinese are tortured by even more doubt and uncertainty as both expectations and apprehensions are intensified by the state of utter dependence and helplessness in which they find themselves by the force of circumstances. Most measures decreed by the "authorities" are received with passivity but rarely without some reserve and a hefty dose of skepticism and wariness about whether the refugees or the administrators will be the real beneficiaries of these dispositions. When aid is provided, there is still fear and suspicion that it may be only a lure or, if this is truly a windfall, that it may not last for long. In the latter case one had better be quick and grab as much as possible as long as the "freebie" is still available. Conversely, if assistance is denied or not immediately forthcoming, the perceived reason may be that it has been withheld maliciously or that "they"—the faceless authorities—are too callous to care. In either case, it serves no purpose to fight or to argue since one is at "their" mercy. Instead, any reaction had better be cautious, subtle, and indirect rather than direct, open or confrontational.

A good way for mainstream agencies to give assistance more efficiently across the cultural barrier could be to use *bilingual, bicultural Southeast Asian* workers. Because they may help to bridge the gap between language and culture, these intermediaries may also bring American providers and Indochinese service users closer together (Tung, 1978).

Contrary to what one would have predicted in view of the potential benefits of using this particular category of personnel, the practice of enlisting the help of Indochinese resettlement workers has been neither common nor systematic. Whenever they were called to serve, it was mainly as translators or in minor clerical positions. Rarely and not until recently has serious thought been given to the possibility of tapping the native workers' experiences in their own cultures and communities to gain access to the Indochinese viewpoint, a most necessary input into any plan or program expected to be responsive to refugees' needs and demands.

With no systematic policy for exploiting this particular resource, it was inevitable that the indigenous workers would encounter problems which undermine their effectiveness and run counter to the purposes for which they were employed. The most basic question certainly is about the interposition of a third party in the process of communication. The risk of distortion, that is inherent with any translation is definitely greater in this case as very few qualified Indochinese who are truly bilingual and bicultural were available for employment when the resettlement programs were started. Also, the Indochinese workers themselves are treading the path of acculturation and struggling with the same issues with which they are supposed to help their clients. What is being relayed to an unsuspecting American supervisor, therefore, may be sometimes not so much objective reality as a subjective, culturally-biased rendition of reality. Further distortion occurs when the interpretation is altered to suit the individual needs of the interpreter, the most frequent being the desire to please the employer and to present oneself in a good light, for example, by hiding or camouflaging the "bad" behavior of the compatriot as it may reflect upon the interpreter (Tung, 1983).

The Indochinese workers' position is also particularly delicate since they may be viewed by their compatriots as adversaries and an extension of the bureaucracy. At the same time, they are expected to act as allies and advocates for their compatriots, taking sides with the latter as well as protecting them against the "system." Not surprisingly, Indochinese workers often feel uneasy, insecure, frustrated, and unhappy, unable to respond to so much expectation when they can do so little and never as much as they would like. Practically all of them will have to fight an uphill battle, trying to reconcile the conflicting loyalties owed to their American employers and their fellow countrymen.

Working

The *work environment* is another opportunity to observe the effect of cultural differences. Given traditionally strong work ethics, no Southeast Asian ever questions the necessity of working. In fact, the majority welcomes the chance to work as the means to ensure their subsistence and to respond to the enticements of a consumer society in which people seldom seem to be satisfied with what they have.

Given a choice, most Indo-Chinese refugees prefer to work for or with their compatriots. The greatest number, however, work with Americans or other persons who are not Indo-Chinese. This has often proven to be more advantageous because of better opportunities for career development, greater choice of occupations, and more generous financial and other benefits. Asked about such jobs, however, they generally complain that their occupations are rarely commensurate with their qualifications, past work experiences, and accomplishments. Mention is also often made of the fast pace of work and the usual intensity with which Americans perform their jobs, which contrasts with the more leisurely tempo of most jobs in their homeland.

The major problem, however, rarely verbalized or even conceptualized, is their feeling of being drained and tense and unable to relax when working with Americans. Indeed, their sense of insecurity and anxiety is constant and almost natural if one remembers that it is most stressful to always strive to observe, to understand and to reconcile oneself to a milieu of which one has yet to make sense. For example, they appreciate the generally informal work atmosphere in the U. S., but they also deplore the absence of subtlety and tact in most personal relationships, in contrast with the finely tuned and complex social rapport which take place in the home country. They enjoy the frankness and simplicity of most interactions with Americans but also miss the serenity and security of a family-like ambiance in most work environments in the old country, with less overt competitiveness and almost no need for assertiveness. Finally, the American *emphasis on efficiency* and *results* is sometimes experienced as brazen *materialism* and disregard for feelings and higher values, while criticisms and negative comments are often taken personally and perceived as attacks on their pride and assaults on their dignity.

One should always remember that refugees are easily fearful and anxious because of their self-perceived disadvantage stemming from their *foreignness*. In addition, they are apprehensive about losing their jobs which have been so hard to obtain. Equally as important is the *threat of real or perceived racial discrimination*. The inner tension, however, rarely manifests itself except in the most subtle manner, namely, by making them withdraw and retreat from most commerce with non-Indo-Chinese colleagues. Refugees feel they must keep the lowest profile possible, for example, by not voicing their opinions, especially if negative, to the point of not even protesting when they are the victims of gross injustices. This unhappy situation will not be eased until the refugees have enough understanding of the system and gain sufficient confidence in themselves to feel less vulnerable and more comfortable in a milieu with which they must identify in some measure.

In general, this stage may be reached in two or three years, and this is where most Indochinese now find themselves. For the majority, America is a good place to live and to work, maybe not quite like home but no longer as strange or forbidding as when they first arrived. In fact, most of them are "in the full swing of things" and very much a working part of the American community even if they often prefer the company of their own people. At minimum there is the appearance of assimilation in the way they dress, talk, and act which is reflective of other Americans. As a result of a newly acquired affluence, many have moved out of their ethnic enclaves to other areas which are more convenient, comfortable or prestigious, to more predominantly American neighborhoods. The majority work and live well while contributing to the community in a significant manner with the products of their labor (Montero, 1979).

Barriers have not totally disappeared however. Handicaps may derive from the distinctive, *non-Caucasian* physical features of Southeast Asians which preclude total social integration. Their experiences may be too recent to permit any real change of heart of deeply ingrained values and beliefs. Perhaps being an exile is not the best motive for wanting to change and for taking on a new identity. In any event, the struggle is far from over even for those most disposed to becoming assimilated. In the process all have tried different tactics to resolve the challenges of adjustment. These are often variations on a common theme—discussed next—and describing the different choices offered to refugees as they try to plan strategies by which they can adapt themselves to the new environment.

Working It Out: Strategy and Choices

There is no doubt that most refugees realize that once they have settled in their new country, they must attempt to reach some kind of accommodation with the new order. It would be farfetched to describe a uniform or exemplary pattern in their behavior as they react to the conflicting pressures and demands of their new existence. It seems, however, that the majority simply try to attain a compromise between the need to conform to the host society and the desire to retain a distinct identity; both drives are equally urgent and inspired by equally strong reasons.

The *wish to conform* is logical and easy to understand if one just remembers that essentially Indochinese are pragmatists who fully realize that they are aliens and displaced persons. They consider themselves uninvited guests who are not certain that they will always be welcome in a foreign country. The best protection, therefore, would be to try to "blend in with the crowd," to be as inconspicuous as possible lest they be singled out, discriminated against, and possibly persecuted or rejected. Hence the desire is to comply, to conform, and to "bend with the wind," with a noticeable reluctance to stand up, speak out, object, or disagree too forcefully. Even when they would like to defend their rights, they fear that their actions will be construed as manifestations of ill-will or mischief and possibly used against them.

The drive to conform also comes from cultures and traditions which idealize peace and harmony and advocate arrangement and accommodation, not confrontation or the direct forcing of any issue, as the best way to solve conflict and disagreement. As the traditional saying goes, "Go with the tide when riding a river, conform to the (house) customs when entering a home." As a matter of principle, refugees who see themselves as mere guests in this country feel obliged to go along with whatever the rules are of the host nation.

However, many other forces work in the opposite direction, pushing for resisting changes and for maintaining their primary identity as Indochinese. One point to remember is that these persons are *refugees, not voluntary migrants*; the distinction is essential. Very few Indochinese had been prepared for the drastic changes which followed their emigration, and even fewer were willing to accept the consequences of their *forced uprooting* and *exile*. They suffered through the many upheavals of expatriation which brought losses, demotion and disruption and very few of the benefits—real or expected—which often motivate voluntary expatriates to migrate. The refugees are now free and no longer threatened as they were when they lived under the communists. In terms of creature comforts there is no doubt that their lives are much better in this new land. Still this is an *existence in exile* which they would not have chosen had it been possible to make a choice at the time they fled. For this reason and for a long time after their transplantation, they continued to feel regret and remorse. They longed for the past and the old country with little regard for the present and not much hope for a future, which seems to promise only separation and exile. Rarely if ever can there be found among the refugees the eagerness and receptivity often shown by the true voluntary immigrants who aspire most fervently to absorb and become absorbed into the new culture; this is what the voluntary immigrants want and chose by leaving the old country.

Such sentiment is readily expressed in direct pronouncements during private conversations and also in public speeches, or in articles, poems, and fiction that are found daily in a very active refugee press. The gist of these messages consists of an exaltation of the old country with its traditions and cultural heritage and idealized reminiscences about the past, the homeland, and bitter views of the refugees' present existence and environment.

The Refugee Community

Nostalgia for the old country also manifests itself in various actions which seek to preserve the past and to maintain a distinct identity while the refugees try to reconstruct a more familiar environment. Most obvious is the regrouping of refugees which occurred almost immediately after the initial dispersion decreed by the U. S. administration (North, 1979). This led to the formation of many good-sized Indo-Chinese communities in California, Texas, and Louisiana, which made most Indo-Chinese feel warm in their hearts, as if somehow the homeland is accessible again.

One also notices the flurry of activities, formal and informal, which take place all year long in most expatriate communities—meetings, conferences, cultural events, traditional festivities, and other communal celebrations (Dorias, Pilo-Le, &

Huy, 1987). All are the products of often frantic efforts by the refugees to rebuild communities like the ones they remember and miss so much and to organize themselves into some structure which will keep them together. Associations abound, often built on the bases of special affinity or some common denominator rooted in their past—political (new and old political parties); geographic (provincial associations); religious (Buddhist, Catholic organizations); professional (legal, medical professions); school affiliation (alumni associations of Vietnamese schools and universities); and military service branches (navy, air force, marines). The number of these associations, generically known as Mutual Assistance Associations (M.A.A.), is staggering even though their strength is rarely equal to the ambitions of their founders and members. At any rate, their existence and their survival against many odds reflect a real and deeply felt need by most refugees for assurances that they still have a distinct identity, even in this distant land.

Most organizations are fraternal and are rarely involved in anything besides benevolent activities. Only in recent years have efforts gone into the organization of Southeast Asians as "hyphenated Americans," willing and able to go into the U. S. political arena to make the most of their rights and responsibilities as American citizens. But even when they work toward objectives related to local and national American politics, their organizers never forget to insist that they use the newly forged political instruments for the good of the homeland, for example, Vietnam and Vietnamese compatriots outside the USA, in Vietnam or in the many Pacific refugee camps.

Last but not least, wherever one finds a sizable refugee population, there exists a very active and often sizable network of Indochinese professionals and small businesses catering almost exclusively to an Indochinese clientele. Physicians, pharmacists, dentists, lawyers, real estate and insurance agents, grocery stores, restaurants, beauty salons, video stores, nightclubs, book shops, magazine and book publishing ventures—an array of trades and commerce offer their services and products to a highly appreciative ethnic community. In most locations the system has developed quickly and extensively because it answers the needs of a rapidly expanding and increasingly affluent community. In the process this network has also created thousands of new jobs—providential niches for the new immigrants who are not yet ready to go "mainstream"—and provided opportunities for Southeast Asian entrepreneurs to try their hands at business ventures with a minimum of apprehension and risk since they will be working in a relatively familiar and friendly environment.

The situation, however, is not all rosy. In spite of partial success and some progress, the idea and ideal of an Indochinese community this side of the Pacific remains as elusive as ever. Talks about unity and concerted moves are often heard but not always put into action. Dissension, *divisions*, and internal bickering erode most of the energy which should be channeled into more constructive enterprises and which dilute the effectiveness of many collective endeavors.

Among the many reasons which may explain the relative failure of most community building efforts are material obstacles such as distance and cost. Also, most newcomers are still too absorbed in the struggle for survival to have much time and energy to devote to public causes. As communities go, theirs are still too young to possess the resources or experiences of Hispanics or other Asian-American groups to be able to organize themselves effectively. The major obstacle, however, especially for the Vietnamese and the Cambodians, resides within themselves and lies within their culturally derived difficulty in working cooperatively with each other in the absence of a formal, preexisting social structure. They all deplore the conflicts and disputes which are riddling their associative enterprises, yet they seem unable to overcome the traditional reserve and hesitation in trusting "strangers"—people outside their familiar circle of relatives and friends. They maintain an inveterate tendency to question everybody's motives.

Very evocative evidence can be found of the above in the findings of an unpublished research study by William T. Liu, Elena Yu, and this writer, under the aegis of the Asian American Mental Health Research Center from 1977 to 1979, on the Vietnamese refugees in the San Diego, California: area (Lin, Yu, & Tung, 1977-79). For example, almost all the subjects interviewed professed a desire to live near a concentration of Indochinese refugees. Many, however, made clear that they would rather not live "too close" to their compatriots, except their relatives and friends. The most frequent explanation for this singular reserve was that they were afraid of possible "problems" if they were surrounded by fellow countrymen some of whom may be nosy, fussy and "unpleasant."

On the other hand, when asked about their ties with the American community at large, the majority confessed that they had little or no interaction with their American neighbors or work associates. Some stated that they had some contact at work, but very few had any sustained relationship with Americans. *None of them saw himself or herself as American, even in the future.* All felt more comfortable with their own people, and none looked forward to initiating a personal relationship or progressing towards anything beyond a casual acquaintance with Americans.

In fact, the majority of refugees stay away from most social activities except with their Indo-Chinese communities and generally avoid "unnecessary" contacts with the host society. Withdrawal as a self-protection device has been observed most frequently in the early stages of the resettlement. Even five or seven years later, it has not disappeared completely because few refugees knowingly submit themselves to the risk of being reminded of being "different" and "inadequate." Such defense may sometimes be extreme and turn into isolation or reach pathological dimensions if by withdrawing, the subject keeps exclusively to his or her own world of fantasies, delusions or paranoia. In most instances, however, the retreat does serve a useful purpose; it provides a temporary refuge and security from stressful situations which may be too much for some people to handle.

The Refugee Family: Asset and Liability

Among other benefits, security and retreat are precisely what are being offered by the most important element of the support and defense system favored by the Indochinese in their struggle for adjustment: *the family*. In the world of Southeast Asians, family should always be understood as the extended kinship organization and a multigenerational grouping, united by a precisely engineered network of mutual loyalties and responsibilities which form the bases of its strengths and values, especially useful in the present circumstances.

Materially, the family offers the force of a group, the benefits of economic association, and frequently the convenience of communal living arrangements. Psychologically, it represents continuity and stability and also means security and protection, thanks to the assurances of solidarity and the promises of mutual support and assistance.

As for the task of adjustment, the presence of the family has proved to be a mixed blessing. On the positive side, the family often facilitates change and adaptation by providing a most helpful relief which allays some of the anxiety which arises in the process of confronting the new environment. It may even contribute directly to adjustment through the sharing of common experiences and learning from other members of the group. On the negative side, the family atmosphere may be too comfortable or so reclusive that its members have little desire and no real possibility of going out and trying to cope with a far too threatening outer world. In practice the protection is never so perfect that the reality of the external world is not felt and its impact not totally deflected. In many cases in fact, the message about differences and changes will be conveyed through the involuntary offices of some of the younger family members whose transformation unmistakably reflects the influence of the new environment and reminds the rest of the family that indeed they are living in a different time and a different place.

This eventuality, more and more often, has resulted in numerous and continuous conflicts and tensions arising between the older and younger generations of refugees. The latter model their postures, mores and behavior on those of the new society, and the former desperately cling to the ways of living and thinking of the old country (Carlin & Sokoloff, 1985). The division may be acute at times, with the parents on one side trying to enforce the old traditions as a means of vicariously fulfilling their dreams of holding onto the past. The children are on the other side, uncomprehending and unconvinced that there could be something better than what they are experiencing every day in their lives in the U. S.

There is no doubt that families are the refugees' greatest strength and asset. They can also be the breeding ground for new problems and the source of additional troubles, many of which have already emerged and many more of which will continue long after most other difficulties have subsided.

Questions and Suggestions

Indo-Chinese rank in number second only to Cubans as the largest group of *refugees* who ever came to the USA. They constitute a special group and present a *special challenge* to assimilation as *the most sizable mass of Asians ever admitted* to the U. S. in a short period of time. They also came at a particular juncture—in the wake of an unpopular conflict and an economic recession—which made for a less than unanimous and enthusiastic response from an ambivalent community. In this venture we see for the first time in American history a direct and extensive involvement of the United States government which assumed more initiative and responsibility in the more recent resettlement operations, instead of relying entirely on the voluntary agencies, as in other previous programs (Taft, North, & Ford, 1979).

A number of statistical studies and reports have tried to gauge the results of these efforts essentially in terms of measurable economic achievement and of the problems which came to the attention of the service agencies. Surveys have also been made on some of the qualitative results of adjustment (Caplan, Whitmore, & Choy, 1990). As could be expected from the special nature of the subject matter, much less clearly defined results were obtained. Conclusions are, therefore, mostly impressionistic appreciation, which almost invariably lead to an overly optimistic picture of the situation.

One decade after their arrival, Indo-Chinese refugees have made great strides towards becoming an integral part of their adopted country, though they continue to maintain a great part of their identity as a group. What is unclear is how much this has occurred as a result of the various maneuvers, choices, and decisions that were made by the refugees themselves, by the U. S. government, or by the voluntary agencies, or in spite of the efforts of these various parties. It may also be interesting to know how much of what we see is appropriate or desirable in attaining the goals of adjustment and acculturation and how successful have resettlement operations been. Other questions one may ask: What is adjustment? What is integration? How much assimilation or identification with the host country is enough? And from the community viewpoint: *How much difference, diversity or pluralism* is tolerable or desirable?

There are no easy answers to these questions when reason mixes with politics, logic with emotions, and cold facts with humanitarianism. But this may be more a reason not to be content solely with intuition and experimentation. Should the decision be made to intervene in a thoughtful manner, then the issues must be tackled more openly and more systematically, with an eye to including all relevant factors and elements. Up to now, paradoxically, the most critical element (the refugees themselves) has been left out of most of the planning. They were rarely consulted or really heard. Not much attention has been given to their special needs or sensitivities. It may not be too late, even at this point, to be a bit less arrogant or paternalistic and to involve in our planning the refugees and migrants themselves who are the very subjects of our efforts. Only in this manner can we hope to make the resettlement a truly cooperative venture, at the end of which the new Americans will feel comfortable enough to call this land their own, not because they have been so told but because they have so chosen after having voiced their opinions and worked on reshaping their own lives in the best American traditions.

References

Caplan, N., Whitmore, J. K., & Choy, M. (1990). *The boat people and achievement in America*. Ann Arbor, MI: University of Michigan Press.

Carlin, J., & Sokoloff, B. (1985). *Mental health treatment issues for Southeast Asian refugee children*. In T. Owen (Ed.), *Southeast Asian mental health: Treatment, prevention, services, training and research*. Bethesda, MD: National Institute on Mental Health.

Dorias, L. J., Pilo-Le, L., & Huy, N. (1987). *Exile in a cold land: A Vietnamese community in Canada*. New Haven, CT: Yale Center for International and Area Studies.

Lin, W., Yu, E., & Tung, T. M. (1977, August-1979, September). *Refugees as immigrants: The case of Vietnamese* (Grant No. 29102-2). Washington, DC: National Institute on Mental Health.

Montero, D. (1979). *Vietnamese-Americans: Patterns of resettlement and socio-economic adaptation in the U. S. A.* Boulder, CO: Westview Press.

North, D. (1979). *The geographical distribution of Indochinese refugees in the United States*. Washington, DC: New Transcentury Foundation.

Taft, J., North, D., & Ford, D. (1979). *Refugee resettlement in the U.S.: Time for a focus*. Washington, DC: New Transcentury Foundation.

Tung, T. M. (1978, October-December). *The Indochinese mental health paraprofessional: What do we want?* U.S. Department of Health, Education and Welfare grantee conferences in Chicago, Atlanta, San Francisco, and Seattle.

Tung, T. M. (1979). *Perspectives: Vietnamese views on resettlement and adjustment*. Paper presented at the 87th Annual Convention of the American Psychological Association, New York, NY.

Tung, T. M. (1983, April). *Caught in the middle: Problems of the Indochinese resettlement workers*. Paper presented at the 4th Conference of the National Association for Vietnamese-American Education, Tysons Corner, VA.

U. S. Department of Commerce. (1991, June 12). *Census Bureau releases 1990 census counts on specific racial groups*. News release Number CB91-215, Washington, DC: Bureau of the Census.

U. S. General Accounting Office. (1990, March). *Asian Americans*. GAO HRD-90-36FS, pp. 14-16.

U. S. Department of Health and Human Services. (1980). Indo-Chinese refugee assessment, a report to the secretary. Washington, DC: Office of the Inspector General.

Chapter Six

A Challenge to the Mental Health Systems:
Central American Refugees

Leland K. Hall, Sr.

Nearly a decade ago, the District of Columbia was composed of a highly culturally diversified population of approximately 606,900 people—399,604 (over 65 percent) of whom were Black. An estimated 32,700 were Hispanic (Bureau of the Census, 1991). The current Hispanic population is about eight percent of the city's total citizenry. The nation's capital is one of the major American cities for immigrant (refugee) resettlement—immigrants from all over the world. The most recent influx of foreign settlers has come from Central America, particularly El Salvador where the people were involved in an ongoing civil war for a number of years. The civil war in El Salvador has been a direct causal factor in many families and individuals fleeing their country to a safer and less hostile environment, especially to the United States. Many Salvadoran immigrants enter this country without legal documentation, gaining entry any way they can as long as they can leave the dire effects and impacts that the civil war has had upon them and their families (General Accounting Office, 1989).

El Salvador is a poor country which relies on larger, richer, and stronger countries for its economic stability. This factor places the country in a position where the political influence of larger nations coerces and entices the El Salvadoran leadership to adopt the political ideology of those larger nations. The common people who know little of the political interplay among "super nations" find themselves fighting for *some* kind of political freedom. This reality has caused many people to find it difficult to remain in El Salvador due to the insecurity and political pressure under which they have had to live.

A version of this chapter was presented at the Clinical Social Work Conference, National Association of Social Workers, San Francisco, California, Sept. 11, 1986. A condensed version was included in *Hospital and Community Psychiatry*, a journal of the American Psychiatric Association, November, 1988, Vol. 39, No. 11, Washington, D. C., titled, "Providing Culturally Relevant Mental Health Services for Central American Immigrants." Published here with the author's permission.

As previously stated, El Salvador struggled with civil war for a number of years. This war placed a great deal of pressure on the people to join either of the opposing forces and supply manpower and resources. Young men and sometimes young women were recruited to serve the warring factions as fighters and informants. As is evident, the common folk (peasants) were caught in the middle. If they did not comply with the demands of the opposing forces, they might pay for their resistance with their lives and sometimes the lives of other family members.

According to Dr. Ricardo Galbis, a Latino psychiatrist, common folk who were not responsive or sympathetic to the different political factions' positions in El Salvador were faced with the possible consequences of torture or death, or both. Lists of non-supporters were kept by the government and the guerrillas, and many people were killed to demonstrate that they (both sides) meant business. Children saw their parents, siblings, and friends killed, and they sometimes witnessed their mothers and sisters being raped. In some cases the children themselves were also victims of physical and sexual abuse. When some people could no longer tolerate this oppression and violence, they arranged to escape to "freedom" in the United States. An example of the mass exodus of people that occurred is a small town in El Salvador called Inticupa where the political pressure was so great that a majority of the town's population now live in the District of Columbia (Galbis, 1986).

Though the United States represents freedom and new opportunities to immigrants and is somewhat of a "mecca" for Central Americans, the journey into this country, and ultimately to the District of Columbia, is one that is full of many ordeals and dangers. Some immigrants make several attempts to resettle in other parts of the United States before finally traveling to and resettling in the District of Columbia.

For some years Salvadorans have traveled "directly" to the District of Columbia and resettled with those members of their families who were already established. The cost of this intercontinental journey has often been as much as $1000, beginning with travel from El Salvador, through Mexico (mainly by foot), and swimming across the border (the Rio Grande) into Texas. It is at the U. S. border where about 20 percent of the refugees are captured by customs agents. The Salvadorans who are intercepted tell the authorities that they are from Mexico so that they will not be sent back to El Salvador. They know that many of those who were returned were imprisoned, tortured, or killed by government authorities.

Those Salvadorans who manage to safely reach the United States are transported across country by car, truck, train, and airplane. But even though they reach U. S. soil, the remainder of their journey is anything but safe. Periodically, immigrant transport vehicles are involved in severe accidents which kill many of the occupants. Some are smuggled across the country in closed, airtight trucks (some refrigerated) which at times break down and are abandoned by the drivers, leaving the occupants trapped in the trucks to suffocate. This is quite a high price to pay for "freedom." If the immigrants are fortunate, and many are, they arrive in the District of Columbia where they seek the help of the local Central American Refugee Center

A Challenge to the Mental Health Systems

in locating their families or someone who can assist them with resettlement (Vargas, 1984).

Resettlement Adjustment

Resettlement in the District of Columbia is not a very smooth transition for most people, and can be traumatic for immigrants. the change in lifestyle is an unexpected "cultural shock" since most had been peasant-farmers who had lived in rural communities where the language, values and customs were well known to them. Vargas (1984) explains that people who migrate to a country whose socio-political and cultural systems and language differ from that of their country of origin generally face stress in the transitional process of readjustment. Although the immigrants may settle in a Latino or Hispanic community where they speak similar languages, there exists a great diversity among a community's subcultures, that is, in the political, social, and religious values. For example, Latinos who emigrate from Spain to the United States are culturally closer to Europeans' cultures than to the cultures of Latinos who come from Central America or the Caribbean (Anders, 1986).

There are many Central American refugees who have settled in the District of Columbia since the early 1980s, and new family members continue to arrive yearly. This process causes the acculturation of these families to be inconsistent because adjustment occurs at different times for the various family members. Most often family cohesion is disrupted, and parents begin to feel a loss of control over their children. At the same time, children have difficulty coping with the change in their parents' effectiveness as authority figures. It is well known that children seek parental controls over their behavior (Anders, 1986). In addition, children of immigrants are more easily acculturated and acquire far better English language skills than their parents. This situation can also be a source of frustration and a symbol of parental impotence (Vega and Miranda, 1985).

Comparatively, immigrant children have more exposure to the "American way" than their parents or other adult immigrants. They must attend schools where they become involved with other children in educational and social activities. This exposure aids the children in assimilating more easily into the culture of their newly adopted country. On the other hand, the adults are forced to learn about this society mainly from their children. This is contrary to their cultural values, that is, children should learn from parents, not vice versa. One result, Vega (1985) notes, is that parents may experience psychological distress when they feel they are losing parental control over their children.

Many adult immigrants feel their authority beginning to erode as soon as they arrive in the United States. This is particularly true for the male's role of authority since the woman's role as provider tends to increase since she can acquire employment much more easily than the man. These immigrant women are able to secure employment that also pays higher salaries than their men. This fact alone causes a change in the attitude of one toward the other. In the eyes of the men their value and stature as men are reduced since most of them are not trained in skilled occupations. Most men were farmers in their homeland, but there is little or no demand for such skills in the nation's capital area.

Given the menial employment they are able to find, the wages immigrant men earn are usually sub-minimum, and in many instances they are exploited by employers. This is particularly true for those who entered the country illegally. This exploitation is widespread in the lower wage labor market because employers and immigrants know that if undocumented persons are found, they will be deported. (This is true for women as well as men.) This reality is what the immigrants want to avoid. Therefore, they accept whatever menial, low visibility work they can find in order to survive and remain in the United States.

Since the male immigrants' self-esteem is negatively affected when they are able to find only low-paying employment, they often resort to alcohol for relief and escape. Economic strain produces frustration and tends to disrupt other aspects of their adjustment process. Men who are fortunate enough to find employment help their families secure those resources that supply their basic human needs, that is, food, clothing, and, shelter. But those who have very menial jobs or are unemployed can be observed in groups drinking alcohol and milling around on the street corners of Latino communities.

On the other hand, Latino women are somewhat more fortunate. They are often in demand as domestic workers and baby-sitters for middle-class women and mothers who are gainfully employed and involved in their own careers.

Evolving Problems

Psychological Stress

As previously stated, most Salvadoran immigrants come to the United States to either escape being drafted into the military or because they feel they can no longer survive in their country's austere economy. Once they decide to leave for the United States, they have already resolved to make a new life in a culture quite different from that which they leave.

They are now confronted with the fact that women are more in demand for employment than men. The males' authority is challenged; and because of the women's new-found independence, many male-female relationships begin to deteriorate. Having been the heads of their families in Central America, and having used physical abuse as an acceptable means of controlling their families, some men continue this behavior in the United States. This behavior is not socially acceptable in this country. For some, more antisocial behavior may occur because of the rage

A Challenge to the Mental Health Systems

resulting from having been brutalized, and also for feelings of having no sense of control over their new environment. Family violence, especially child abuse and wife battering, is a common result of these feelings (Vargas, 1984).

If mental health, health, or social intervention is warranted, the men (and most women) will not seek public assistance, primarily because of the language, social, and cultural barriers that exist. In addition, immigrants are not familiar with the public health and social service systems of the District of Columbia, and in many cases they are afraid to seek help. In fact, one of the reasons immigrants are afraid to seek assistance from public agencies is because of their negative perceptions of public authorities in their own countries. If learning about how to access the public service systems is difficult for natives of the District of Columbia, one can imagine how much more difficult it must be for those who do not speak the language or understand the rationale for existence of the systems in the first place.

Children of the illegal immigrants must attend school just as do children who are United States citizens. Many immigrants may not understand mandatory education because in their countries of origin, children are kept home when they are needed to work and help support their families. However, it is through the mandatory public education system that many of the social service needs and health problems of this population are discovered. For example, some children suffer from post-traumatic stress disorders caused by the atrocities they witnessed before leaving El Salvador. They demonstrate the trauma they have experienced through school art classes in which they draw graphic pictures of the military devastation and violence which they remember (Schemick, 1986). Once it is realized that a child is having such deep-seated emotional problems, the child is referred to the Latino Community Mental Health Center for evaluation.

When some Salvadoran men realize that the transition from El Salvador has been accomplished, they too suffer post-traumatic stress and other types of stress when they begin to feel that they have "deserted" their people back home. Symptoms include the re-experiencing of traumatic events, shunning responsibilities, personal withdrawal, recurrent nightmares, flashbacks, and feelings of guilt from surviving when others did not (Vargas, 1984). Forgetting such incidents is difficult, and some of the men periodically become aimless. The assimilation process occurs slowly for some men, and depression and despondency set in, causing them to feel futile and pessimistic.

Family Adjustment

After refugee family members have settled, it is quite common for relatives and close friends to pursue the same path. For example, a male moves to an area seeking employment and a better way of life; after finding a job and settling into a residence, he begins to send for members of his immediate family. As the family prospers, more members of the extended family arrive to live with the first "pioneers" until they "get on their feet," after which they move into a home of their own. The cycle begins again until all who care to move to this new location are accommodated. In the District of Columbia this same pattern of resettlement is now being practiced by other Central Americans, Africans (primarily Ethiopians) and Asians.

When a person leaves his place of birth to go to another culture to live, the availability of money for resettlement is often limited. Hence, the immigrants usually find living quarters in the least expensive sections of the city. This is certainly the case for Salvadorans who have immigrated to the District of Columbia. In many cases there are several people living in one small apartment since living space is scarce and overcrowding is the rule, not the exception. It is because of the immigrants' need for inexpensive places to live that many landlords exploit them, allowing more people to live in smaller quarters (for a high price) than is permitted by law.

Mental Health Services

The massive influx of immigrants into Washington, D. C. has caused many problems for the city's public mental health, health and social service agencies since there are no adequate programs and services to meet the immigrants' mental health, health, and social service needs. Existing public services are barely adequate to meet the needs of the city's permanent residents, most of whom are low income Blacks. This situation exists not only because of the influx of immigrants but also because of the growing population of homeless people whose large numbers are partially a result of the liberal policies and programs established for this population.

In addition, there is a scarcity of bilingual, Spanish-speaking personnel working in the public sector's mental health, health, and social service agencies. Although there are Latino programs in mental health, health, social services, and economic development, these programs are not presently closely coordinated. There are several reasons for this inadequacy, the most prevalent being the ethnic and cultural differences within the Latino community itself. The lack of service coordination has caused many needy individuals to fall between the inevitable cracks. However, these service agencies have helped to identify some of the unique service needs of this culturally diverse population.

Considering the difficulties that immigrants encounter when migrating to the District of Columbia, one has some conception and appreciation of the stresses and pressures they must experience in their quest for "freedom." Once they have settled in (the mission of escape is complete), they begin their adjustment to this strange new environment. As stated earlier, many immigrants who have witnessed atrocities to their families and friends and sometimes had these experiences themselves may suffer from post-traumatic stress disorder—vivid memories of the horrible experiences suffered in El Salvador. When emotional factors such as these are displayed, these refugee-immigrants are in need of some mental health intervention, interven-

A Challenge to the Mental Health Systems

tion which is designed specifically to meet the psychological and emotional needs of this population.

The District of Columbia has a publicly-supported, community-based mental health center that services a large population of the city including the largest growing Latino community. This center has the responsibility for offering mental health programs designed to meet the unique needs of the large, multicultural service area population. Typically, Latinos will not voluntarily come into this facility for assistance. The center has very few Spanish-speaking personnel, and more than 85 percent of their client population is Black. Other reasons affecting services to this population are partially based on cultural considerations: persons seeking such services can be stigmatized; they experience an absence of referral networks; some Hispanics may choose to tolerate deviant behavior among family members rather than refer them for treatment or institutionalization (Vega, et. al., 1985). Because of these factors the center is working with the leadership of Latino agencies to try to develop and design realistic and effective services and programs for Latinos.

In its efforts to more adequately meet the mental health service needs of Latinos, the city, through its community-based center has contracted with two small, Spanish-speaking, Latino community-based mental health and social services agencies. The contract requires these agencies to develop and implement mental health services and programs that are relevant to the mental health needs of the Latino population. In addition, there is a day treatment program for Latinos located on the grounds of the District of Columbia's "state" hospital (St. Elizabeth) where clients receive treatment for their mental health disorders and where they are helped to acquire confidence in their continuing efforts to acculturate themselves into this society.

The largest of the two community-based, Latino mental health agencies has an active alcoholism program which is a member of the National Alcoholics Anonymous (AA) network. To some extent the program is used as a means to ascertain the causal factors that trigger adverse child behavior, domestic violence, spousal and sexual abuse, and other emotional disorders. It was through this method of case findings that the center successfully sought funds from the National Institute of Mental Health and the local government's Department of Human Services to identify and work with Latino families experiencing domestic abuse and emotional problems.

Present Latino mental health services are making an impact upon the lives of some of those people whom they assist. However, the programs and services are designed much in the same configuration as those traditional services operated by the city for its other residents. Services and programs for Latinos are designed in a way that does not "fit" their specific service needs. Latino service programs should be designed and instituted in a culturally sensitive fashion that is unique to their mental health service needs.

There are other social service and educational programs in the Latino community which have vested interests in the welfare of the Latino people. However, each program is narrowly focused on a particular aspect of community service needs (prenatal care, for example), and their interface with other human service programs is often blurred. It is here, between and among the Latino programs, that close collaboration is needed to identify, document and design services and programs that effectively impact the mental health service needs of this population. These agencies are in daily contact with the pulse and heartbeat of the Latino community. However, they struggle to acquire the needed resources to adequately service the people from their own vantage point. The qualitative outcome of their efforts is therefore inconsistent.

There are other public and community-based agencies trying to help established programs to assist the Central American immigrant in making an adequate adjustment to the style of life in the District of Columbia such as how to understand and respect urban law. For example, programs are designed to teach the immigrant that the District of Columbia police are not an occupation force, like the police in Central America, but serve to protect the people and secure the community. As a means of creating a comprehensive plan for Latino programs, a *common Latino agenda* has been attempted in the Washington, D. C. area. The *agenda* is trying to bring positive public attention to the Latinos' problems and their quest for equal services. These efforts are necessarily difficult to achieve because of the diversity of the sub-cultures that comprise the Latino community and the differences in the levels of expectations of the people.

Recommendations

Many Latinos feel that there are specific programmatic steps that should be taken to establish services and programs that will comprehensively meet their mental health needs.

First, it is agreed that public mental health programs should employ more Spanish-speaking personnel so that clients can effectively communicate with staff. It is well known that this population needs more personalized relationships with service agencies such as mental health centers. A more open system of mental health services for Latinos is feasible given an inclusive planning process.

Second, a program of reciprocal, ongoing training should be designed and established whereby Latinos can be oriented to the need for merging Latino and American (U.S.) cultures with the multiple values of their native subcultures. In so doing, the unknown for all will become known, and the interface between the Latinos and the service agencies will not be so conflicting.

Within the context of helping immigrants move through the mental health, health, and social service systems of the District of Columbia, the worker must be aware of the Latinos' previous public agency experiences. Governments of Latin countries typically function more like occupational forces than providers of human services. Rather than the government's taking a farmer's crops after a harvest, the United States government taxes their wages so that general revenue will be available to assist the less fortunate in this country. Understanding this process can help Latinos to begin to learn our American way of lending a helping hand. They must also adjust to this culture's basic lifestyle including, for example, crossing the street properly, not carrying weapons, not drinking alcohol on the street, and so on.

Third, socialization and psychological programs operated by Latinos should be defined and designed with the comprehensive involvement of established public mental health, health and social service administrations. Given the different experiences that many Latinos have had in going to the service centers, it is obvious that what is interpreted as a psychosocial or socialization program for Latinos requires distinctions from those developed for native-born citizens. New definitions of such programs must be devised so that services can be problem and issue specific to the Latino population.

Fourth, greater emphasis must be placed on orienting and treating the Latino family. Family therapy and multi-family therapy can be designed so that the common problems and difficulties of coming to and settling in the District of Columbia can be discovered. Families involved in this kind of therapy can begin to develop an appreciation of the fact that an individual's mental stress and mental illness are shared in a family and in a community. Also, programs for alcoholism within the Latino community should be expanded, and the treatment type should be combined with family therapy. In this way problem-specific therapies for Latinos can be designed and implemented within their own communities.

Fifth, there are two public systems that some feel can make major inroads into the Latino community. It is felt that these two systems can uniquely enhance the acculturation process of the Latino people. The systems are *public health* and *education* (Espino, 1986). The concept of utilizing public schools as multi-service centers for the Latino community has merit. All immigrants are in need of some medical care, and school-aged children have to attend public school. The school is the milieu in which many of the physical and domestic problems are identified, and it is the place to which almost all Latinos in the city can relate. Therefore, various services could be located in school facilities where familiarity could facilitate comprehensive service delivery.

Parents could take their under-school aged children to a clinic located in the school for medical services, and they could also receive services for themselves. They could attend evening orientation and educational classes to learn English and learn about the community's systems, as well as obtain counseling from mental health or health care professionals. Social service referrals and commodity foods can be located at such sites, and the people could receive intake, screening, and referral services for those goods and services they may need to survive in their newly chosen home. Close collaboration among public agencies could take place in such facilities because of their convenient locations and worth to the people living in the community.

These recommendations will take some time to be realized. However, the level of intercultural sensitivity on the part of public agencies, local Latino agencies, and the immigrants themselves has to be heightened so that the thrust and fairness of sharing resources can be instituted successfully to assure effective service delivery.

References

Anders, A. (1986, July). Interview with the Director of Hispanic Affairs and U. S. Virgin Islands Services, Saint Elizabeth's Hospital, Washington, DC.

Espino, C. (1986, July). Interview with the Coordinator of Child, Youth, and Family Programs, Andromeda Community Mental Health Center, Washington, DC.

Galbis, R. (1986, July). Interview with the Executive Director, Andromeda Community Mental Health Center, Washington, DC.

General Accounting Office (GAO). (1989, March 9). Refugees and U. S. asylum seekers from Central America. [Testimony by N. R. Kingsbury].

Nava, J. O. (1986, July). Interview with the Coordinator of Spanish Programs, Mental Health Services Administration, Washington, DC.

Schemick, N. (1986, July). Interview with the Administrative Director, Andromeda Community Mental Health Center, Washington, DC.

U. S. Department of Commerce. (1991, June 12). *News Release*. Washington, DC: Bureau of the Census.

Vargas, G. E. (1984, August). Recently arrived Central American immigrants' mental health needs. *Research Bulletin*. Washington, DC: Spanish-Speaking Mental Health Center.

Vega, W. A., & Miranda, M. R. (1985). *Stress and Hispanic mental health, relating research to service delivery*. U. S. Department of Health and Human Services, Public Health Service, Alcohol, Drug Abuse and Mental Health Administration.

Chapter Seven

Understanding the Plight of Cuba's Marielitos:
A Mental Health Perspective

Roberto J. Velásquez & Michaelanthony Brown-Cheatham

> The costly burden of the Mariel boatlift has plagued the United States far too long. The time has come to make the difficult decisions to finally resolve the problems of Mariel. (Larzalere, 1988; p. 443-444)

It has now been two decades since the last massive wave of Cuban refugees, known as the "Marielitos," arrived on the shores of the United States. While the majority of these Marielitos have successfully integrated into American society and its institutions, many continue to bear or exhibit the emotional scars (e.g., depression, substance abuse, or post-traumatic stress disorders) of this ordeal. For example, in 1992, it was still common to find articles in the popular media concerning the mental health or legal problems of the Marielitos and the difficulties that they have encountered in acculturating to this society. Larzalere (1988), in examining the legal problems of this wave, found that "... since the 1980 Mariel boatlift, about 10,500 Marielitos have been convicted of crimes committed in the United States" (p. 434). Thus, while the migration officially ended in 1982, the mental health issues of the Marielitos continue to linger. In addition to the overrepresentation of Marielitos in the prison and correctional systems of this country, Marielitos are also significantly represented in a variety of clinical settings including community mental health centers, substance abuse treatment programs, and inpatient psychiatric facilities.

For mental health professionals, the Mariel exodus presented a series of issues and problems not encountered in previous waves of Cuban or non-Cuban (e.g., Vietnamese) refugees (Westermeyer, 1989a, 1989b; Williams & Westermeyer, 1986). For example, within a relatively short period of time, mental health professionals from throughout the country had to be mobilized to respond to the various mental health needs of the Marielitos. Using unproved methods and procedures, these professionals had to: (a) devise methods to quickly assess, diagnose, and treat the variety of psychiatric symptoms or disorders manifested by the Marielitos, (b) develop collaborative working relationships with other mental and non-mental health professionals, and (c) become quite flexible and innovative in their delivery of mental health services to the Marielitos within the context of social and political pressures. In many instances these mental health professionals were unprepared to manage this massive and sudden migration because of the lack of previous experience with refugees (Cohen, 1986; Perez, 1982). Perez (1982) summarized the struggles of mental health professionals by stating that "the emergent nature of the [crisis] did not allow the time for the systematic development [and implementation] of standardized [mental health] procedures. Furthermore, political factors inherent in an immigration of this sort exerted powerful pressures on all ... [of those] involved" (p. 43).

The purpose of this chapter is to present an overview of the mental health issues that continue to impact this population. This chapter is divided into five sections. The first section presents a brief overview of the history of the Mariel exodus. While it is beyond the scope of this chapter to discuss the social, political, economic, and historical nuances of this migration, it is nonetheless critical to present some aspects of the controversy surrounding this migration. The second section describes the unique plight of the Marielitos who came from Cuba to the United States. For example, unlike previous waves, at least 50 percent of this wave were interned in makeshift refugee camps that were coordinated by the military. These camps were overcrowded (Perez, 1982) and resembled the social conditions of prisons including prostitution, rape, assault, gang formation, and a black market (Gamarra, 1982).

The third section presents an overview of mental health research on the Marielitos. With the exception of Szapocznik, Cohen, and Hernandez' (1985) book that focused on the mental health care of children and adolescents, there has been no other attempt to systematically organize the extent of mental health research on the Marielitos. The fourth section describes the mental health problems most commonly associated with the Marielitos. Clearly, this wave was less prepared to adapt to American society and more at risk to develop mental health problems than previous waves. The final section presents a series of recommendations for mental health professionals who continue to work with Marielitos and for individuals who are involved in generating policy concerning all refugees and immigrants. From the outset, it is important to describe the authors' assumptions concerning the psychological adjustment of the Marielitos. First, it is our belief that the Mariel exodus represented an "extreme" psychosocial condition that increased the vulnerability to psychopathology in Marielitos. For example, Westermeyer (1989) states that "migration can precipitate psychiatric disorder, exacerbate it, and in some unusual cases, relieve it" (p. 5). Second, children, adolescents, adults, the elderly, the educated and uneducated, the skilled and unskilled, and married and unmarried individuals can experience the same migration process in different or unique ways (Westermeyer, 1989). Third, duration of resettlement is an important factor in the psychological readjustment of the Marielitos. Gamarra (1982) noted that the longer that the Marielitos were institutionalized in a refugee camp, the greater the probability of their developing psychological dysfunction or maladaptive behavior patterns. Fourth, the attitudes of previous waves of Cubans significantly impacted the psychological adjustment of the Marielitos. Previous waves of Cuban refugees, known as the "old" Cubanos or "golden exiles," were less open to accepting these "new" Cubanos into their communities (Boswell & Curtis, 1984; Gamarra, 1982). Finally, understanding the level of "acculturative stress" (Berry, Kim, Minde, & Mok, 1987) in Marielitos is a key to the effective mental health treatment of this population. Berry, Kim, Minde, and Mok (1987) noted:

> There is often a particular set of stress behaviors which occurs during acculturation, such as lowered mental health status ... feelings of marginality and alienation, heightened psychosomatic symptom level, and identity confusion. Acculturative stress is thus a reduction in the mental health status of individuals, and may include physical, psychological, and social aspects. (p. 492-493)

The Controversy Surrounding the Marielitos: An Overview

Since 1959, or since the rise of the Castro government, there have been a least six documented periods of Cuban immigration to the United States (see Azicri, 1982; Boswell & Curtis, 1984; McCoy & Gonzalez, 1986). Collectively, this has amounted to approximately one million Cubans who have migrated to the United States over the last 40 years (Bernal, 1982; Bernal & Gutierrez, 1988). Yet, no migration has been as politically or socially controversial as the most recent migration of Cuban refugees, known as the "Freedom Flotilla," "Mad Exodus," or "Mariel Boatlift" of 1980 (Bach, Bach, & Triplett, 1981; Gamarra, 1982; Hernandez, 1985; Larzalere, 1988; Llanes, 1982; Pedraza-Bailey, 1985). Between April and September of 1980, approximately 125,000 Cuban nationals fled the country of Cuba through the port of Mariel (and the Peruvian Embassy) for the United States. According to Bach, Bach, and Triplett (1981), "if there is one characteristic of the 'Freedom Flotilla' ... that distinguishes it from all preceding waves, it is frustrating ambivalence with which the new exiles have been received in the United States" (p. 30). Pedraza-Bailey (1985), describing the chaos or madness of this migration, noted that unlike other waves this one lacked proper protocol.

> From Miami, thousands of boats manned by relatives sped across the 90 miles of sea to Cuba's Mariel Harbor. At times, they succeeded in bringing their families, other times they brought whomever angry officials put on the boats. (p. 22)

Some of those who were sent involuntarily included "social undesirables" such as prisoners, homosexuals, and the mentally ill. Boswell and Curtis (1984) have estimated that "... more than one million additional Cubans would have left ... had Mariel not been closed to further migration by Castro in September, 1980" (p. 53).

While there remain many controversial issues stemming from this migration, the most salient relates to the caliber or type of Cuban who arrived in 1980. In contrast to previous waves, especially those of the early 1960s, who represented the social, economic, and political elite of Cuba (Boswell & Curtis, 1984), this wave was characterized as socially marginal, uneducated, unskilled, emotionally dysfunctional (i.e., psychological misfits), and sexually deviant (e.g., homosexuals, prostitutes, and sex offenders). Also, this wave was composed of up to 40 percent Black Cubans (Dixon, 1983a, 1983b). Bernal (1982), in contrasting this migration to previous migrations (including those of other Hispanic groups including Mexicans and Puerto Ricans), noted that "... Cuban migration of the 1960s was overrepresented by Whites and therefore were less likely to experience racial barriers, [was] disproportionately composed of the upper and middle classes of [Cuban] society; these sectors had educational resources, business know-how, financial backing, and a set of values shared by the dominant U. S. culture...." (p. 189).

Pedraza-Bailey (1985) noted that, "After twenty years of celebrating the achievements of Cuban exiles, the press [and other media] contributed to this damaging portrayal. It focused on the criminals, the homosexuals, the many Blacks; categories of people to whom Americans accord too little respect" (p. 22).

Since 1980, researchers from various disciplines have attempted to understand the social, economic, political, and legal implications of the Mariel Boatlift (e.g., Ascher, 1981; Azicri, 1982; Bach, Bach, & Triplett, 1981; Boswell & Curtis, 1984; Briquets, 1983; Dixon, 1983a, 1983b; Fernandez, 1982, 1984; Fernandez & Narvaez, 1987; Larzelere, 1988; Lega, 1983; Pedraza-Bailey, 1985; Portes & Mozo, 1985; Portes & Stepick, 1985; Rivera, 1982). Azicri (1982) and Portes and Mozo (1985) examined the impact of the Marielitos on the political structure of the Cuban American community, while Bach, Bach, and Triplett (1981), Fernandez (1982, 1984), and Pedraza-Bailey (1985) compared the demographic characteristics of this wave to those of previous waves. Portes and Stepick (1985) examined the labor market experiences of the Marielitos, while Dixon (1983a, 1983b) considered the socioeconomic adaptation of Black Marielitos, or Afro-Cubanos, in comparison to White Marielitos.

Understanding the Plight of the Marielitos

Stein (1986) has noted that "there is a tendency to see all [Cuban] refugees ... as a homogenous group.... Most groups are subdivided into many waves and vintages that may differ greatly [and] have different experiences...."(p. 10). This is truly the case for the last wave of the refugees, the Marielitos. Figure 7-1 outlines the plight of the Marielitos.

For example, the Marielitos represented the wide spectrum of the Cuban general population including individuals who had been interned in the prison,

The Plight of Cuba's Marielitos

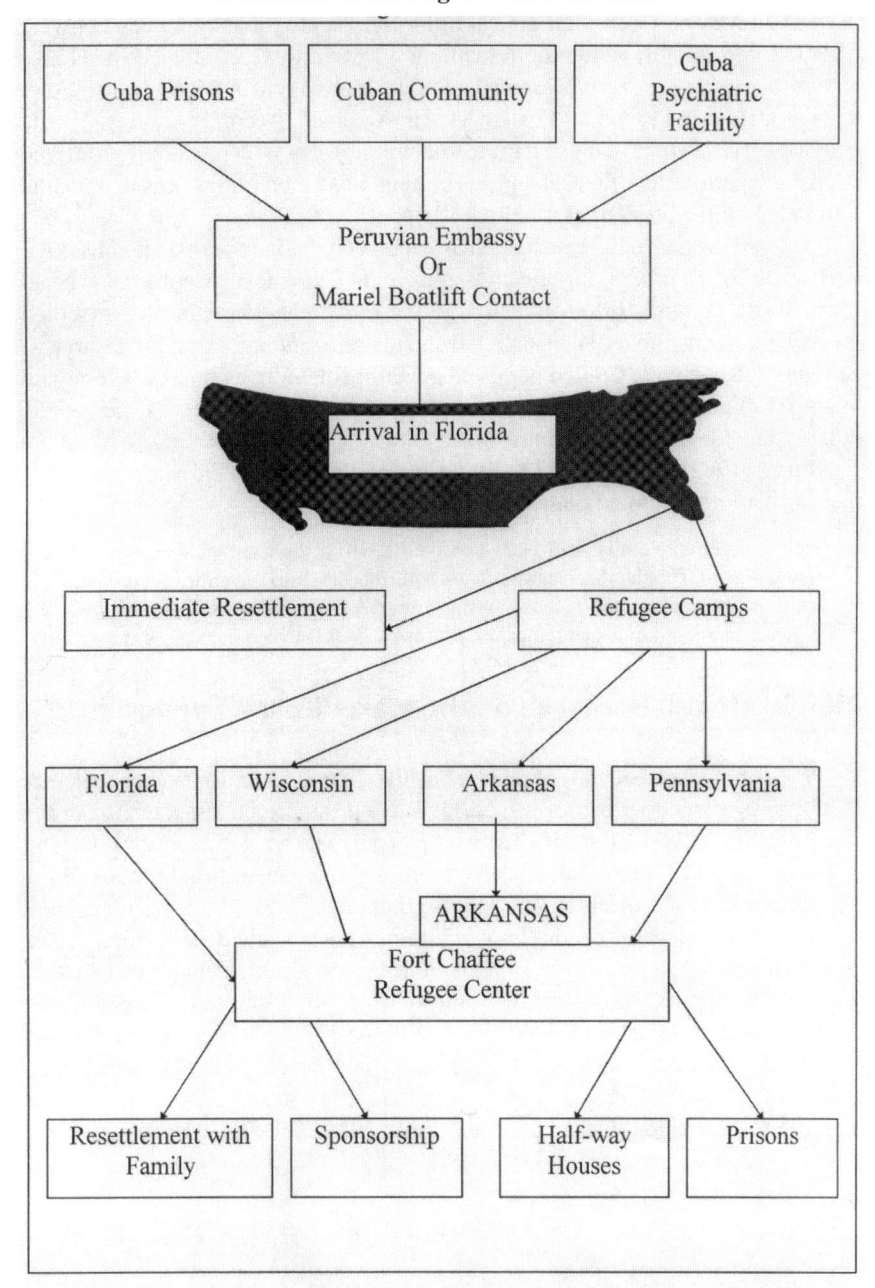

Figure 7-1
Flowchart of the Plight of the Marielitos

```
┌──────────────┐   ┌──────────────┐   ┌──────────────┐
│ Cuba Prisons │   │Cuban Community│   │    Cuba      │
│              │   │              │   │ Psychiatric  │
│              │   │              │   │   Facility   │
└──────┬───────┘   └──────┬───────┘   └──────┬───────┘
       │                  │                  │
       └──────────────┐   │   ┌──────────────┘
                      ▼   ▼   ▼
              ┌──────────────────────┐
              │  Peruvian Embassy    │
              │         Or           │
              │ Mariel Boatlift Contact│
              └──────────┬───────────┘
                         ▼
                ┌─────────────────┐
                │Arrival in Florida│
                └─────────────────┘

┌──────────────────────┐         ┌──────────────────┐
│Immediate Resettlement│◄────────│  Refugee Camps   │
└──────────┬───────────┘         └────────┬─────────┘
           │                              │
    ┌──────┼──────┬──────────┬────────────┤
    ▼      ▼      ▼          ▼            ▼
┌───────┐┌─────────┐┌──────────┐┌──────────────┐
│Florida││Wisconsin││ Arkansas ││ Pennsylvania │
└───┬───┘└────┬────┘└────┬─────┘└──────┬───────┘
    │         │          │             │
    │         │      ARKANSAS          │
    │         │          │             │
    └─────────┴──► Fort Chaffee ◄──────┘
                  Refugee Center
                        │
        ┌───────┬───────┼────────┬─────────┐
        ▼       ▼                ▼         ▼
┌──────────────┐┌──────────┐┌─────────┐┌────────┐
│Resettlement  ││Sponsorship││Half-way ││Prisons │
│ with Family  ││          ││ Houses  ││        │
└──────────────┘└──────────┘└─────────┘└────────┘
```

correctional, and psychiatric systems of Cuba. While the initial exodus began through the Peruvian Embassy, the majority of all Cuban refugees escaped through the port of Mariel. Upon their arrival in Florida, approximately 50 percent were resettled immediately while the remaining 50 percent were interned in refugee camps such as Ft. McCoy in Wisconsin, Ft. Indiantown Gap in Pennsylvania, Eglin Air Force Base in Florida, and Ft. Chaffee in Arkansas. According to Bach, Bach, and Triplett (1981), "... many sent to the four military camps for processing ... arrived amidst allegations that the Cuban government was emptying its jails and mental hospitals into the boats of Mariel harbor" (p. 30).

Toward the end of the resettlement process, Ft. Chaffee became the consolidation center for all other refugee camps and handled the most unsponsorable of all Marielitos (Gamarra, 1982). Eventually, the remaining Marielitos were settled through family members, sponsorship through humanitarian and religious organizations (U. S. Catholic Conference), and government half-way houses. Those with known criminal records continued to be interned in the federal prison system, most notably the Atlanta Federal Penitentiary.

Perez (1982) summarized the culture shock that awaited the Marielitos upon their arrival in the United States:

> The refugee population had been uprooted ... from their accustomed cultural environment. They had been transported several thousand miles to an unknown camp run by what was (for them) a foreign army. They were required to remain in the camp ... until an immigration and relocation process ... could be completed. (p.41)

Mental Health Research on the Marielitos: A Synopsis

A comprehensive review of mental health research on the Marielitos indicates that in comparison to previous waves this wave has received less attention in the literature. Since 1980, a total of 17 articles and only one book (Szapocznik, Cohen, & Hernandez, 1985) have specifically examined the mental health issues of the Marielitos. Table 7.1 offers an overview of these resources.

Upon closer inspection, this body of literature can be divided into three types. The first type focuses on the early years of Marielito resettlement (Marina, 1980; Spencer, Rodriguez, Szapocznik, & Santiesteban, 1981). The second type focuses on the socio-demographic characteristics of the Marielitos (Gamarra, 1982, 1984; Peterson, 1982; Velásquez, 1982) with an emphasis on predicting adaptation, assimilation, or acculturation. The third type focuses on some aspects of service delivery to Marielitos (Cohen & Szapocznik, 1985; Gil, 1983; Hoffman, 1987; Perez, 1982; Szapcoznik & Cohen, 1986).

Table 7.1
Mental Health Research on the Marielitos: An Overview

Author(s):	Primary Purpose of Article
Marina (1980)	Attempted to predict the acculturation of the Marielitos
Spencer, et. al. (1981)	Discussed issues in the mental health care of Marielitos
Bernal (1982)	Discussed family therapy approaches for the treatment of Cubans including Marielitos
Gamarra (1982)	Studied 1,000 Marielitos at Ft. Chaffee, AK; examined the psychological adaptation of this group
Perez (1982)	Examined the delivery of mental health services to Marielito minors at Ft. McCoy, WI
Peterson (1982)	Examined the attitudes of 37 Marielitos toward employment
Velásquez (1982)	Attempted to determine the psychological adaptation of 1,000 Marielitos at Ft. Chaffee, AK
Dixon (1983)	The socio-economic adaptation of Marielitos was examined, with a section devoted to mental health
Gil (1983)	Discussed issues in the delivery of mental health services to Marielitos
Fernandez (1984)	Discussed rates of mental disorders among Marielitos at Ft. Chaffee, AK
Queralt (1984)	Discussed mental health issues unique to Cubans and Marielitos
Boxer & Garvey (1985)	Examined the reliability of psychiatric diagnoses for 109 Marielitos in the federal prison system
Gamarra (1984)	Discussed continuing mental health issues of Marielitos
Hoffman (1985)	Discussed the need for "acculturation specialists" to work with Marielitos
Szapocznik, et. al. (1985)	Only book to focus on the mental health issues of the Marielitos; specifically examined the problems of Marielito adolescents and included a model for the delivery of mental health services to this special group
Szapocznik & Cohen (1986)	Described a culturally sensitive mental health program for unaccompanied Marielito minors
Hoffman (1987)	Discussed the application of Hispanic Alcoholics Anonymous to alcoholic Marielitos
Bernal & Gutierrez (1988)	Discussed clinical issues in the treatment of Cubans —including Marielitos

Mental Health Problems of the Marielitos

Over the years, several researchers (Keller, 1975; Kunz, 1973; Lin, 1986; Stein, 1986) have outlined models or frameworks for understanding the psychological experience(s) of the refugee. Keller (1975) for example, presented at least eight generic stages of the refugee experience. These include (a) perception of threat, (b) deciding to flee, (c) a period of extreme danger and actual flight, (d) reaching safety, (e) refugee camp behavior, (f) settlement or resettlement, (g) adjustment and acculturation, and (h) residual stages and changes in behavior caused by the refugee experience.

Kunz (1973, 1981) distinguished between two types of migrants: those who are "pulled" to leave their own country (for economic, educational, or political gain) and go to a new country, and those who are "pushed out" of their country due to political persecution or oppression. Following this line of reasoning, Kunz also noted that there are anticipatory refugees who anticipate danger before it actually occurs in their homeland and are able to leave with intact families and economic and personal resources. These individuals are also able to make preparations for a new life in the host country. Acute refugees, on the other hand, flee their country on a moment's notice due to a current political or economic crisis (e.g., the Mariel Boatlift). These individuals have not planned or prepared for an exodus, nor have they considered what their future holds for them in a new country. Clearly, the acute refugees are more susceptible to mental illness because they lack accurate information about the host culture or society. The earlier waves of Cuban refugees, especially those of the early 1960s, appear to have elected to leave the country while the Marielitos, for the most part, were forced to leave their homeland.

Using the *Diagnostic and Statistical Manual of Mental Disorders* (DSM-III and DSM-III-R; American Psychiatric Association, 1980, 1987), which is the official system of diagnostic classification in the United States, Table 7.2 presents some of the most common symptoms and disorders experienced by the Marielitos during and after their departure from Cuba. The primary purpose of this table is to illustrate the fact that refugees are not immune from a wide range of mental health disorders.

Table 7.3 presents a framework for understanding the relationship between stress and psychological prognosis in the Marielitos. For example, it is possible to determine the prognosis of Marielitos in mental health treatment by assessing the levels of stress encountered by individuals prior to, during, and after the Mariel exodus.

Note: There are numerous combinations and permutations of stress levels by migration experience which are unique to each Marielito.

Table 7.2
Psychopathology of the Marielitos

Psychopathology
DSM-III-R Disorders   Symptoms

*Adjustment Disorders   *Grief
*Mood Disorders   *Lethargy
*Substance Use Disorders   *Apathy
*Anxiety Disorders   *Insecurity
*Conversion Disorders   *Ambivalence
*Dissociative Disorders   *Entitlement
*Schizophrenia   *Alienation
*Organic Disorders   *Mistrust
*Sexual Disorders   *Weight Loss
*Sleep Disorders   *Fear
*Impulse Control Disorders   *Isolation
    *Personality Disorders   *Nightmares
                                   *Marginality
                                   *Regression
                                   *Substance Abuse
                                   *Paranoia
                                   *Helplessness
                                   *Anger/Aggression

Note: These disorders are based on the *Diagnostic and Statistical Manual of Mental Disorders* (DSM-III and DSM-III-R).

Table 7.3
Relationship Between Marielitos' Stress and Psychological Prognosis: A Framework

Migration Experience

Levels of Stress	Pre-Mariel	Mariel Exodus	Post-Mariel	Prognosis
Low	Low	Low	Low	Good
Moderate	Moderate	Moderate	Moderate	Fair
High	High	High	High	Poor

Recommendations for Mental Health Professionals

The following list of recommendations are proposed for mental health professionals who are currently working with Marielitos or those who will be involved with future waves of refugees:

1. Mental health professionals should be aware and sensitive to the cultural, social, and political backgrounds of their clients. For example, family and group interventions with Cuban refugees can be effective in alleviating the intensity, frequency, and duration of mental health disorders.

2. Mental health professionals should be aware of the role of acculturative stress in the psychological functioning of Cuban refugees.

3. It is paramount that mental health professionals differentiate the political and clinical issues in working with Cuban refugees. While it is clear that these issues overlapped in working with the Marielitos, the overlap of political and clinical issues can oftentimes compromise the effectiveness of mental health professionals leading to transference dilemmas.

4. Mental health professionals need to understand the inherent differences within the waves of Cuban refugees. For example, Cuban adolescents faced different mental health issues from those of Cuban adults, just as Cuban women did from Cuban men. Clearly, the special needs of all subgroups must be considered in the delivery of mental health services.

5. Mental health professionals need to further recognize their roles as advocates in the resettlement process. They must recognize that their roles in the resettlement process are varied or multifaceted and differ from roles in traditional mental health settings (e.g., private practice). This would include working as consultants to individuals and organizations.

6. Special training is necessary for refugee camp staff on the roles of mental health professionals in the resettlement process. It is clear from the Mariel exodus that camp staff were oftentimes not aware of the special roles of mental health professionals such as psychologists, social workers, and psychiatrists.

7. Mental health professionals should make every effort to obtain comprehensive histories of all Cuban refugees including psychiatric background. The purpose of these evaluations is to determine premorbid psychosocial adjustment of Cuban refugees. From the authors' experiences it is clear from working with the Marielito that those who had lengthy psychiatric

or criminal histories were more likely to experience greater difficulties in adjusting or adapting to the norms of mainstream society.

8. There is a need for follow-up studies on the psychological adaptation and acculturation of the Marielitos to American society. For example, there remains a paucity of research on the prevalence of mental disorders in this population.

Recommendations for Mental Health Policymakers

The following list of recommendations are suggested for individuals who are directly involved in the development of policy for refugees and immigrants:

1. Establish a national mental health center on immigration. Staff at this center would be responsible for developing policy on the delivery of mental health services to immigrants and refugees of varying nationalities. This center would also serve as a national clearinghouse for research on refugees and immigrants. This would include the development of a network of qualified or certified mental health professionals who have been specifically trained in counseling techniques that focus on the psychological aspects of migration (e.g., trauma). This would include the development of "quick response teams" composed of mental health professionals from various disciplines to respond to unexpected migrations.

2. Establish "state of the art" refugee resettlement facilities that would include educational, social, occupational, cultural, and mental health components. For example, the refugee camps that were established during the Mariel boatlift resembled correctional facilities or prisons. This type of environment was found to be highly detrimental to the psycho-social adjustment of Cuban refugees.

3. Limit refugee internment to less than three months. In the case of the Mariel exodus, individuals were interned for up to one and a half years (excluding individuals who were interned in the federal prison system for crimes). It appears that after three months, the Marielitos began to assimilate a "prison mentality" that ultimately impacted their adjustment to American society. One would speculate the extent to which crowding influenced the emergence and intensity of these observed behaviors. It appears that the longer the Marielitos were interned, the greater their susceptibility to a variety of mental health disorders, ranging from anxiety disorders to schizophrenia.

4. Develop local transitional support services to assist immigrants in their integration into the community. For example, in the case of the Marielitos,

many were sponsored out to half-way houses throughout the United States. Unfortunately, the quality of these programs varied from setting to setting with respect to the delivery of mental health services.

5. The emphasis of refugee resettlement programs should be a tripartite prevention model, for example, primary prevention (education), secondary prevention (detection), and tertiary prevention (treatment). The experience of the Mariel exodus clearly reflects secondary and tertiary interventions. Primary prevention programs would focus on "stress inoculation" and education.

Summary

The purpose of this chapter is to sensitize mental health professionals to the plight of one particular group of refugees, the Marielitos. Given the recent fall of communism in the Eastern bloc countries such as the Soviet Union, it is possible that the next wave of Cuban refugees will significantly overshadow all previous waves including the Mariel boatlift of 1980. It is our responsibility to see that history will not repeat itself in the treatment of future Cuban refugees as occurred with the Mariels of 1980. Rumbaut and Rumbaut (1976) used a metaphor that has applied to all Cuban migrations:

> [Janus]... had two faces, which enabled him, to see in opposite directions simultaneously.... The face that looks back sees displacement, separation, uprooting, loss, nostalgia, and in a certain sense, even death.... The face that looks forward sees new horizons, unknown environments, strangers... unfamiliar customs... languages, real and imaginary perils, a vigorous challenge.... (p.396)

Consequently, these challenges present the Cuban refugee with an opportunity to establish a new identity from an experience that combined the traumas of premature death and rebirth (Rumbaut & Rumbaut, 1976).

References

American Psychiatric Association. (1980). *Diagnostic and statistical manual of mental disorders, (3rd ed.)*. Washington, DC: American Psychiatric Association.
American Psychiatric Association. (1987). *Diagnostic and statistical manual of mental disorders. (rev. 3rd ed.)*. Washington, DC: American Psychiatric Association.
Ascher, C. (1981). *The United States' new refugees: A review of the research on the resettlement of Indo-Chinese, Cubans, and Haitians*. Washington, DC: National Institute of Education. (ERIC Document Reproduction Service No. ED 212 731).
Azicri, M. (1982). The politics of exile: Trends and dynamics of political change among Cuban-Americans. *Cuban Studies, 11*, 55-73.
Bach, R. L., Bach, J. B., & Triplett, T. (1982). The flotilla "entrants": Latest and most

controversial. *Cuban Studies, 11*, 29-48.
Bernal, G. (1982). Cuban families. In M. McGoldrick, J. K. Pearce, & J. Giordano (Eds.), *Ethnicity and family therapy* (pp. 187-207). New York: Guilford.
Bernal, G., & Gutierrez, M. (1988). Cubans. In L. Comas-Diaz & E. E. H. Griffith (Eds.), *Clinical guidelines in crosscultural mental health*. New York: John Wiley.
Berry, J. W., Kim, U., Minde, T., & Mok, D. (1987). Comparative studies of acculturative stress. *International Migration Review, 21*, 491-511.
Boswell, T. D., & Curtis, J. R. (1984). *The Cuban/American experience: Culture, images, and perspectives*. Totowa, NJ: Rowman & Allanheld.
Boxer, P. A., & Garvey, J. T. (1985). Psychiatric diagnoses of Cuban refugees in the United States: Findings of medical review boards. *American Journal of Psychiatry, 142*, 86-89.
Briquets, S. D. (1983). Demographic and related determinants of recent Cuban emigration. *International Migration Review, 17*, 95-119.
Cohen, R. (1985). Roles and functions of mental health professionals in refugee camps. In J. Szapocznik, R. Cohen, & R. E. Hernandez (Eds.), *Coping with adolescent refugees: The Mariel boatlift* (pp. 100-124). New York: Praeger.
Cohen, R., & Szapocznik, J. (1985). CAMP: An emergency relief model using a problem-solving approach. In J. Szapocznik, R. Cohen, & R. E. Hernandez (Eds.), *Coping with adolescent refugees: The Mariel boatlift* (pp. 39-56). New York: Praeger.
Dixon, H. (1983a). *A look at the socio-economic adaptation of the Mariel Cubans*. New York: New School for Social Research. (ERIC Document Reproduction Service No. ED 229 466).
Dixon, H. (1983b). *An overview of the Black Cubans among the Mariel entrants*. New York: New School for Social Research. (ERIC Document Reproduction Service No. ED 233 104).
Fernandez, G. A. (1981). Comment—The flotilla entrants: Are they different? *Cuban Studies, 11*, 49-54.
Fernandez, G. A. (1984). Conflicting interpretations of the freedom flotilla entrants. *Cuban Studies, 14*, 49-51.
Fernandez, G. A., & Narvaez, L. (1985). Bibliography of Cuban immigration/adaptation to the United States. *Cuban Studies, 15*, 61-72.
Fernandez, G. A., & Narvaez, L. (1987). Refugees and human rights in Costa Rica: The Mariel Cubans. *International Migration Review, 21*, 406-415.
Gamarra, E. A. (1982). Comment—The continuing dilemma of the freedom flotilla entrants. *Cuban Studies, 12*, 87-91.
Gamarra, E. A. (1984). Reply to Gaston A. Fernandez. *Cuban Studies, 14*, 53-56.
Gil, R. C. (1983). Issues in the delivery of mental health services to Cuban entrants. *Migration Today, 11*, 43-48.
Hernandez, R. E. (1985). The origins of the Mariel boatlift. In J. Szapocznik, R. Cohen, & R. E. Hernandez (Eds.), *Coping with adolescent refugees: The Mariel boatlift* (pp. 3-21). New York: Praeger.
Hoffman, F. (1985). Clinical sociology and the acculturation specialty. *Clinical Sociology Review, 3*, 50-58.
Hoffman, F. (1987). An alcoholism program for Hispanics. *Clinical Sociology Review, 5*, 91-101.
Keller, S. L. (1975). *Uprooting and social change: The role of refugees in development*. Delhi, India: Manohar Book Service.

Kunz, E. F. (1973). The refugee in flight: Kinetic models and forms of displacement. *International Migration Review, 7*, 125-146.

Kunz, E. F. (1981). Exile and resettlement: Refugee theory. *International Migration Review, 15*, 42-51.

Lazalere, A. (1988). *Castro's ploy—America's dilemma: The 1980 Cuban boatlift.* Washington, DC: National Defense University Press.

Lega, L. I. (1983). The 1980 Cuban refugees: Some of their initial attitudes. *Migration Today, 11*, 23-26.

Lin, K. M. (1986). Psychopathology and social disruption in refugees. In C. L. Williams & J. Westermeyer (Eds.), Refugee mental health in resettlement countries (pp. 61-73). New York: Hemisphere.

Llanes, J. (1982). *Cuban Americans: Masters of survival.* Cambridge, MA: Abt Books.

MacCorkle, L. (1984). *Cubans in the United States: A bibliography for research in the social and behavioral sciences, 1960-1983.* Westport, CN: Greenwood.

McCoy, C. B., & Gonzalez, D. H. (1985). Cuban immigration and Mariel immigrants. In J. Szapocznik, R. Cohen, & R. E. Hernandez (Eds.), *Coping with adolescent refugees: The Mariel boatlift* (pp. 22-38). New York: Praeger.

Marina, D. R. (1980). Predicting the Cuban entrants' acculturation rate. *Clinical Psychologist, 34*, 22-23.

Pedraza-Bailey, S. (1985). Cuba's exiles: Portrait of a refugee migration. *International Migration Review, 19*, 4-34.

Perez, R. (1982). Provision of mental health services during a disaster: The Cuban immigration of 1980. *Journal of Community Psychology, 10*, 40-47.

Peterson, M. F. (1982). The flotilla entrants: Social psychological perspectives on their employment. *Cuban Studies, 12*, 81-85.

Portes, A., & Mozo, R. (1985). The political adaptation process of Cubans and other ethnic minorities in the United States: A preliminary analysis. *International Migration Review, 19*, 37-63.

Portes, A., & Stepik, A. (1985). Unwelcome immigrants: The labor market experiences of 1980 (Mariel) Cuban and Haitian refugees in South Florida. *American Sociological Review, 50*, 493-514.

Queralt, M. (1984). Understanding Cuban immigrants: A cultural perspective. *Social Work, 29*, 115-121.

Rivera, M. A. (1982). *An evaluative analysis of the Carter administration's policy toward the Mariel influx of 1980.* Unpublished doctoral dissertation, University of Notre Dame, Notre Dame, IN.

Rumbaut, R., & Rumbaut, R. D. (1976). The family in exile: Cuban expatriates in the United States. *American Journal of Psychiatry, 133*, 395-399.

Spencer, F., Rodriguez, A. M., Szapocznik, J., & Santiesteban, D. (1981). *Cuba crisis 1980: Mental health care issues.* Paper presented at the annual meeting of the Southeastern Psychological Association, Atlanta, GA.

Stein, B. N. (1986). The experience of being a refugee: Insights from the research literature. In C. L. Williams & J. Westermeyer (Eds.), *Refugee mental health in resettlement countries* (pp. 5-23). New York: Hemisphere Publishing Corporation.

Szapocznik, J., & Cohen, R. (1986). Mental health care for rapidly changing environments: Emergency relief to unaccompanied youths of the 1980 Cuban refugee wave. In C. L.

Williams & J. Westermeyer (Eds.), *Refugee mental health in resettlement countries* (pp. 141-156). Washington, DC: Hemisphere.

Szapocznik, J., Cohen, R., & Hernandez, R. E. (Eds.). (1985). *Coping with adolescent refugees: The Mariel boatlift*. New York: Praeger.

Velásquez, R. J. (1982). *Predicting Psychological adaptation for recent Cuban refugees*. Unpublished manuscript, Arizona State University, Tempe, AZ.

Westermeyer, J. (1989a). *Psychiatric care of migrants: A clinical guide*. Washington, DC: American Psychiatric Press.

Westermeyer, J. (1989b). *Mental health for refugees and migrants: Social and preventive approaches*. Springfield, IL: Charles C. Thomas.

Williams, C. L., & Westermeyer, J. (1986). *Refugee mental health in resettlement countries*. Washington, DC: Hemisphere.

Chapter Eight

Ethopia's Exodus of Human Resources:
Adjustment and Acculturation Issues

Maigenet Shifferraw & Getachew Metaferia

Historically, Ethiopians have fiercely challenged foreign aggression and kept the country independent from European colonizers, except for the five years of occupation by Fascist Italy (1936-41). In spite of its long history of independence, however, Ethiopia's record on democracy and human rights is not at all impressive. Emperor Haile Selassie's government, which played an important role in the development of the country, failed to provide conditions for democracy to flourish. That government was overthrown in June, 1991. The 17 years under military rule were noted for famine and economic and political crises, as well as gross human rights abuses. Hence, the government was the catalyst for the exodus of millions of Ethiopians—unprecedented in the country's long history.

According to a 1985 report by the World Bank, Ethiopia has deficiencies in trained human resources in every field (Spolar, 1987). This could be due primarily to the exodus of considerable numbers of skilled and trained citizens who settle or find temporary refuge in other countries.

Of course, the exodus of Ethiopians is not composed exclusively of the above-categorized groups of Ethiopians. An estimated 2 million Ethiopians, including those with little or no formal education, have left the country since 1974. Most of these Ethiopians are in the neighboring African countries. Some, mostly the educated, have migrated to Western Europe and North America (*Ethiopian Community Center News,* Fall, 1983).

In 1986, the authors conducted a survey of the exodus and adjustment of those trained and experienced Ethiopians who settled in the United States. "Trained and experienced" Ethiopians are defined as persons with the following formal educa-

---

This chapter is reprinted by permission of the authors, copyright by Getachew Metaferia and Maigenet Shifferraw, 1992. Versions of this paper were presented at the 1988 Annual Conference of the African Studies Association in Chicago, and included in *The Ethiopian Revolution of 1974 and the Exodus of Ethiopia's Trained Human Resources*, the Edwin Mellen Press, 1992.

tion and/or experiences: (a) four years of college education and above; (b) two years of college education, with technical and vocational skills; and (c) less than two years of college education, but with working experiences in their country at mid- or high-level, policy-making positions. This valuable resource of trained personnel played a vital role in the development of Ethiopia. On the other hand, the exodus of this human capital has negatively affected the development of the country.

When dealing with adjustment issues of Ethiopians in the United States, especially within the group of trained and experienced people we studies, we cannot ignore the historical circumstances that precipitated their exodus and their decision to settle in a different environment. Generally speaking, the majority of educated and trained Ethiopians led satisfying lives prior to the 1974 Ethiopian revolution. Some said that they were better off socially, professionally, and psychologically in Ethiopia than in the United States. Almost all Ethiopians who had studied in the United States prior to that time returned to their country upon completion of their studies. This research focuses on how Ethiopians in the United States are adjusting to a new environment.

Currently, a large number of trained and experienced Ethiopians are living in the United States. Most Ethiopian graduates from American institutions of higher education prefer to remain in the United States rather than return to their country where the political condition is volatile and unpredictable. Similar to many other Third World immigrants in the United States, many trained and experienced Ethiopians hold jobs that are incompatible with their training and/or experience, largely because of survival considerations. The question, then, is what exactly are the major *push* and *pull factors* that forced these people to decide to leave their country and resettle in the United States, even when this host country has not offered them jobs in which they can utilize their training and skills and be more productive?

The *first objective* of this research, therefore, was to find the *push* and *pull* variables which influenced the exodus of trained and experienced Ethiopians from Ethiopia to their resettlement in the United States. The *second objective* of this research was to study the conditions of this group of Ethiopians in the United States—their social integration into American society and their psychological and economic adjustment to their new environment, including the utilization of their training and professional experiences. This study also attempted to identify probable economic and political developments which might persuade this particular group to return to their country and help retain the developed human resources in Ethiopia. In this paper we deal primarily with the second objective of the research, that is, adjustment issues regarding the utilization of trained and experienced Ethiopians in the United States.

In the first part of the paper we briefly discuss the methodology we used to collect the data for the research. We also highlight the findings of our research regarding the *push-pull factors* that contributed to the exodus of the respondents to this survey. The second part of the paper deals with adjustment issues regarding this group of Ethiopians studied in the United States. In the last part we discuss the summary and conclusions of this study.

Framework and Method of Data Collection

Several studies about what is called the "brain drain" from developing countries have indicated some common *push-pull factors*. The *push factors*, according to these studies, include lack of economic incentives, political problems, and limited professional satisfaction with fewer opportunities for upward mobility in one's own country. The existence of these opportunities in other countries is thought to *pull* people to countries that offer them.

Having this theoretical framework in mind, we developed several questions in order to identify the common *push-pull factors* that might have contributed to the immigration to the United States. We also developed questions that evaluate issues of their social, cultural, and economic adjustment in the United States. The following questions were used as a basis for the study.

1. Are the lack of professional opportunities or the lack of monetary rewards at home, and the perceived presence of the opportunities and rewards in the United States, factors in Ethiopians leaving their country and resettling in the United States?

2. What are the attitudes of Ethiopians toward the political circumstances their country, and what are their estimates of probable developments in the future that might interest them in returning to Ethiopia?

3. What are the major adjustment problems faced by trained and professionally experienced Ethiopians currently residing in the United States? To what degree are they satisfied or dissatisfied professionally, economically, and socially in their new home, and to what degree do they feel that they are integrating into American society?

The validity of these questions and the explanatory power of each proposed causal factor were determined by comparing and contrasting the profiles of respondents who: (a) had different levels of professional success; and (b) had come to the United States at different times, such as before and after the 1974 Ethiopian revolution. Based on these variables, the respondents' attitudes were compared with generalized political attitudes and values, as well as with specific attitudes toward the past and present (military) regimes in Ethiopia. The following is an explanation of the methods used to collect data for the research.

Methodologies Used To Collect Data

In the spring of 1986 a questionnaire was sent to Ethiopians in the United States who fit our definition of training and experience. After the responses or questionnaires were collected and analyzed, selected individuals were interviewed. The interviewees were community leaders, former government officials exiled in the United States, current officials, former and current political activists, and representatives of the major opposition groups and liberation fronts currently stationed in the United States. The purpose of the interviews was to qualitatively gather information that was inadvertently missed through the questionnaire. Any gap created because of the inherent weaknesses of the survey method was filled through the interviews.

In addition to the above methods of gathering data, we also gained more information as participant-observers since both researchers are Ethiopian and participate in various social and professional Ethiopian gatherings. This access increased our chances of collecting information through continuous observations, and through informal discussions with individual Ethiopian friends as well. Hence, participant-observer and informal discussion enhanced the methodology of data gathering and gave us more insight into the predicaments of exiled compatriots.

Selection of Respondents

There does not exist any systematic and complete enumeration of Ethiopians in the United States. According to estimates by various Ethiopian community centers, there were about 40,000 Ethiopians in the United States in 1986. The exact number of trained and experienced Ethiopians who fit our definition is unknown. Thus, no sampling frame exists for the selection of a strict random sample. Because we encountered this sampling problem, we decided to conduct an opinion survey of "X" numbers of trained and experienced Ethiopians in the United States. The findings of this research, therefore, are limited to the opinions of respondents to the survey and interviewees, plus the participant-observations and informal discussions held with other Ethiopians.

In order to select respondents from different segments of the Ethiopian population in the survey, the following method was used. Variables for stratifying respondent categories were selected with a view toward assuring that all segments of the trained and experienced Ethiopian population were represented. The variables that were selected wee gender, ethnicity, age, profession, and political affiliation to assure that respondents to the survey were heterogeneous and to minimize the chances of their composition being biased in any significant way. Then, working through a network of personal contacts, 50 Ethiopians were identified as contacts for the research. We call these 50 people *key contacts.*

The *key contacts* were selected on the basis of the following criteria: (a) suitability to our definition of trained and experienced manpower; (b) activity in community work and/or knowledge of a considerable number of Ethiopians that fell within our definition of trained and experienced manpower; and (c) ability to help us in approaching Ethiopians, with the variables selected, to stratify respondents to be included in the research. The *key contacts* agreed to identify respondents who would fit our criteria. We provided them with guidelines regarding the selection of respondents.

Pre-Testing the Questionnaire

The questionnaire was designed and sent to the *key contacts* for pre-testing. We asked the *key contacts* to send us their comments about the questionnaire. We wanted to know if other issues of importance were inadvertently excluded, or if trivial issues were identified. Out of the 50 questionnaires we sent for pre-testing, 35 (70 percent) were returned. The questionnaires were carefully completed, with comments and suggestions included. We then refined and prepared the final questionnaire to be sent to possible respondents.

Questionnaire Administration

When the final questionnaire was completed, we called our *key contacts* and asked them to provide the names and addresses of respondents whom they had selected for the survey, based on the criteria. Most *key contacts* did not provide lists of respondents because many possible respondents were unwilling to give their names and addresses to researchers. However, they were agreeable to receiving the questionnaires from the *key contacts*. Because of the sensitivity of the research, there was an element of suspicion among possible respondents in sharing their views about the current conditions in Ethiopia and their reasons for leaving; therefore, these circumstances compelled us to depend upon our *key contacts*.

In April, 1986, we sent 600 questionnaires to our *key contacts* to distribute to possible respondents; a few additional ones were sent directly to possible respondents. Respondents were given a month to complete the questionnaires and return them. Two days after the questionnaires were mailed, the *key contacts* reminded the possible respondents to complete and return the questionnaires.

Out of the 600 questionnaires we sent out, either directly or through our *key contacts*, 136 were returned unopened. This meant that (a) our *key contacts* returned the questionnaires to us because they were unable to distribute them, for various reasons; (b) some respondents likely received duplicate questionnaires since many of our *key contacts* knew the same people; or (c) possible respondents had changed their addresses. Of the remaining 464 questionnaires, 244 (52.5 percent) were completed and returned. Therefore, the data gathered through this questionnaire method are the opinions of 244 trained and experienced Ethiopians who live in the United States.

As mentioned earlier, the total population of Ethiopians in the United States at the time of this survey (1986) was estimated to be 40,000, and the number of trained and experienced Ethiopians in the United States, as defined in this research, was unknown. Nonetheless, the opinions of the 244 Ethiopians who did respond to our survey are significant in shedding light on the questions developed as a basis for this study.

Profiles of Respondents

The gender makeup of the respondents was 52 females and 192 males. Most respondents have four years of college education or more. More than half (57.7 percent), for example, have Masters' degrees or above. Out of this number, 38 (15.6 percent) hold Ph.D. or M. D. degrees. Before the revolution in Ethiopia, the majority (63.9 percent) worked in Ethiopia as executives, administrators, or managers, and as professionals and/or experts. Most had achieved higher education in the social sciences, economics, engineering, and business. At the time of the survey, respondents lived in 32 of the United States, with the majority residing on the East Coast. More than 10,000 Ethiopians, for example, were said to reside in the Metropolitan Washington, D. C. area (which includes areas of Maryland and Virginia). Some respondents resided in the East Coast states of New York, New Jersey, Pennsylvania, and Massachusetts. The West Coast respondents, the second most popular region for Ethiopian resettlement, comprised 20.9 percent of our survey. Most lived in the states of Washington and California (which today have the second largest Ethiopian communities).

The majority of our respondents, 217 (88.9 percent), were above the age of 30. There were only 27 between the ages of 21 and 30 though a large number, 109 (44.6 percent), were above the age of 36. The age distribution of respondents is important because most of those who were above the age of 36 had uninterrupted elementary and secondary school education in Ethiopia. Their education was uninterrupted because most had finished secondary school before the late 1960s. Beginning in the late 1960s, students in Ethiopia were becoming radical, and schools were periodically closed by the government to curb student agitation and demonstrations. After the revolution the students' education was often interrupted for campaign duties, so many students did not have the opportunity to finish their schooling on schedule. Most respondents who were 36 years of age and older had work experiences in Ethiopia during the previous government's reign and/or after the revolution. Most of the rest, who were below the age of 36, had work experiences only in the United States. The respondents above the age of 30 were the well-educated and experienced group. The loss of this age group, especially those who are trained and experienced, can hamper a country's development.

As indicated in Table 8.1, a large number of respondents have a Bachelor's degree or above (87.5 percent of the total respondents). Of those who have Masters' degrees, 42.3 percent are female, and 43.2 percent are male. Those respondents who have a Ph.D or M.D. are 15.6 percent of the total. The majority of the respondents, 81.6 percent, received their last degree in the United States. Other places for the last degree achieved by respondents were Ethiopia, 7.4 perecnt; Western Europe, 6.1 percent; Eastern Europe, 1.2 percent; the Middle East, 1.2 percent; and other African countries, 0.8 percent. The majority of respondents (43) had achieved higher education in the social sciences (political, anthropology, sociology, geography, and history). A significant number (30) of the respondents had achieved higher education in engineering (civil, mechanical, electrical, and chemical); 32 in economics; and 28 in business.

Why Leave the Homeland?

Out of the 244 respondents to the survey, 72 left Ethiopia after the 1974 revolution, and 172 left before the revolution. The majority of our respondents were, therefore, those who had opted to stay in the United States after completing their education. Respondents were asked what major factors affected their decision to leave Ethiopia or influenced them to remain in the United States. We also asked for respondents' opinions, in the survey as well as in the interviews, why there is an exodus of trained and experienced Ethiopians out of their homeland. This question

Table 8.1
Respondents' Levels of Formal Education by Gender

Level of Formal Education	Female No.	%	Male No.	%	Total No.	%
12th grade completed, plus experience	0	0	1	.5	1	.4
Some college education, plus experience	3	5.8	5	2.6	8	3.3
Two years vocational and technical training	5	9.6	17	8.9	22	9.0
Bachelor's degree	22	42.3	48	25.0	70	28.7
Master's degree	22	42.3	83	43.2	105	43.0
Ph.D. and M. D.	0	0	38	19.8	38	15.6
Total	52	100.0	192	100.0	244	100.0

was raised many times throughout the informal discussion we had with some Ethiopians. The current political conditions in the country, more specifically the absence of democratic and basic human rights, was the answer most frequently given by respondents. Since democracy is a controversial concept, we asked our respondents to explain what they meant by democracy so that we could establish a framework within which we could analyze the situation in Ethiopia.

We derived a framework for our analysis of this research from the following basic concepts of democracy which our respondents advocated:

1. Protection of the individual's basic rights, such as guaranteeing due process of law, freedom of expression, and self-actualization;

2. Protection of equal rights among citizens regardless of socio-economic class, gender, religion, race and/or ethnicity, and political opinion;

3. Provision for opportunities for all citizens to satisfy basic needs.

Respondents argued that the rights and liberties identified above can only be achieved through a democratic process. They said that such a process cannot exist when power is in the hands of a military dictatorship and other oppressive special interest groups. In such regimes, respondents pointed out, citizens cannot freely participate in the process of establishing a democratic society. Therefore, in light of the above concepts democracy should mean not only free elections, free press, and free speech, but, according to our respondents, should also include protection— the conscious and systematic assurance of the above democratic rights of citizens, denial of which reflects the curtailment of democracy. These respondents argued that individuals' rights should be abridged only when their exercise clearly becomes detrimental to society's interests. It is the absence of these democratic rights that inhibits most respondents from returning to their country.

According to this finding, the major *push factor* for trained and experienced Ethiopians out of their country is the lack of democracy, as defined above. This reason given by respondents as a *push factor* makes our respondents involuntary emigrants (or refugees) seeking freedom from political persecution, directly or indirectly. Another study done on Ethiopians in the United States also identified this factor (Cohen & Negash, 1986). What is interesting is that most of the respondents, except those who came with a refugee status, do not like to be referred to as refugees. Even those who were granted political asylum disdain such labeling. In the interviews, for example, respondents' immigration status was a sensitive issue to raise. Even though those respondents who had migrated before the revolution did not return to Ethiopia for reasons similar to those of the refugees, they always sought to distinguish themselves by saying that they were residents, not refugees. The word "exile" is somewhat more acceptable and more dignifying than "refugee" to them. The term "refugee" is associated with having a lower status. The term "immigrant" usually is a reference to voluntary migration, and our respondents believe that they are not voluntary emigrants; neither do they consider themselves immigrants.

Although most of our respondents (172) left Ethiopia prior to the revolution and had a less dramatic experience when compared to most of those who were exiled after the revolution, they said that they have opted to stay in the United States because they distrust the Ethiopian government and fear the political situation in Ethiopia (96 out of 172 of them stated this reason). They are, therefore, political refugees. These terms and what it means to be referred to as a political refugee have a psychological impact on the adjustment of our respondents. They live with the anticipation of returning home when the political problems are drastically minimized.

While most respondents emphasized that the political condition in Ethiopia was the principal cause of their exodus, we cannot underestimate the economic and other opportunities the Unites States offers as underlying reasons for coming to this country. For example, in the survey we asked if respondents were financially better off in the United States than in Ethiopia. Though the majority of our respondents said "yes," some indicated that this was not their major reason for leaving their homeland. We made a cross-reference of their responses to this question with their work experiences in Ethiopia. For those who had not worked in Ethiopia, we anticipated that the response would be positive since they had not earned a living for themselves while they were in Ethiopia. However, the majority of those who had worked in Ethiopia also said that they were financially better off in the United States; this includes even those who were not working in their field of study. Therefore, definite monetary gain from living in the United States is indicated by more respondents.

Despite perceived and/or actual monetary gains respondents might have in the United States, there is a clear indication that there have been problems of professional, social, and cultural adjustment. There were very few voluntary migrants, or "immigrants," who came with jobs offered to them prior to their departure from Ethiopia, or a third country of transitory stay. Most came to or opted to stay in the United States without first being assured of jobs.

Having highlighted the research findings regarding the major *push factor* for the exodus of trained manpower from Ethiopia to the United States, below we discuss how this group is adjusting to its new environment.

Ethopians in the United States: Adjustment and Survival

Efforts in a Different Environment

As Gordon (1964), one of the recognized scholars in the study of immigrants in the United States, described in his book, *Assimilation in American Life: The Role of Race, Religion and National Origin,* American society is a mosaic of ethnic groups based on race, religion, and national origin. Despite these differences among immigrants, they share a certain degree of similarity in the nature of the *push factors* that contributed to their immigration. The common *push factors* are mainly the need for political and religious freedom and/or the economic opportunities perceived to exist in the United States. The initial *push factors* of Ethiopians, mentioned earlier, and their subsequent adjustment experiences are therefore not unique but similar to those of most current immigrants to the United States.

While the early immigrants to the United States were mainly Europeans who did not have much educational training and most of whom were unskilled or semi-skilled, recent refugees coming to the United States have usually had more schooling and more professional backgrounds. Refugees in the United States from Cuba and Vietnam, for example, include a cadre of well-educated people. Among this wave of trained and experienced Third World refugees, Ethiopians are currently one of the largest African exile groups. It is important, therefore, to examine how these new immigrant minorities, that is, Ethiopians, are adjusting once they settle in the United States. The adjustment issues that are raised and examined revolve around professional, cultural, social and economic considerations.

Adjustment Issues Related to Profession

The goal of many Ethiopian students in the United States prior to the 1974 revolution in Ethiopia was to arm themselves educationally in order to advance professionally in their own country. The drive to complete college or higher education was partly a result of social pressure and expectations from family and friends, and obviously a requirement for scholarship recipients. Education was also one of the key factors for upward social and economic mobility; thus, it was an incentive for individual effort. In Ethiopia, higher education has been considered one of the means to improve one's status and living conditions, and to maximize opportunities.

When the number of Ethiopian students in the United States increased in the early 1970s, many came independently—without sponsorship. To supplement their incomes, many engaged in part-time jobs; the kind of work they did was immaterial to them since their goal was to successfully finish their education. It was common to see Ethiopian students working on Masters' or Ph.D. degrees and at the same time working part-time as busboys, or parking lot attendants, or waiters and waitresses. These jobs were primarily seen as means to ends—which minimized the potential frustration in performing such work..

Now, since the 1974 revolution in Ethiopia, many have opted to remain in the United States. The part-time jobs assumed while pursuing higher education are becoming permanent jobs in order to survive economically—for some. Professional jobs in America are generally getting more and more scarce, particularly for minority immigrants. And since those respondents who had not completed their schooling did not seem to be under any time pressures to return to Ethiopia, postponing the completion of schooling has become common. Many (16 percent) have had to take any job available, or take more than one job, not only to support themselves but also to support their families in their homeland who continue to endure harsh economic conditions in Ethiopia. As indicated in an article in the *Washington Post* ("Executive Immigrants," 1986), "When a former Ethiopian cabinet minister drives a cab to support his family, pride takes a back seat" (p. C5). Therefore, looking for professional jobs or improving one's skills through continuing education programs becomes secondary, especially for those who have family responsibilities.

Due to the nature of this survey, only a small sampling was obtained of Ethiopians fully engaged in the jobs they most commonly perform, such as parking lot attending, taxi driving, and waiting tables. However, the majority who responded to the survey were employed in jobs pertinent to their training and experiences. The majority (62 respondents) said their occupation was not related to their fields, and declined to identify the type of job in which they were employed.

Table 8.2 shows the educational achievement levels of the 240 respondents who supplied the data in this study—along with their employment statuses.

Sixty-two respondents represent 26 percent of those who noted that their work was "not at all" related to their jobs; they indicated that they work in the service areas of taxi driving, parking lot attending, and waiting tables. According to data from questionnaires, it is apparent that the higher the respondents' education levels, the closer their jobs are related to their training. However, interviews with community leaders in several cities indicated that despite their higher education, many Ethiopians were unable to find jobs commensurate with or even close to their training. The consequences were frustration and economic strain.

Table 8.2
Respondents' Educational Background and Relation to Current Job

Level of Education	Close	Somewhat	Not at All	Unemployed	Total #	%
12th grade	0	0	1	0	1	.4
Some college	3	1	4	0	8	3.3
2 years technical and professional	8	2	10	1	21	8.8
B.A./B.S.	24	16	24	6	70	29.2
M.A./M.S.	55	25	21	1	102	42.5
Ph.D./M.D.	31	5	2	0	38	15.8
Total	121	49	62	8	240	100.0

As indicated earlier, most respondents (172, or 75 percent) did not initially come to settle permanently in the United States. This, their goals and aspirations were totally different before they arrived here. Some may have specialized in areas which might not be relevant in the United States; therefore, they were unprepared for the American job market. Others had skills marketable in the United States but for various reasons, including racism, they were unable to find jobs in their areas of expertise. For example, an Ethiopian taxi driver with a Master's degree in business management had applied for dozens of jobs, but had had no success. He concluded that racism was the obstacle. An Ethiopian-trained social worker was employed as a housekeeper in a Washington suburb since she had not been able to get a job commensurate with her education. A former Ethiopian airlines pilot was meagerly employed as a car lot attendant since no American airlines would accept his credentials. Many told us they had had to hide their educational backgrounds and work experience in order to obtain menial jobs (such as housekeeping) since American employers are not comfortable hiring professional people for such work. Therefore, there is a general dissatisfaction with not using one's training and skills in a more productive way. In order to adjust to the circumstances, many are trying different avenues to use their talents. This educational waste is a loss for Ethiopia because the wasted education could have been utilized in Ethiopia if the political situation had improved. The waste of the education of Third World immigrants in the United States, however, needs further, in-depth study.

Dictated by reality, many Ethiopians who came to the United States prior to the Ethiopian revolution are trying to adjust to conditions here which they had not expected before they arrived. The hope of returning home after the completion of schooling is fading. They are accepting the reality that their resettlement in the United States is not temporary. So, they have started to establish themselves, many into business ventures. Common businesses owned by Ethiopians are in the service area such as real estate, restaurants, and taxicabs. After years of interruption, only a few have resumed their studies in the hope that the completion of further higher education might guarantee professional jobs, and result in the psychological satisfaction that successful completion of higher education brings.

For those respondents who were in Ethiopia after the revolution and who experienced harsh conditions under the military regime, coming to the United States to avoid political repression and find personal safety were their primary goals; getting professional jobs was secondary. As time passes and as jobs in line with their training and skills become unavailable, frustration is inevitable. Those who are not engaged in private enterprise often continue, in vain, to search for jobs. The few established Ethiopian community centers in the United States try to provide information on job opportunities, which is helpful for some with lower levels of education but not for highly trained professionals. The difficulty with not having meaningful jobs relevant to their training and experience has negatively affected the adjustment process of most Ethiopians.

Cultural Adaptation and Integration

Because of the increasing number of Ethiopians residing in the United States, there now exists what is called the "Ethiopian community." Many Ethiopian community leaders and some American observers have shared with us their view that the Ethiopian community is a closed society, especially in those cities where there is a large Ethiopian population. These Ethiopians tend to associate most often with each other, thus limiting their interaction with Americans and, equally as important, with potential employment contacts.

This may not be uncommon in the United States when a particular ethnic group grows in number and establishes its own enclave. The association, understandably, is mainly with one's compatriots because of the many things they have in common. However, the offspring (secondary generation) of these Ethiopian immigrants do interact extensively with Americans and may quickly integrate as they are socialized by schools and influenced by their peer groups. The Ethiopian's case is no different than other immigrants' (voluntary or otherwise) in American history. As do other immigrant groups, they tend to cling to each other and form their own community supports. Their socialization and interaction with other groups are often limited due to cultural idiosyncrasies.

Ethiopians have formed group self-help associations called "equibs." Equib members contribute money to association treasuries which then distribute the money to the membership, on a rotational basis. They also help each other when a member has a death in the family—contributing additional funds, comforting each other, keeping company, and bringing food and drink to the home of the aggrieved. An offshoot of the equib association resulted in one group in Washington, D. C., financing ventures in real estate and courier services. Such equib associations, which are common in Ethiopia, are taking root among Ethiopians in several cities in the United States.

This survey used several indicators to identify whether respondents interacted frequently with other groups. For example, we asked if the majority of their friends were Americans, Ethiopians, or other foreigners; whether they attended church primarily with Ethiopians; and whether they preferred Ethiopian entertainment to others. Most respondents preferred Ethiopian friends, attended church with predominantly Ethiopian members, and chose Ethiopian entertainment and restaurants when available.

The respondents' social interaction with Americans outside of their work places was limited. Those engaged in professional jobs did interact with Americans and other nationalities, depending upon the kind of jobs involved, but they preferred to associate mostly with other Ethiopians, unless the Ethiopian community was so small that they had to relate to Americans and others. Those who operated private businesses, especially those catering to Ethiopians, had very little contact with Americans. Therefore, the attraction to associate with Ethiopians only became greater. An Ethiopian who worked in an Ethiopian restaurant in Washington, D. C., said that she sometimes feels that she still lives in Ethiopia because her contact with non-Ethiopians was so limited. She said that her supervisor at work, most of the patrons in the restaurant, her roommate, and practically all her associates were Ethiopians. She eats mainly Ethiopian food, patronizes Ethiopian entertainment, and has few American friends whom she invites to her home; and she has never been invited to an American home.

In the survey, respondents were asked if they felt that they were successfully integrating into American society. We compared their responses with the length of their stay in the United States. Table 8.3 shows the results.

According to the above table, 86 or 36 percent of the respondents do "not at all" feel integrated into American society. In fact, 41 of them had lived 11 years or more in the United States while 45 had lived in the United States less than 10 years. Thus, the length of the respondents' stay in the United States did not significantly influence their feelings of integration into American society. One respondent who had lived in the United States more than 20 years, and had a son attending college, observed that he lived with "one leg in the United States and the other in Ethiopia." He has not accepted his stay here as a permanent status and hopes to return to Ethiopia one day. Although he very much appreciates the United States' allowing him and others like him a place in this nation, his ambivalence and unsettlement is similar to that of many other refugees in the United States who have been reluctant to put down deep roots because they yearn to return to their homeland. Cuban refugees in the United States, for example, seemed not to accept as permanent their resettlement here until they resigned themselves to the impossibility of repatriation in the near future. Similar predicaments are faced by Ethiopians who have resettled in this country.

Table 8.3
Feeling of Integration into American Society by Length of Stay in the U. S.

Length of Stay in the United States	Yes	Somewhat	Not at All
Less than 5 years	5	19	25
5-10 years	10	25	20
11-15 years	28	48	31
16-20 years	8	6	7
21 years and above	0	3	3
Total	51	101	86

N=238

Based on the researchers' observations, responses to the survey, interviews, and data analyses, following is a description of how the Ethiopian community tries to maintain it culture, and also pass along some of its culture to its children.

Cultural Maintenance

Ethiopians in the United States, especially those in large communities, are trying to maintain their culture by: (1) opening Ethiopian restaurants, although the economic interests are necessarily a consideration; (2) establishing churches and celebrating religious holidays; (3) establishing newspapers and journals; (4) listening to Ethiopian music; and (5) engaging in familiar sporting activities such as soccer games. Through these means of cultural maintenance, their Ethiopian values are maintained, and their cultural identity is nurtured.

Further interviews explored to what extent Ethiopians are involved (individually as well as collectively) in maintaining their culture and transmitting it to their new generations.

A community leader had mixed feelings about the strong cultural identity Ethiopians claim to maintain. He argued that because of a lack of strong cooperation among Ethiopians, particularly because of differences based on political lines and regionalism, it has not been easy to transmit cultural values that embrace all Ethiopian ethnic groups. The divided groups have also been unsuccessful in forging strong community-based cultural socialization of the young. Homes, according to this interviewee, were apparently effective places for the transmission of Ethiopian culture.

On the other hand, an Ethiopian political activist thought that Ethiopians are nationalists and that while the bonds to their culture are tight, he believed that this nationalism and bonds to the culture were pivotal forces for transmitting culture to their children. He noted that the Ethiopian restaurants are not only business endeavors but are, more or less, fortresses for Ethiopians. They bring Ethiopians together as a community.

This issue of cultural maintenance in general is debated privately among Ethiopians because there are those who believe that their culture is transmitted to the young, and the home is still a strong place for that transmission of culture. There are others who say that younger Ethiopians—those born in the United States—have lost their culture so fast that parents are disappointed with the rapid pace at which their children are "Americanized."

In this study the majority of respondents (67.4 percent) did not attend any kind of church services. About 30 percent attended church services regularly, and another 2.6 percent did so occasionally. Most who are churchgoers attend Ethiopian Orthodox churches (19.2 percent) while others attend different churches such as Greek and Egyptian Orthodox, Catholic, and Protestant. One respondent belongs to the Islamic faith. The number of Ethiopian churches in large cities in the United

States has increased lately, serving mainly the resident Ethiopian community. For example, there were eight Ethiopian churches in Washington, D.C., and its vicinities. This is a drastic change from a decade earlier when none existed; currently, more than 26,000 Ethopians reside in the Greater Washington Metropolitan Area (Ethiopian Community Development Council, Inc., 1990).

While Ethiopians in the United States try to maintain their native culture, at times it becomes too expensive and unrealistic. An example of this expense are weddings among Ethiopians in cities where there is a large Ethiopian community. Some weddings may cost in the neighborhood of $10,000 and more. These weddings become quite expensive when trying to accommodate two cultures. On the one hand, it is part of Ethiopian culture to share happiness with relatives and friends. This does, at times, increase the number of invited guests to more than 500, depending on the popularity, "connections," and length of stay of the bride and/ or groom in the community in a particular city. The food served is mostly a combination of Ethiopian and American dishes, making the weddings even more expensive. These costly weddings have been criticized by some Ethiopians, as well as other observers, for being too lavish and expensive for people who live in exile. In addition, the famine situation in Ethiopia and the starving faces of Ethiopian children seen on American television, especially during the time of this survey, are constant reminders of the situation in the homeland.

While we were working on this research, a United Nations official in New York observed that we Ethiopians do not make good exiles. He said, "You are trying to live in America with an Ethiopian culture which makes great demands on you." (This person had lived in Ethiopia and maintains many Ethiopian friendships.) Other hardships he mentioned, beyond wedding expenses, were the commitments of many Ethiopians to help their relatives, either by bringing them over here or supporting them at home. To fulfill these social and family obligations, many Ethiopians hold two or three jobs, thereby creating enormous personal stress. Sixteen percent of our respondents, as explained previously, were second wage earners. The second jobs were mainly taxi driving, parking lot attending, and waiting tables.

Acculturation of the Children

About 45 percent of the respondents have children. The majority of their children were in preschool or elementary school. Most respondents were rearing their children to adopt the good points of both Ethiopian and American cultures. Some stressed that their children learn Ethiopian languages, eat Ethiopian food, and watch Ethiopian cultural shows. But the children are, as are most other children of immigrants in the United States, more American than Ethiopian or any other immigrant group's culture. Some prefer hamburgers over spicy Ethiopian dishes. They prefer rock and roll over Ethiopian songs. Some resent their language and refuse to speak it because their American peers might ridicule them. This seems to be especially true where the number of foreigners in a particular community is limited.

Sometimes Ethiopian parents also unintentionally forget the stresses experienced by their children who are trying to cope with two cultures. On one hand, the children attend American schools and are socialized into American culture. On the other hand, most parents prefer to rear their children in the Ethiopian cultural context. The children are, therefore, products of two different worlds. Parents continue to observe their culture and do not become fully acculturated and integrated into the American way while the children are socialized into the American lifestyle in the school systems.

This point is illustrated by the experience of an Ethiopian family on a Thanksgiving Day. This family we interviewed had two children, ages four and six. For this Thanksgiving Day the mother had prepared Doro watt (chicken stew), a dish popular on Ethiopian holidays, and had invited relatives. When the family was prepared to have their lunch, one child cried when he saw Ethiopian dishes on the table. The surprised parents asked the boy why he was crying. He complained that there was no turkey prepared, that he had an assignment from school to draw the turkey they would have for Thanksgiving and report in class about the occasion. The family was troubled and called another Ethiopian family and asked if they had prepared turkey for Thanksgiving. The other family also had no turkey for the day, but they did have turkey legs—so the boy's mother could prepare turkey for the child. The mother prepared the turkey legs and served dinner hours later—everyone had had to wait for the meat to be cooked. However, when the turkey legs were ready, the little boy was still not satisfied since it was not a whole turkey served with cranberry sauce, sweet potatoes, and pumpkin pie—the usual Thanksgiving dinner for Americans. After a long attempt at appeasement, the boy finally settled for turkey legs.

This example demonstrates two points. First, some parents are not sensitive to the cultural conflicts that their children face while growing up in a culture foreign to their parents. Second, because of the insensitivity of some teachers in many American schools, the cultures of children outside the dominant culture are not given due consideration, especially in schools where the number of minority students is not significant. In the above case the teacher could have used the boy's different background as a learning experience and could have asked to report on what Ethiopians eat at home on holidays. This approach could have benefited the whole class in general and the boy in particular by making him proud of his culture and also would have gone a long way in building his self-confidence. Such cultural insensitivity in American schools is generally one of the problems of minority immigrants in the United States. But in spite of the pressures they experienced in learning and living in two cultures, young Ethiopians show high levels of performance in their educational pursuits. This is because of their parents' positive attitudes towards education and their desire to have the nest for their children in "the land of opportunity".

Economic and Psychological Pressure in Exile

So far most trained and experienced Ethiopians in the United States have been leading a transitory life in anticipation of returning to their country. This anticipation does not seem likely to materialize in the near future. Hence, they are coming to grips with this reality and shaping their lives in such ways as completing schooling, establishing families, and looking for permanent and professional jobs, all of which have been very stressful for many.

Added to these stresses are the economic and political conditions in Ethiopia, especially the famine situation, which have caused untold psychological pressure on both individuals and the community-at-large. Many people have told us that whenever they see pictures of the famine on television, they are unhappy about going to work for fear of being asked and reminded about the famine in their homeland. Some Ethiopian school children are ridiculed with jokes about hunger in Ethiopia. For some Ethiopians, the agony that has befallen their country has increased their commitment to help relatives as they wonder about the fate their country is facing. During the drought of 1984-85, and the hunger that followed, many were involved in raising funds and collecting material which they sent home to help their compatriots. Most would have preferred working in Ethiopia, had the situation permitted, to help ameliorate the problems that face their countrymen.

The economic conditions in Ethiopia have created enormous pressure on Ethiopians in the United States. There is an increasing need for financial support of immediate and extended families back home. Close to 80 percent (195) of the survey respondents said that they support their families in Ethiopia. Some had brought their brothers and sisters over to educate them in the United States. About 48 percent of the 244 respondents have invited family as temporary visitors.

Table 8.4 shows the number of respondents who help their families back in Ethiopia, and those who have brought their immediate families to visit with them.

As the stay of respondents in the United States is extended, their invitations to parents increase. The reasons given vary. Some said that they could not return home

Table 8.4
Family Visitations and Support

	Support Family to U. S. N	Support Family to U. S. %	Invited Family to U. S. N	Invited Family to U. S. %
Yes	195	79.9	117	49.0
No	48	19.7	123	50.4
No Response	1	.4	4	1.6
Total	244	100.0	244	100.0

for various reasons, one of which is distrust of the military government which might wantonly restrict exits from the country. Others said that it is easier to invite parents to the United States than visit them in Ethiopia. Some gave medical reasons for inviting parents to come here or stated that parents would be visiting other countries, especially in Jerusalem during the Ethiopian Easter. Therefore, they could extend their trips into the United States.

Family obligations in general have put pressure on many Ethiopians. Some, in fact, postpone or terminate their education, as well as postpone establishing their own families (marriage and children) because they are obliged to assist families at home or those members also residing in the United States.

Summary and Conclusions

The exodus of trained and experienced Ethiopians to the United States increased after the 1974 revolution in Ethiopia. The majority of those who were pursuing their education in the United States opted to stay here. According to our study, the major *push factor* for their exodus, or for their staying in America, is the lack of democracy, specifically the lack of due process of law and the lack of basic human rights, in Ethiopia. These circumstances have made them "involuntary immigrants" or refugees seeking political freedom and avoiding oppression in their own country.

Most Ethiopians who have attained higher education usually lived better professionally, socially, and psychologically in their own country. In the United States the majority are engaged in low-level jobs for survival considerations. This has created problems of psychological, social, and professional adjustment among many highly-educated Ethiopians. In recent years many are trying to cope with their situations by engaging themselves in private businesses or other self-help programs. This waste of educational resources and manpower is a phenomenon that needs in-depth study.

Similar to other immigrants, Ethiopians are forming their own communities, and the integration process into American society has lagged, even for those who have lived in the United States 10 years or longer. Though Ethiopian communities have been formed in several large United States cities, all suffer in one degree or another from the difficulty of forming all-inclusive, strong community organizations because of political or regional differences which create inter-group suspicions. When an organization is formed by an individual or a group, that organization is automatically labeled as belonging to this or that political or regional group, so its motives are questioned. As a consequence, those who need its services are hampered in their adjustment to their new country without the support of a strong community organization. A strong community-based organization is also necessary for creating a viable force that would have to be reckoned with by policy makers.

Many other ethnic groups in the United States have fought the prejudices they face by uniting and forming strong community-based organizations. In the case of Ethiopians this has not yet been successful.

The political situation in Ethiopia has not changed to the satisfaction or our respondents. Hence, their returning home is not likely in the near future. Therefore, the only alternative they have is to adjust to the environment in which circumstances have placed them.

The United States is a land of immigrants, and studying the experiences of other immigrants and their adjustment process is relevant for the Ethiopian community. More research in the area of adjustment issues of Ethiopians, as current minority immigrants, should be encouraged. This is not to say that these studies will help the current generation of immigrant Ethiopians who are struggling to survive, but they would help the children who are being reared under the influence of their parents' cultural backgrounds. The exodus of Ethiopians, unparalleled in the history of Ethiopia, needs also to be documented, and thus deserves study of its own.

References

Cohen, P., & Negash, G. (1986, July). *Refugees and asylum applicants: Implications of the case of migrants from Ethiopia for United States Policy.* Missoula, MT: University of Montana.

Ethiopian Community Center. (1983, Fall). President's message. *ECC NEWS.* Washington, DC.

Ethiopian Community Development Council, Inc. (1990). *The development needs of Ethiopian refugees in the United States, Part I: Analysis.* (Contract report, 233-88-0057). For the U. S. Department of Health and Human Services. Washington, DC: Ethiopian Community Development Council, Inc.

Executive immigrants: Surviving in the USA. (1986, February 25). *Washington Post,* p. C5.

Gordon, M. M. (1964). *Assimilation in American life.* New York: Oxford University Press.

Spolar, C. (1987, December 15). Prejudices leave educated foreigners in menial jobs. *Washington Post,* p. A27.

Part Four

The Multicultural Public Education Challenge

Racist scholars obliterated the influence of whole African civilizations. For whites, Afro-centrism contains within it an uncomfortable truth.

—Jerry Alder,
"African Dreams"
Newsweek, September 23, 1991

Black history, long ignored by all but a handful of black scholars, became, in decades after World War II, perhaps the most exciting and innovative genre practiced by historians of the United States.

—Roger Daniels
Coming to America
(New York: Harper Collins, 1990)

Challenges of a Changing America

Chapter Nine

Multiculturalism:
A Paradigm for Educational Reform

Aaron B. Stills & Constance M. Ellison

Overview

As we enter the 21st century, we will find that ethnic children of diverse cultural backgrounds will be the dominant clientele in the American school system. Moreover, a substantial proportion of those entering the labor force over the next decade will be of non-European descent (Workforce 2000, 1987). In part, the face of the nation is changing. We can no longer sit back and deny the fact that pluralism and cultural diversity is a reality. As a nation, we have traditionally maligned diversity instead of acknowledging, valuing, and appreciating it (Grant & Melnick, 1977). As a plan of action, we need to begin addressing the reality of pluralism and cultural diversity as a national strength in order to meet the changing dynamics of our society and the challenges of the decade to come (Boykin, 1990). To view this nation as an unidimensional/mono-cultural one, in its own right, creates insensitivity to the many divergent groups which have themselves built upon our nation's strengths and resourcefulness.

One institution that consistently, whether overtly or covertly, denies the existence of diversity is our nation's education system. As such, we must begin to re-evaluate, restructure, and re-define the pedagogical philosophies, goals, and objectives of American education in order to prepare all children more realistically for the challenges and demands of the 21st century. Thus, our children must, for the most part, be prepared to operate and function in a multicultural society. Quite obviously, our educational goals and objectives must reflect upon and be predicated along such multicultural realities. No longer can our school system continue to operate along a fictitious monocultural framework.

Introduction

Recently, a major concern of the school system across the country is how to effectively incorporate educational curriculum and program activities for students of diverse cultural backgrounds. This has been a concern mainly because students from diverse backgrounds bring with them to the school context certain expectations and orientations reflecting their own unique cultural conditioning, socialization practices, and preferred style of learning. These specific dimensions at times are not in accord with the institutional norms and expectations of the school. When children of diverse backgrounds do not conform to these traditional institutional norms and expectations the hypothesis has been that these children come to the school environment ill-equipped to meet the demands and challenges of the school as a direct result of being either "culturally disadvantaged" or "cognitively deficient." However, when middle class white students are not conforming to these norms and expectations, it is often thought that there is a problem with the method of instruction or that there is a mismatch between the curriculum content and the child's level of development (Hale, 1977). We cannot continue to perpetuate and give lip service to this deficit hypothesis as it is applied to the educational performance of students from diverse backgrounds.

Although educators are now realizing to some degree that to be different is not synonymous with being deficient or disadvantaged, these expressions are still implicitly implied within the learning context. To speak of any child as culturally disadvantaged, or cognitively deficient, merely because of his/her diverse origin is damaging not only to the child but also to society at large for it deprives the nation of the contributions that can be made by each of the divergent groups that make up our nation (Stent, 1973). Moreover, it undermines the integrity and uniqueness of the diverse groups. Educators and society at large must stop operating along the assumption that all that is wrong with children from diverse backgrounds rest with these children and their immediate environment exclusively. They must begin to accept the reality that a significant proportion of the responsibility rests with the school system and its inability or unwillingness to understand, accept, and cultivate diversity in the school context. Moreover, educators must begin to be more cognizant that culture and socialization practices determine how one thinks, behaves, and feels in a broad range of situations. These practices have a very pervasive and potent influence and the school context is by any means an exception. Finally, educators must not ignore the possibility that children from diverse backgrounds may not be conforming because they are placed in an environment that does not nurture and perpetuate their own unique style of learning in the classroom. These are age old concerns, but even today, still quite prevalent.

As can be surmised, there is an urgent need for our nation's school system to address pluralism and cultural diversity not only as a priority, but also as an asset. Subsequently, these institutions must establish curriculum content, contexts, techniques, and programs that create an "I'm O.K." atmosphere. Thus, a special effort must be made by school officials, educators, and society at large to create a multi-cultural environment within the schools that is culturally enriching. By introducing cultural enrichment education to all children, this new awareness of diverse cultural systems will afford schools the opportunity to develop positive cognitive and social frameworks for relating to their own cultural and the culture of others. Moreover, it will provide an atmosphere that would make learning a rewarding, enlightening, relevant, and familiar experience. This type of atmosphere will be one that will promote self-confidence, self-awareness, self-respect, and most importantly a sense of cultural identity and integrity apart from what is global. Additionally, it will afford students of diverse backgrounds the opportunity to implement their own preferred and unique style of learning reflective of their past experiences and socio-cultural orientation (Banks, 1981; Bennett, 1986).

Culture and the School Context

The concept of culture has been defined in many ways, and along many dimensions. However, the general theme that has been professed is that culture entails the ways a particular group categorizes reality in terms of language, beliefs, values, customs, kinship patterns, skills, and dietary customs. As Giroux and McLaren purport (1986), culture embodies a set of practices and ideologies from which groups draw to make sense of the world. Similarly, Sue (1981) argues that cultural identity affects the culturally different individual world view. He explains that world views are composed of our attitudes, values, opinions, and concepts. They may also affect how we think, make decisions, behave, and define events. Along the same framework, Boykin (1986, 1991) and Ogbu (1986) provide an analysis of ethnic minority culture and its relationship to the culture of the "dominant" Euro-American culture.

To understand the world views of many ethnic minority groups, as Boykin would profess, we have to understand how these groups go about negotiating their way through three separate realms of experiences: (1) Mainstream: sharing and accepting many of the values of the majority group that are oppressing them; (2) Ethnic Minority Culture: maintaining cultural identity and integrity; and (3) Minority: adaptively coping with racism and oppression. On the other hand, Ogbu (1986) would argue that the world view of many ethnic minority groups would be a direct result of a natural consequence of belonging to an oppressed minority in a caste system where by birth different roles are assigned to different subgroups. Many ethnic minorities are born into a lower caste system. Here, the message is communicated that their life will eventually be restricted to a small or poorly rewarded set of social roles.

Students from diverse backgrounds have world views that may be diametrically opposed to and different from that of the education system. This presents a problem for them because educators, as Giroux and McLaren (1986) assert "view the classroom as one dimensional plan upon which a set of rules and regulative practices are enacted." Thus, educators are oftentimes inattentive and insensitive to the cultural fabric and texture of the school's diverse clientele (Boykin, 1991). Instead of being idealistic, educators must develop a more realistic and accepting attitude towards diversity. They in part need to develop a better understanding of and an appreciation for culture and educators as well as students should be able to demonstrate, be proud of, and have integrity for cultural identity and diversiveness.

The cultural aspects of the school-aged youth should not be overlooked or taken for granted by educational providers. If educators fail to recognize the existence of cultural diversity, inappropriate conclusions can be drawn about curriculum and programmatic planning. The school environment must be conducive to learning for all children. It is important for teachers, counselors, and administrators to be culturally aware and give consideration to ethnic group differences.

Educators must also be sensitive to the fact that specific cultural variables have tremendous implications for children's reaction to and involvement in classroom social structure, routines, and expectations. On such variable that must be considered is cognitive/learning style. It must be stressed that culture, or for the most part, socialization practices correspond with variations in cognitive/learning style. This correspondence has been born out in the work of Vygotsky who has stressed the importance of cognitive socialization in the development of basic intellectual skills. Research in the Vygotskian tradition has demonstrated the important ways in which parent-child interaction shapes early cognitive development. In part, what is emphasized is that children do not learn in isolation but parents seem to play a vital and pivotal role in shaping certain key elements of children's cognition (Greenfield, 1984; Rogoff & Gardner, 1984).

This is not to say, however, that universal cognitive processes do not exist. On the contrary, what must be understood is that children of diverse cultural backgrounds may develop "intellectual adaptations to the special demands of their environment" (Ginsburg, 1986). Moreover, educators must be more cognizant of the fact that many of the conventional teaching practices may be in conflict with children's cognitive and learning style. What must be considered in the classroom arena is the diverse background of the clientele, the school services, and the possible misfit between the child's cognitive experiences and classroom practices. These differences in cognitive make-up among diverse learners must not be viewed as deficiencies but be recognized as strengths that are valuable and enriching to the school context and that can be built upon to facilitate and enhance the learning process.

The rationale behind cognitive/learning style is congruent to the rationale for multicultural education. One goal of multicultural education is to foster children's multicultural competencies so they can function in a variety of cultural settings. If classroom expectations are limited by monolithic cultural/cognitive orientations, then we obstruct success for learners who are governed or not governed by another cultural/cognitive orientation.

In all then, the education system has a responsibility to recognize and respect the world view (i.e. attitudes, customs, and values) of diverse learners and be conversant of the strong association between world views and cognitive/learning styles and their probable impact on achievement and learning outcomes in forming the basis for multicultural decisions, activities, and instructional practices.

Multicultural Concept

The concept of multiculturalism, over the last few decades, has sparked increased interest among researchers and educators. Quite recently, however, we find many education systems in the U.S., as well as abroad, permeating this concept into their school curricula. Here, culturally skilled teachers and administrators are equipped with the necessary training and knowledge to develop educational curricula and programs which reflect the cultural values and norms of students from diverse cultural backgrounds. Gay (1988) asserts that "the essence of multicultural education is the diversification of the content, contexts, and techniques used to facilitate learning to better reflect the ethnic, cultural, and social diversity of the U.S." Its intent, as Gay professes, "is to improve the academic success of a broader spectrum of students, to develop knowledge and appreciation of cultural pluralism, and to better equalize social, economic, and political opportunities among ethnic and cultural groups."

One issue of considerable debate has been how to conceptually and operationally define multicultural education. These debates have been predicated on how to define multicultural educational goals, content, and practices as well as the social groups that will seek to service (Gibson, 1984; Bennett, 1986; Sleeter, 1991). For example, some researchers and educators view multicultural education as specifically addressing bilingual bicultural education (Garcia, 1976; Troike, 1981; Brisk, 1982), race and ethnicity (Gay, 1983; Bennett, 1986; Phinney & Rotheram, 1987), and race, gender, and ethnicity (Baptiste & Baptiste, 1979).

Although impressive results have been obtained from each of the above approaches, multiculturalism must not be an euphemism for addressing certain oppressed groups at the expense of others. It must be viewed as a non-exclusive concept addressing all diverse and oppressed groups with society—those groups that have not experienced equity from the education system. One of the most promising and progressive analysis of multicultural education quite recently focuses on multiple forms of oppression simultaneously such as race, ethnicity, language, gender, social class, and disability (Banks, 1989, 1991; Stills, 1988; Sleeter & Grant, 1988; Sleeter, 1991; Schniedemind & Davidson, 1983). This multidimensional approach to multicultural education appears to be more viable and can be viewed as an appropriate conception of multicultural education given that most conflicts and oppressive circumstances have different causes and manifest themselves differently depending upon the individuals' race, ethnicity, culture, gender, and other socioeconomic factors.

Our schools are faced with educating students of diverse grouping. Schools must make a concerted effort to focus on diversity and must identify and develop base-line expectations, content, goals, and practices for learning and behavior that are expected for all students. This leads to a consideration of special knowledge and methods of program intervention on behalf of these specialized groups that may vary from population to population.

As the concept of multiculturalism continues to be explored, two pertinent questions need to be addressed, namely (1) what are the barriers to establishing a multicultural environment within the school context?; and (2) is multicultural education a national necessity and a viable alternative to educational reform?

Barriers to establishing a multicultural environment within the school context would include, but are not limited to the following:

◆ Failure to make it a national goal and practice;

◆ Resistance to change traditional and normative ways of operating on the part of school officials and society at large;

◆ A lack of commitment;

◆ Lack of sensitivity to cultural and other oppressed group needs;

◆ Poor change agent skills of school professionals;

◆ Failure to recognize that the U. S. is not a homogeneous or monocultural nation;

◆ A lack of understanding of and training in devising and implementing multicultural teaching strategies; and

◆ The inability of educational policy makers to come to terms with cultural pluralism and diversity, and the lack of educator's knowledge and discourse in multicultural education policy and practice.

Addressing whether or not multicultural education is a national necessity and a viable alternative to educational reform has yet to be sufficiently answered on a national level and in some respects has been used as a lip service mechanism or as a political ploy. It is no surprise that the education system in the U.S. is heavily influenced by national goals. Over the last decade or so various reports have been generated suggesting alternative methods of how to better improve education in America (i.e., *A Nation at Risk*). The First Bush Administration issued the "America 2000" Report mimicking the same initiative. One common theme that can be drawn from these reports is that they lack ecological and trans-contextual validity. In addition, consistent throughout these reports is a demand for a national commit-

Multiculturalism

ment to excellence in American education with the underlying question being: "How can we do what we have traditionally done, more effectively?" Thus, the level of analysis that these reports are operating from is to work within the already existing monolithic system and go from there instead of a commitment to or concern with the transformation and restructuring of this system.

What has to be emphasized is that these reports continue to negate, whether intentionally or non-intentionally, two very important issues: (1) the issue of individual, social, and cultural differences that characterize the diversity of American society; and (2) that excellence in American schools cannot be achieved without educational equity in order for all students to reach their fullest educational potential and that achieving educational excellence requires an impartial, just education system. With this in mind, multicultural education, with its core being equity, must be viewed as a national necessity and a viable alternative to the existing system if educational reform is to be effective. Thus, those committed to education reform must attempt to address multiculturalism as the nucleus by which reform efforts, policies, and strategies are embedded, immersed, and articulated. Moreover, multicultural education, as Gibson (1984) states, must be viewed as a process whereby an individual is given an opportunity to develop competencies in multiple systems of standards for perceiving, evaluating, behaving, and doing. This type of process is more congruent with that notion of cultural pluralism and diversity which runs rampant throughout

To be an effective process, multicultural programs should reflect the contributions and cultural interests of the various diverse groups in attendance. Most importantly, parents, students, community leaders, politicians, education reformers, educational researcher, curriculum developers, and school officials should be a viable part of the planning process.

In all then, although some have paid lip service to and have practiced, and theorized about this multicultural educational ideology, realistically, we still have not deviated very much from an assimilation framework. We still find for the most part Anglo-European social dominance ideology being consistently infused and perpetuated and that children, regardless of their diverse backgrounds, are socialized and educated along traditional monolithic cultural patterns. The education system, and educational policy makers must begin to accept divergent groups on their own terms and work to achieve its educational goals by serving as a meaningful agency which encourages diversity among individuals. This would enable culturally divergent groups to continue to be their best possible selves by utilizing their own distinct culture.

Multicultural Curricula

Research literature in both the psychological and educational domains has demonstrated that students learn best if the instructions or teachings are related or extend to their experiential continuum. In spite of this, the school curricula are still dominated by a monolithic, Eurocentric approach. Banks (1992) concurs by asserting that the dominated Eurocentric curriculum "reinforces the status quo, makes students passive and content, and encourages them to acquiescently accept the dominant ideologies, political and economic arrangements, and prevailing myths and paradigms used to rationalize and justify the current social and political structure" (p. 130). The traditional classroom instructions and teachings are not, for the most part, related to the experiences of a significant percentage of the student population.

It stands to reason, therefore, that if we are to develop effective and meaningful multicultural programs within our school, curriculum reform is not only a necessity but also an inevitability. The essence of multicultural education, as Gay (1988) professes, is the diversification of the content, context, and techniques used to facilitate learning to better reflect the ethnic, cultural, and social diversity in the United States. As such, multicultural education must be the foci of the school curricula. Although over the years we have seen great stride in many school systems to incorporate multicultural education into their school curricula, to date these efforts still need to be questioned from operational and methodological perspectives. Most of these attempts have been incorporated along general guidelines instead of being systematically integrated throughout the entire school curriculum (Gay, 1988, 1983; Banks, 1989). In order to meet the diverse needs of all students, the concept of multiculturalism must be permeated throughout the entire school curriculum development, implemented, and evaluation (Gay, 1988).

Moreover, an effective multicultural curriculum must include equitable illustrations of the life experiences of all diverse groups in this country. Thus, we must not continue to emphasize the traditional core curriculum as if it is the only alternative for educational attainment and enhancement. Furthermore, we can not continue to advocate that any deviation from the standards prescribed for assimilating the traditional core curriculum represents a deficiency on the part of the learner. It is plausible that for students of diverse backgrounds it is not a question of deficiency but instead the knowledge acquired from the traditional core curriculum, and the form it takes are disabling academically as well as socially (Sleeter & Grant, 1988). Thus, as Sleeter and Grant (1988) assert, "students who are disabled by their school experience do not experience congruence between school knowledge and the knowledge they bring to the school with them."

Designing a multicultural curriculum is not an easy task. For the most part, it requires a basic sensitivity, respect, understanding, and acceptance for ethnic, social, and cultural integrity and diversity. Additionally, it requires an understanding that variations in learning experiences have an effect on student achievement and performance outcomes. Thus, it stands to reason that the more diversified the learning content and activities within the school environment, the greater the

Multiculturalism

chances are that a significant proportion of students will be interested in, and successful at learning. Educators can not continue to assume that they have a monopoly on education and educational experiences. A multicultural curriculum can make provisions for all students to identify, practice, and cultivate their own unique and preferred style of learning.

Geneva Gay (1988) explained that multicultural curriculum should be reviewed critically to insure that ethnic and cultural diversity permeates all academic components. Gay offered the following questions as a means of assessing curriculum development review:

◆ Does the curriculum rationale reflect sensitivity to and celebration of various kinds of diversifying factors among students?

◆ Does the pluralistic content included play a center role and function in understanding the disciplinary subject matter?

◆ Is the pluralistic content used as the context or arena for major skill development?

◆ Will students from different ethnic and cultural backgrounds find the proposed instructional materials personally meaningful to their life experiences?

◆ Has a variety of culturally different examples, situations, scenarios, and anecdotes been used throughout the curriculum design to illustrate major intellectual concepts and principles?

◆ Are the culturally diverse content, examples, and experiences included comparable in kind, significance, magnitude, and function to those selected from mainstream culture?

◆ Are the performance expectations (goals and objectives) for diverse learners similar to those for mainstream students?

◆ Are the suggested methods for teaching content and skills, and the proposed students learning activities responsive to the learning styles and preferences of different students?

◆ Do the evaluation techniques allow different ways for students to demonstrate their achievement? Are these sensitive to ethnic and cultural diversity?

◆ Will the proposed learning activities continually stimulate and interest different kinds of students?

◆ How do the content and learning activities affirm the culture of diverse students?

◆ Will the self-esteem and confidence of diverse learners be improved by the curriculum methods and materials? (Gay, 1988)

These questions can assist in establishing an assessment foundation on which to build school-wide reform programs that can better accommodate diverse learners and improve student academic success.

Model

Use of a multicultural perspective requires that effective multicultural curriculum, programs, and teaching strategies serve as vehicles for innovation and change in order to provide an environment supportive of multicultural teaching and learning. Regarding programs, cultural awareness activities that are appropriate for enhancing a multicultural environment within the schools should be implemented. Such programs and activities should include but are not limited to the following:

◆ Programs that de-emphasize ethnocentrism. Here, the primary focus should be on valuing, understanding, respecting, and accepting cultural diversity. Such programs should expose learners to other cultures in order to minimize the development of stereotypes, prejudice, and inflexibility with emphasis placed on developing a positive meaning of culture, understanding the cultural perspectives of others from their own unique frame of reference, developing a conceptual understanding of groups and labels, and the powerful impact of culture;

◆ Programs that will help learners develop the skills and abilities necessary to deal positively and effectively with culturally diverse individuals;

◆ Programs that consist of delivery systems and techniques for training teachers, counselors, and school administrators to become more multicultural in their presentation and approach. Primary focus should be on the development of a pedagogical philosophy that embodies a commitment to multicultural education and cultural pluralism, and training for teachers competencies, lessons, and strategies for classroom use;

◆ Programs that will incorporate multicultural resources from the community at large using community as a viable resource in the classroom;

◆ Programs designed to provide a framework for better understanding cultural diversity through art, music, language, social organizations, and world views;

◆ Programs that would provide knowledge of the social, cultural, and economic contexts of the learners' life and social circumstances.

Multiculturalism

Multicultural education should be also be permeated throughout the total school curriculum, which is directed towards and meets the needs and abilities of all learners. As such, the curriculum should be designed to:

◆ Help learners increase their academic achievement and performance levels across all content areas including basic skills. Specific emphasis must be placed on the learners' own unique style of learning and acquisition of strategic skills;

◆ Be sensitive and relevant to the learners' socio-cultural background and experiential learning experiences;

◆ Enable learners to analyze concepts, issues, events, and themes within both an interdisciplinary and multidisciplinary framework using perspectives from diverse cultural groupings;

◆ Promote and facilitate talent development. The primary focus should be to develop academic talent in as many learners as possible by starting "where they are" regarding their knowledge, attitudes, and skills. Thus, talent development must begin from the learners' own vantage points;

◆ Be client-centered. The primary focus is on understanding the learners' needs and addressing them as proactively as possible;

◆ Provide experiences for all learners that will better equip them with skills, knowledge, and attitudes necessary to live in a pluralistic/culturally diverse society;

◆ Facilitate more active involvement of the learner. Learners bring to the classroom environment a repertoire of knowledge, skills, attitudes, and values acquired through experiential and socio-cultural involvement and interaction. A passive learning environment breeds boredom, unfamiliarity, and discontentment. What must be stressed is that learners are active constructors of their own knowledge;

◆ Provide learners with opportunities to work together in a cooperative fashion. Cooperative learning environments have been shown to contribute positively to intergroup relations, and particularly for improving and enhancing relations among culturally diverse learners. Cooperative learning is a good example of how schools can build on the learning of all students working collaboratively together towards a common goal. Its arrangements in the classroom encourage students of all ages, cultural groupings, and ability levels to learn by assimilating their ideas, knowledge, abilities, and skills, and creating new knowledge through interacting with others; and

◆ utilize the community as an effective learning environment. This entails drawing on cultural institutions within the community to provide content information, instructional programs, and learning materials.

Finally, effective teaching strategies (i.e., procedures and approaches) must be used as a catalyst for transmitting and activating classroom endeavors. Such strategies should include but are not limited to the following:

◆ Developing instructional skills and techniques based on the needs of learners. This will assist learners to reach their fullest potential and develop their own unique talents;

◆ Being sensitive, fluent, and skilled at interpreting the unique cultural styles and motifs of culturally diverse learns-styles such as language, gesture, and behaviors;

◆ Helping learners to understand and comprehend academic skills, learning/cognitive styles, ideas, and information;

◆ Assist learners in understanding and developing values and social skills, and to understand themselves and others;

◆ Assist learners in developing repertoires of effective strategies for acquiring knowledge and information;

◆ Acquire knowledge of the social, cultural, and economic context of learners' life to develop more effective, efficient, and suitable teaching practices;

◆ Skill development in translating multicultural perspectives and knowledge into programs, curriculum, practices, activities, and behaviors of classroom instruction;

◆ Develop competencies in making educational goals, objectives, curriculum content and material, and learning activities meaningful to the frame of reference of all learners;

◆ Making sure that teaching styles and learning styles of the learner are congruent;

◆ Strategies should be based on the goal of preparing learners to live harmoniously and communally in a pluralistic/culturally diverse society;

◆ Strategies should allow students to assert their individuality to foster a classroom climate that discourages cultural disrespect;

◆ Make available materials, resources, and experiences that correspond to learners' interest, skills, and abilities; and

♦ Develop mechanisms that can assess, monitor, and evaluate learners' progress and success.

Conclusion

This nation consists of persons of different ethnic backgrounds, socioeconomic levels, religions, gender, languages, and age groupings. It is essential that educators be more responsive to and aware of the cultural diversity that exist in this county and develop skills and competencies for adapting effectively to the diverse clientele that they service. This entails implementing a multicultural educational perspective throughout the total educational and learning process.

The overall goals of multicultural education are to design systems of education that are inclusive rather than exclusive by providing an equitable education for all students and to ensure that these students develop their fullest potential for academic and vocational success while, at the same time, preparing them for the social, political, and economic realities that individuals experience in culturally diverse and complex human encounters. Implementing an approach to multicultural education entails a strong commitment to educational equities for all students. This will be a way of moving schools to the realities of cultural pluralism and diversity, and the incorporation of a multicultural perspective into the education process. Moreover, it entails a commitment by the education system to begin reevaluating, redefining, restructuring, and reinvigorating traditional educational goals, objectives, curricula, programs, and teaching instructional strategies to be more responsive to multicultural perspectives and ideologies. By skillfully permeating the multicultural perspective across all the dimensions of the education process, educators can meet a wider range of students' aptitudes, interest, participation, and knowledge than they do now. Further, educators must also focus their endeavors toward the knowledge, attitudes, skills, and characteristics needed for multicultural teaching if the clientele that they service is to be properly and efficiently trained.

Based on current demographic studies, there is no question that the demographic configuration of this nation is drastically changing as we venture into the 21st century and beyond. Although we have made some progress towards achieving the goals and objectives of multicultural education as a means of imparting knowledge and teaching acceptance and respect for diverse cultures, particularly within our education system, we still have a ways to go. There still exists a reluctance to constructively and realistically understand, recognize, and appreciate the existence of cultural pluralism. The primary goals of the education system is that of providing meaningful and relevant educational experiences for all American youth. As we continue to address educational reform in this country, we must continue to seriously consider multicultural education as a viable alternative to traditional monocultural education if reform efforts are to be successful. This alternative approach to education will direct our schools, as well as our students to be oriented towards 21st century realities where our society will become increasingly racial and culturally pluralistic. In all then, there is a great need at present for awareness and acceptance of cultural diversity in order for our youth to meet the challenges and demands of the years to come. Acceptance of multiculturalism has the potential to enrich not only the schools but the nation as well.

References

Banks, J. A. (1991). *Teaching strategies for ethnic studies*. Boston, MA: Allyn & Bacon.
Banks, J. A., & Banks, C.A. (Eds.) (1989). *Multicultural education: Issues and perspectives*. Boston, MA: Allyn & Bacon.
Banks, J. A. (1981). *Multiethnic education: Theory and practice*. Boston, MA: Allyn & Bacon.
Baptiste, H. P., & Baptiste, M. L. (1979). *Developing the multicultural process in Classroom Instruction*. Washington, D C: University Press of America.
Bennett, C. I. (1986). *Comprehensive multicultural education: Theory and practice*. Boston, MA: Allyn & Bacon.
Boykin, A. W., & Ellison, C. M. (1991). The multiple ecology of African-American socialization. In R. Taylor (Ed.), *The social economic status of black youth in the U.S.*, Hollywood, CA: Sage Publication.
Boykin, A. W. (1986). The triple quandary and the schooling of Afro-American children. In Y. Neisser (Ed.), *The school achievement of minority children: New perspectives*. Hillsdale, NJ: Erlbaum Associates Publishers.
Brisk, M. (1982). Language policies in American education: An historical overview. In M. Montero (Ed.), *Bilingual education teacher handbook*. Cambridge, MA: Evaluation, Dissemination and Assessment Center for Bilingual Education.
Garcia, R. (1976). *Learning in two languages*. Bloomington, IN: Phi Delta Kappa Educational Foundation.
Gay, G. (1975). Organizing and designing a culturally pluralistic curriculum. *Educational leadership*, 33, 176-183.
Gay, G. (1988). Designing relevant curricula for diverse learners. *Education and urban society*, 20(4), pp. 327-340.
Gay, G. (1983). Multiethnic education: Historical developments and future prospects. *Phi Delta Kappan*, 64, pp. 560-563.
Gibson, M. (1976). Approaches to multicultural education in the United States: Some concepts and assumptions. *Anthropology and Education Quarterly,* 7(4), pp. 7-18. Reprinted in *Anthropology and Education Quarterly,* 15(1), 1984.
Ginsburg, H. P. (1986). The myth of the deprived child: New thoughts on poor children. In. Y. Neisser (Ed.), *The school achievement of minority children: New perspectives*. Hillsdale, NJ: Erlbaum Associates Publishers.
Grant, C. A., & Melnick, S. L. (1977). In praise of diversity: Some implications. In M. Gold, C. Grant, & H. Rivlin (Eds.), *In praise of diversity: A resource book for* multicultural *education*. Washington, DC: Teacher Corps; Association of Teacher Education.
Giroux, H., & McLaren, P. (1986). Teacher education and the politics of engagement: The case for democratic schooling. *Harvard Educational Review*, 56(3), pp. 213-238.

Hale, J. E. (1977). Demythicizing the education of Black children. *First World,* (May/June), pp. 30-35.

Johnson, N.B., & Parker, A. E. (1987). Workforce 2000: Work and Workers for the 21st Century. Indianapolis, IN: Hudson Institute.

Ogbu, J.U. (1986). The consequences of the American caste system. In U. Neissen (Ed.), *The school achievement of minority children: New perspectives.* Hillsdale, NJ: Erlbaum Associates Publishers.

Phinney, J. S., & Rotheram, M. J. (1987). *Children's ethnic socialization: pluralism and development.* Beverly Hills, CA: Sage Publication.

Sleeter, C. E. (1991). *Empowerment through multicultural education.* Albany, NY: State University of New York Press.

Sleeter, C. E., & Grant, C. A. (1988). *Making choices for multicultural education.* Columbus, OH: Charles E. Merrill.

Stent, M. D., Hazard, W. R., & Rivlin, H. N. (1973). *Cultural pluralism in education.* New York: Meredith Corporation.

Stills, A. B. (1988). The development of a multicultural environment within the schools. In C. A. Heid (Ed.), *Multicultural education: Knowledge and perceptions.* Bloomington, IN: Center for Urban and Multicultural Education, Indiana University.

Sue, D.W. (1981). *Counseling the culturally different: Theory and practice.* New York: John Wiley & Sons.

Troike, R. C. (1981). Synthesis of research on bilingual education. *Educational Leadership,* 38, pp. 498-504.

Part Five

The Community Market Place: Intercultural Confrontation

A challenge to all Americans ... to become one community again, to reach across the divisions of race and income and region and age to put our people together again.
—Bill Clinton,
U. S. President-Elect, 1992
(*Washington Post*, October 17, 1992, p. A10)

Chapter 10

African Americans and Korean Immigrants:
Cultures in Conflict

Halford H. Fairchild & Denise G. Fairchild

Two blocks from our home in the West Adams District of Los Angeles is a small neighborhood market. It is owned by a family of Korean immigrants.

On a recent trip to the store we noticed that the proprietors had installed a bullet-proof, plastic barrier that shielded them from their clientele. We asked whether they had been robbed. They responded negatively, saying that the protective cage was a preventive measure.

We also witnessed the displeasure among the predominantly African-American clientele to the merchants' decision. Several were impatient and verbally hostile when the merchants took longer than usual to bag their purchases.

Meanwhile, in the Flatbush section of New York a simmering feud continues between African-American residents and the Korean owners of two neighborhood markets. Are these coincidences? Or, are these inter-ethnic rivalries the inevitable result of social-cultural design? To the extent that these disparate events are similar in origin, they may suggest both the causes and the solutions to such hostile relations. In both instances African-American residents view with resentment the invasion of their neighborhoods by outside merchants. This intrusion is like rubbing salt into the wounds caused by generations of economic despair. (By any measure, the economic status of America's ethnic-minority inner cities has worsened during the 1980s.)

In many buyer-seller relations suspicions occur naturally. Sellers suspect buyers of theft; buyers suspect sellers of overpricing policies. But when the sellers are immigrant Koreans and the buyers are African-American urban dwellers, additional suspicions pervade the relationships including long-standing racial biases that infect attitudes and behaviors. The ideology of white supremacy (the cornerstone of which is Black inferiority), evident throughout the world, and the

---

This chapter is a synthesized version of articles previously published in the *Los Angeles Times*, May 25, 1990; March 24 and May 5, 1991, *Los Angeles Times*, Inc. Reprinted with the authors' permission.

continuing portrayal of African Americans in the media as criminally inclined or pathological reinforce these preexisting biases. Unfortunately, the kernel of truth in these biases imbues them with a false sense of validity.

It is true that African Americans are over-represented among the poor, the violent, and the criminal. Less obvious are the objective life circumstances that produce these symptoms of pathology. In addition, anti-Asian prejudice is a reality that must also be acknowledged. As Americans we have been taught to distrust Asians—through motion pictures about World War II and through other portrayals that dehumanized them. American biases against those with limited English proficiency also impede the formation of harmonious relationships with first-generation immigrants.

These ideological underpinnings of the contemporary conflict between African Americans and Korean immigrants result in justification for inter-ethnic *scapegoating*. Anti-Black prejudice is widespread; anti-Asian bias is a reality in the African-American community.

Human Tragedies

Natasha Harlins, a 15 year-old, African-American school girl died from a gunshot wound to the head after trying to buy orange juice in a South Central convenience store in Los Angeles. A 51 year-old, Korean-American businesswoman, Soon Ja Du, was jailed for allegedly pulling the trigger.

We cannot count all the victims in this uniquely American tragedy. Clearly, Harlins was a victim. Du is both victimizer and victim. Their families and communities are victims—of grief—with the need to mitigate the damage to the relationships between Korean Americans and African Americans.

The 20th Century was marked by the urbanization of African Americans. Structural inequality, exacerbated by residential segregation, has resulted in communities that were and remain hard put to secure the most basic goods and services. The economic impotence of the African-American community opens the way for non-African-American entrepreneurs to fill the commerce vacuum, typically at a price that includes the added cost of doing business in economically depressed areas.

Today, those immigrant merchants are overwhelmingly Korean. In South Central Los Angeles a majority of the convenience stores are owned and operated by Korean-American families. The situation in New York City and in other metropolitan areas is similar. This economic fact underscores the lack of opportunities immigrant Koreans have in America. They continually face discrimination in education and employment. Entrepreneurial ventures offer them a reliable route to economic success.

On the other hand, African Americans have virtually no meaningful opportu-

African Americans and Korean Immigrants

nity to take control of their communities' economies. Lack of education and training, as well as employment discrimination, blocks their economic empowerment. Their economic peril is historically ingrained and appears intractable.

The ethnic diversification of America necessarily carries with it many dangers. In particular, the confluence of African-American and Korean-American cultures invites conflicts—in language, customs, behavioral styles, ideologies, and values. Of course Korean merchants, like any others, face conflicts with customers, workers, and competitors. But when clients and merchants are members of groups who each have long and bitter experiences of racial and ethnic discrimination, the simple act of buying orange juice, as in Natasha Harlins' case, can become an occasion for violence.

Several Korean merchants have been killed in the Los Angeles area. Thus, it is easy to understand why they arm themselves for self-defense. Natasha Harlins may have been the first customer to be killed in a store owned by Koreans, but it is unlikely that she will be the last. Guns in America have increasingly become the *final arbiters* of such interpersonal and intergroup disputes.

The media contribute to the potential for conflict by latching onto images that degrade African Americans and Asian Americans. When a group of people are dehumanized by the popular culture, as African Americans are, it is not surprising to see them as frequent victims of nightsticks and guns. A disturbing and enduring lack of fundamental respect for African Americans connects the beating of Rodney G. King and the murder of Natasha Harlins. African Americans are the most vulnerable, and victimized, group in our society.

But understanding these issues—structured inequality, racism, media prejudice, cultures in conflict—does not make solutions any easier to identify. Clearly, racism must be eliminated, equal opportunity implemented and upheld, sensitivity to different peoples and cultures stressed. However, we need to translate these broad initiatives into individual practices that reduce prejudice, intolerance, and the potential for violent conflict. At some point we need to re-socialize ourselves in a way that views the use of lethal force as a *method of no resort*.

Earlier in 1991, the Black/Korean Alliance in Los Angeles held a breakfast meeting on the steps of City Hall. Established to mediate conflicts between Korean merchants and their African-American customers, this group of business, religious, and community leaders has been successful in avoiding the acrimonious boycotts that characterize Black-Korean relations in New York City. In 1990, the alliance succeeded in getting Korean merchants and their protesting customers to talk to each other, thus defusing a potential confrontation. Currently, it is facilitating the formation of *joint economic* ventures, *religious* and *cultural exchange* programs, and developing a *political* agenda. The group now must contend with renewed animosity in the wake of Natasha Harlins' slaying.

That will not be easy. In early 1991, a group of African-American and Asian-American researchers at the University of California, Los Angeles drafted a proposal to study the nature and causes of conflicts between African Americans and

Korean Americans in Los Angeles. They have also sought to develop guidelines on how to resolve such conflicts. Their challenge is that social science theory in the area of minority-minority conflict is almost non-existent, and new research methodologies need to be developed if meaningful data are to be collected.

Tragedy is certainly not a new theme in America's interracial relationships. If there is anything to be gained from such tragedies as the slaying of Natasha Harlins, they include the increased sensitivity that we are forced to develop toward one another, the need to grapple with differences in cultures, the incentive for non-violent means to resolve conflicts, and recognition that basic features of our society set the stage for inter-ethnic conflict and violence.

The Urban Context

Los Angeles is in a violent confrontation with itself. Its escalating inter-ethnic conflicts are frustrating its efforts to become a world-class city.

Development policies over the last decade have sought to make Los Angeles the magnet of the burgeoning *Pacific Rim* economy. The region's growth has been phenomenal, as measured by trade revenues, number of building permits issued, and aggregate income. The success of Los Angeles' integration into the international economy, however, is not matched by success in integrating its immigrant and ethnic minority populations.

The "new immigration" is comprised principally of persons from Southeast Asia, Mexico, and Central America. They are *pushed* from war-torn countries or countries suffering chronic under-development and poverty, and they are *pulled* by the promise of a vibrant international economy.

Recent events suggest that we are poorly prepared for the increased diversity, as inter-ethnic interactions too often end in tragedy. The consciousness of the city and the nation was shocked by the killing of an unarmed, 15-year-old, African-American school girl by a Korean merchant. African-American and Latino relations came to the boiling point at a local high school where racial epithets were hurled from one group to the other. Innocent children are dying almost daily in ethnic minority gangs' continuing quest for neighborhood control. Racial crimes are setting new records while racial supremacists are coming out of the closet.

All signs point, regrettably, to the continuing escalation of these conflicts and human tragedies. Los Angeles remains the most racially segregated city in the country. Locked out of exclusive, residential communities, South Central Los Angeles is considered the primary *dumping ground* and *launching pad* for immigrant populations. Today, the area is increasingly Latino and Asian, but unlike the *white flight* of the 1950s, African Americans have neither the means nor the motives to take flight.

But African Americans have grown increasingly resentful of other ethnic groups "making it" in America—at their expense. The opening of another Korean store in South Central has exacerbated the wounds of decades of economic dependency.

Economic tensions are also infected by mutually shared stereotypes and intolerance. Newcomers to African-American communities often bring the racial ideology of Black inferiority that permeates much of the popular culture. On the other hand, African Americans may be quick to ridicule the cultural and linguistic practices of immigrant neighbors and merchants.

These groups also compete for limited public resources. African Americans, Asians, and Latinos often find themselves *pitted against each other* for political representation and a share of public goods and services.

Excluded from segregated communities, choked by public and private divestment and neglect, South Central Los Angeles residents live in a breeding ground for inter-ethnic conflict—a social cancer spreading quickly throughout the region.

How then, do we meet and overcome these challenges to America's ideal of a free and open society? Is there a panacea for the interethnic rivalry, violence, and bloodshed?

The crisis of the new immigration forces us to re-examine and reaffirm our American *melting pot* ideals and our efforts toward building a world-class, cosmopolitan city and country. The ideological debate centers on accepting the cultural diversity embodied by the newcomers to America's shores, or retrenching into ethnocentric (and racist) policies of cultural exclusion and homogenization. The restructuring of our social/cultural values must be forged by multi-ethnic coalitions, such as the Asian Pacific Legal Center's plan to offer inter-ethnic relations training. The Los Angeles Black/Korean Alliance is another positive effort to bridge cultural differences.

But these grass-roots efforts, largely funded by volunteerism, are insufficient. We must put on our local and national agenda the question of inter-ethnic and intercultural relationships. We must find a way of resolving disputes, large and small, nonviolently. We must develop and propagate images in the popular media that reverse stereotypes and offer models of positive cross-cultural interaction and understanding. The news media need to focus on positive programs for intercultural exchange as much as they emphasize traumatic interactions.

Positive inter-group relations may also be promoted by changing the land-use policies of our cities. Zoning and transportation policies must take human interaction into consideration. A pedestrian city structured to promote greater contact between merchant and resident, working class and elite, young and old, renter and homeowner, newcomer and old helps to create communities of tolerance and opportunity. We need to redesign our cities to promote a cosmopolitan culture while also creating the land-use efficiency needed to sustain a truly world-class economy.

The silver lining in the crises surrounding the new immigration lies in making us acknowledge and confront our prejudices and our structured inequities. We can use the new immigration to expand the definition of American and Los Angeles culture and to grapple with the problems of linguistic diversity in schools and public affairs. The future of the city and the nation depends upon the successful use of social and physical planning that embraces cultural and racial diversity.

Conclusion

With their long history, solutions to these issues will potentially involve generations of conscious and deliberate action.

First, we must re-socialize ourselves regarding racial differences. Instead of amplifying them, we should recognize that the concept of race is a political invention with little or no scientific basis. We must recognize that the current plight of African Americans is not of their making, but the product of centuries of *de jure* discrimination. We must learn that our attitudes toward Asians are largely the result of superficial media portrayals.

Second, we must learn that cultural differences are a valuable resource. All groups have unique cultural histories and characteristics that are of value to others.

Koreans display a laudatory collective spirit of economic cooperation. It is not so much that wealthy Koreans are "invading" African-American communities as it is that Korean immigrant families are pooling their comparatively meager resources to purchase businesses in economically distressed areas.

African Americans have shown the world a certain moral consciousness, notably exhibited by Dr. Martin Luther King, Jr. Other Blacks have also contributed to the development of modern civilization by the invention—in antiquity—of written script, mathematics, politics, and architecture. Thus, anti-Black biases are unfounded, and the same is true of anti-Asian biases.

A remedy to the current Korean/African-American conflicts must be found. A recognition of the shaping of public opinion by popular media (such as motion pictures), alleviating economic anomie, and a recognition of each group's contribution to modern society are beginning steps toward this positive resolution. We must learn to nourish our ethnic, racial and cultural differences. They illuminate both the diversity and the commonality within our species.

References

Fairchild, H. (1990, May 25). Looking for remedies, not scapegoats. *Los Angeles Times*, p. B7.
Fairchild, H. (1991, March 24). A sad tale of persecuted minorities. *Los Angeles Times*.
Fairchild, H., & Fairchild, D. (1991, May 5). World class tension: Ethnic rivalry heats up Southern California. *Los Angeles Times*, p. M2.

Chapter Eleven

Korean-American Marketing in the African-American Community:
An Exploratory Study in the Nation's Capital

Ernest R. Myers

Since the early 1980s, friction between Asian merchants (particularly Korean-owned grocery stores and Chinese-owned carry-outs) and African-American customers has captured news headlines coast to coast. This societal phenomenon raises a number of questions. What is the nature of this inter-group problem? Do these inter-group, inter-ethnic problems simply express racial bigotry? Are these incidents of conflict a result of intercultural misperception? Has the problem reached the magnitude implied by national media coverage, or are public impressions simply the effect of media hype?

African-American neighborhoods throughout the nation have been the "ecological business sectors of preference" for numerous Chinese and Korean-owned convenience stores, to a perceived saturation point by African Americans in cities where their populations are largest. In New York, Gupta (1983) counted 58 Korean-owned stores on Harlem's 125th Street (all of which opened within a span of a few years), moving one resident to observe, "Everyone's doing business in the Black community except Black people" (p. 53). Harlem residents were early initiators of boycotts against these businesses, accusing them of not employing Blacks and not being responsive to community interests (p. 51). *U.S. News and World Report* noted that 11 Korean-owned shops were firebombed in a single Black neighborhood between 1984-86. In late 1986, local residents picketed a Chinese carry-out in Washington, D. C., forcing its temporary closing because the owner had chased a Black woman from the store with a gun (November 24, 1986). In Brooklyn's Bedford-Stuyvesant neighborhood similar pickets closed two Korean-owned grocery stores in 1988 (*Washington Post*, May 8, 1990). In Los Angeles, Halford Fairchild, a social psychologist of African-American and Asian parentage, has written extensively on *urban* affairs and incidents of confrontation and conflict in recent years between Korean merchants and African Americans (*Los Angeles Times*, 1990, 1991). After nearly a year's picketing of a Korean grocery store in the Flatbush area of Brooklyn, the proprietor acquiesced to community demands and sold out—

to another Korean merchant—in mid-1991 (*Capital Spotlight,* June 6, 1991). In the summer of 1990, the largest, full-service, African-American supermarket in the nation's capital went bankrupt and was quickly purchased by Korean entrepreneurs. A community-based boycott of the store was promptly launched (lasting several months) in efforts to gain the reemployment of African-Americans who had been employed under the store's former ownership, plus other concessions.

Notwithstanding the media's emphasis on problems rather than solutions, nearly a decade of such inter-group, minority-minority conflicts confirm their reality as more than sensational journalism. Moreover, scanning the literature on the topic does not reveal any substantive, empirically-based analysis which would contribute to a sharper understanding of the dynamics involved. The following data analyses are a result of such concerns in exploring preliminary consumer-market research issues and examining the psycho-social factors manifested in these community-based *minority versus minority* conflicts.

Purpose of the Study

In order to investigate the inter-group, interactional influences underscoring the proliferation of conflicts of Asian-American businesses operating in African-American communities, an exploratory study was done between the spring and summer of 1991 in Washington, D. C. This study was originally designed to survey a representative sample of the broad range of Asian businesses in the nation's capital—Chinese, Korean, Japanese, and Southeast Asians. However, in order to manage the research, Korean merchants with membership in the local Korean-American Chamber of Commerce were selected as the focal group. As an exploratory study, the following concerns were highlighted.

◆ What profile data characterize these entrepreneurs?

◆ Where are their businesses located, and where do they reside?

◆ How long have they resided in the United States and in Washington, D. C. in relation to their current residence?

◆ What range of types of businesses do they operate, and how long have they been in business?

◆ Which ethnic/racial groups represent their predominant clientele and ecological business community?

◆ What factors determined their decisions to establish businesses in African-American communities?

◆ In general, what is their perception of their intercultural awareness, and how do they evaluate their merchant-customer interactions?

Korean-American Marketing in the African-American Community

◆ What has been their business experiences as victims of hostile acts and crimes, and what do they perceive to be the causes?

◆ Do they perceive of a need for special police protection for their businesses?

◆ What kinds of relationships or associations do they have with African Americans?

◆ How were they able to start their businesses?

Design of the Study

A six-page questionnaire was developed consisting of 26 major items with six open-ended questions that explored the above-listed concerns. These questions, originally in English, were then translated into Korean by a Korean-American restaurateur who has a social science background. A team consisting of the author, another African-American psychologist, the translator, and the president of the local Korean-American Chamber of Commerce met numerous times to conduct a content analysis of the questions, assure the accuracy of translations, develop an instructional manual for computer analyses of the data (Statistical Package for the Social Sciences [SPSS]), and establish a mailing schedule for the survey.

Approximately 600 questionnaires were mailed (with pre-paid postage return envelopes) to members of the Korean-American Chamber of Commerce who operated businesses in Washington, D. C. An introduction included with the survey forms (in Korean) was as follows.

> *ASIAN AMERICAN BUSINESS COMMUNITY SURVEY*
>
> This is a survey to collect information to better understand Asian business owners and the controversy concerning their clientele, especially Black customer relations. Hopefully, examination of these issues will be useful in developing solutions by and for Asian business persons, community leaders and perhaps the city's police system's community relations unit.
>
> We would greatly appreciate your help in this effort by taking the time (about 20 minutes) to answer this questionnaire anonymously. We *do not* want your name or address so you may respond openly with confidence.
>
> After the *Respondent Profile* section, most questions can be quickly answered by marking a "Yes" or "No" or a mark (x). Thank you for cooperating. Your concerns and cooperation are important to achieve improved community-business relations.
>
> REMEMBER! YOUR IDENTITY (NAME) OR YOUR BUSINESS NAME IS NOT REQUIRED.

Response Rate

By the end of the first week after the mailings had arrived, 30 completed questionnaires were returned, and 235 more followed within a month—a 44 percent rate of response. This successful rate of returns is attributed to: (1) the content of the questionnaires which were responsive to the concerns of Korean merchants, allowing them to ventilate their views; (2) the effective translation of the questionnaires into the Korean language; (3) the assurance of maintaining respondent anonymity; and (4) the mailings indicated the approval of the business association's (Chamber of Commerce) leadership.

Cooperation by the local Korean business leadership was particularly influenced by two factors: (1) the business association's current president had tentatively planned to survey the membership of the local Korean Chamber of Commerce before the author initially approached him; and (2) earlier the head of the community relations unit of Washington, D. C.'s police department had had some dialogue with the association's president related to the survey concerns, such as public safety. Consequently, the author came on the scene somewhat coincidentally in developing the survey design and instruments, and providing coordination required to implement the study.

Results

Length of Time in Business and Merchants' Residence

One-half (or 49.8 percent) 132 of the respondents have operated their businesses for five years or less in the District of Columbia, 59 businesses for less than one year, and 73 businesses for two to five years—the litmus test period for a determination of small business viability. Commendably, 126 of these District of Columbia-based Korean businesses (or 47.5 percent) have flourished beyond five years (See Table 11.1).

Significantly, only 9.7 percent of the Korean merchants responding to the survey (26 out of 265) reside where their businesses are based as shown in Table 11.2. Ninety percent of these merchants maintain domiciles in Suburban Maryland and Virginia rather than in Washington, D. C. (the District of Columbia). As Table 11.2 reflects, 129 (48.7 percent) reside in Maryland, while 108 (40.8 percent) of the respondents live in Virginia. Furthermore, only 26 respondents, or less than 10 percent, hold domicile in the District where their businesses are located.

In 1992, only 800 of the estimated 44,000 Koreans in the Greater Metropolitan Washington Area lived in the District—less than 2 percent. Unlike Los Angeles, there is no "Koreatown" in Washington, D. C. (the District of Columbia). However,

Table 11.1
Korean-American Merchants
Years at Business Locations in Washington, D.C.

Years	Number of Merchants	Percent
Less than 1 year	59	22.3
2 thru 5 years	73	27.5
over 5 years	126	47.5
no response	7	2.7
Totals	265	100

Table 11.2
Korean-American Merchants
Residence in Greater Washington, D.C., Metropolitan Area

Greater Metropolitan Area	Number of Merchants	Percent
Washington, D.C.	26	9.7
*Maryland	129	48.7
*Virginia	108	40.8
Missing Cases	2	0.8
Totals	265	100

* = D.C. Suburbs

the nearby city of Annandale, Virginia, has a "Koreatown" with over 330 businesses. Over one-half of the *current* 98,000 Koreans in the Greater Metropolitan Washington Area reside in Annandale.

Nearly 90 percent of the Korean business respondents have resided in the Greater Metropolitan Washington Area—the District of Columbia, and suburban Maryland and Virginia—for over two years, and 203 respondents (76.6 percent) have been residents of this area for over five years (See Table 11.3).

Sex and Marital Status

The majority of the respondents, as would be expected, were males—three-fourths, or 199. Six, however, declined to identify their sex. Assuming that the respondents to the survey questionnaires were the proprietors of the businesses, a strong number, 60 (nearly 23 percent) are apparently female-operated enterprises, or at least they assume a leadership role (implied by their completion of the survey questionnaires) (See Table 11.4).

Over 90 percent (92.1 percent), or 244, of the respondents are married which is characteristic of the family-oriented business tradition of Korean culture (See Table 11.5).

Challenges of a Changing America

Table 11.3
Korean-American Merchants
Length of Time Residing in Greater Washintgon, D.C., Metropolitan Area

Years of Residence in Area	Number of Merchants	Percent
Less than 1 year	2	0.8
1 thru 2 years	8	3.0
2 thru 5 years	34	12.8
Over 5 years	203	76.6
No response	17	6.4
Missing cases	1	0.4
Totals	265	100

Table 11.4
Korean-American Merchants Sex of Respondents

Sex	Number of Merchants	Percent
Male	199	74.7
Female	60	22.6
Nn Response	6	2.3
Missing Cases	1	0.4
Totals	265	100

Table 11.5
Korean-American Merchants Marital Status of Respondents

Status of Respondents	Number of Merchants	Percent
Married	244	92.1
Single	14	5.3
No Response	6	2.3
Missing Cases	1	0.4
Totals	265	100

Merchants' Education

Table 11.6 indicates that the Korean business respondents to this survey are a highly educated group, surpassing the educational achievement level of the average native-born United States citizen. Over one-half (138, or 52 percent) have earned college degrees. One hundred twenty-five (47 percent) of these were at the bachelor's degree level. These data also indicate that over 90 percent of these merchants are high school graduates.

Table 11.6
Korean-American Merchants Respondents' Education Achivement Levels

Education Level Achieved	Number of Merchants	Percent
Junior High School	9	3.4
High School	71	26.8
2 years of college	34	12.8
4 yesrs of college	125	47.2
Business Technical	5	1.9
Master's Degree	7	2.6
Ph.D. Degree	6	2.3
No Response	7	2.6
Totals	264	100

Religion

A solid one-half, or 50.6 percent, of the respondents indicated Protestant religious affiliation, which is reflective of the strong work ethic of Korean culture. Moreover, 20.8 percent were affiliated with the Catholic Church, resulting in a combined 71.4 percent who practice Christianity (See Table 11.7). In Western society, the Christian belief system is highly associated with the virtue of private enterprise.

Table 11.7
Korean-American Merchants Respondents' Religious Affiliation

Religious Affiliation	Number of Merchants	Percent
Protestant	134	50.6
Catholic	55	20.8
Buddist	20	7.5
Other	23	8.7
No Response	33	12.5
Totals	265	100

Citizenship

The majority, or nearly 56 percent, of the responding merchants have yet to acquire United States citizenship—green card holders—which suggests that a large number are in the process of making immigration resettlements while taking on the challenge of their business operations. Over forty percent (42.3 percent) of the respondents hold U. S. citizenship (See table 11.8).

Table 11.8
Korean-American Mercahnts Respondents' Citizenship

Respondents' Citizenship	Number of Merchants	Percent
U.S. Citizen	112	42.3
Green Card Holder	148	55.8
Temporary Resident	1	0.4
No Response	4	1.5
Totals	265	100

Language Problems

Communication is a key factor in cross-cultural and inter-ethnic relations. Thus, the Korean merchants were asked to respond to the question: "Do you experience language problems with your customers?" Significantly, 147 (55.5 percent) confirmed that language was a barrier in their business operations "sometimes"; only 10 respondents (3.8 percent) indicated that language difficulties with customers occurred often (See Table 11.9). The 91 respondents (34.3 percent) who reported "never" having language problems apparently speak fluent English.

Table 11.9
Korean-American Merchants Respondents Experiencing Language Problems with Customers

Frequency of Problems	Number of Merchants	Percent
Often	10	3.8
Sometimes	147	55.5
Never	91	34.3
No Response	17	6.4
Totals	265	100

Merchants' Education and Association with African-American Entrepreneurs

The greater the degree of levels of educational and professional achievement of the Korean businesspersons, the more they indicated having some association with African-American business persons. This is particularly shown in Table 11.10, especially for those merchants with business, technical, and college backgrounds. Five, or 100 percent, of the Korean entrepreneurs with doctoral degrees, for example, indicated some association with African-American business persons.

Across all educational levels more than half (55.5 percent) of the responses were situationally-dependent, particularly those at the undergraduate level of college

Table 11.10
Korean-American Merchants Respondents' Education by Association with Black Entrepreneurs

Respondents' Educational Achievement	Respondents Who Associate with Black Entrepreneurs		
	No Association	Some Association	Totals
Junior High School	3	3	6 (2.4%)
High School	18	51	69 (27.9%)
2 Years College	10	23	33 (13.4)
4 Year College	37	84	121 (49.0%)
Business/Technical	1	4	5 (2.0)
Master's Degree	3	4	7 (2.8%)
Ph.D. Degree	0	5	5 (2.0)
Totals	73 (29.6%)	174 (70.4%)	247 (100%)

completion; 43 of these respondents were nearly half (45.1 percent) of the survey sample in this column. Interestingly, the high school graduates equally accepted or rejected the notion of hiring African Americans, as Table 11.11 shows.

Table 11.11
Korean-American Merchants Respondents' Education and Potential Hiring of African Americans

Respondents' Educational Achievement	Potential Hiring of African Americans			
	No	Depends on Situation	Yes	Totals
Junior High School	1	3	1	5 (2.9%)
High School	10	28	11	50 (28.9%)
2 Year College	9	16	5	30 (17.3%
4 Year College	21	43	14	78 (45.1%)
Business/Technical	1	3	0	4 (2.3)
Master's Degree	3	2	0	4 (2.3%)
Ph.D. Degree	0	1	0	1 (0.6%)
Totals	45 (26.0)	96 (55.5%)	31 (17.9%)	173 (100%)

Are the educational levels of the Korean merchants and their views on hiring African-Americans associated? Although 26 percent of the respondents flatly declared that they would not employ African Americans in the future, Table 11.11 shows that about 18 percent were affirmative, and over 55 percent responded that it would depend upon the situation. One limitation of the survey was a lack of further exploration in the questionnaire's content—not inquiring beyond the noncommittal response of "it depends on the situation." Significantly, 35 percent of the businesses surveyed, or 93 respondents, *avoided this question* entirely—173 of the 265 business persons answered the question of the possible hiring of African Americans in their enterprises in the future.

The relationship between the following two questions was considered crucial in terms of the Korean merchants' perceptions of potential African-American employees in their businesses, and any indications of their past business-related associations with African-Americans. The questions were: (1) Do you associate with any African-American business persons in your business? (2) If you have not employed any African-Americans, are there circumstances in which you would do so in the future? Fifty-three (31 percent) of the respondents reported having no association with African-American business persons. Of this group, 18 (34 percent) rejected any future potential for hiring African-Americans, while 28 (53 percent) felt that maybe they would, "depending on the situation" (undefined circumstances). Another seven (13 percent) would definitely do so in the future.

Conversely, 117 (69 percent) of the Korean merchants had some past or current association with African-American business persons. Of this group, 27 (23 percent) would not hire African-Americans in the future. However, 67 (57 percent) would continue their "equal employment opportunity" practices by hiring African-Americans, "depending on the situation," and 23 (20 percent) were committed to definite employment of African-Americans in the future.

Significantly, 170 (64 percent) of the 265 Korean merchants who responded to the survey questionnaire answered these questions. Thus, 95 (36 percent) of the respondents declined to reveal whether they had business associations with African-Americans, and whether they would hire African-Americans in the future (See Table 11.12).

The merchants in Washington who also lived in the city were less likely to employ African Americans—9 out of 26—than the merchants who lived in the suburban areas (Maryland and Virginia). More precisely, the merchants employing African Americans were as follows: store owners residing in Washington, 35

Table 11.12
Korean-American Merchants:
Would Respondents Hire African Americans in the Future?

Any Association with African-American Persons	No	Depends on Situation	Yes	Total
No	18 (34.0%)	28 (53.%)	7 (13.0%)	53 (31.0%)
Yes	27 (23.0%)	67 (57.0%)	23 (20.0%)	117 (69.0%)
Totals	45 (26.3%)	95 (55.5%)	30 (17.5%)	170 (100%)

percent, versus store owners living in Maryland or Virginia, 40 percent (See Table 11.12a). Significantly, more than two-thirds of the population of Washington, D. C., is African Americans.

The survey sought to detect intercultural differences and self-awareness on the part of the Korean business community concerning the business respondents' sensitivity to African-American culture. The researcher expected that this observation would identify awareness and sensitivity as indicators in understanding the interpersonal relations and cultural conflicts among Korean merchants, their predominantly African-American customers, and the African-American communities surrounding the businesses. The question posed was: Do you feel you understand and are sensitive to African-American culture? While 68 (nearly 26 percent) felt adequately sensitive and 33 (nearly 13 percent) felt very sensitive, 145 (nearly 55 percent) felt less than adequately sensitive, that is, 30 rated themselves as insensitive or without understanding of African-American culture, and 115 marked the "somewhat" or "little sensitivity" response choice (See Table 11.13).

Table 11.14 indicates that 31 percent of the Korean merchants felt positive

Table 11.12a
Korean-American Merchants:
Location of Respondents' Residence by Those Employing African Americans

Location of Respondents' Residence	No	Yes	Missing Cases	Totals
D. C.	17	9	0	26 (9.9%)
Maryland	74	51	1	127 (48.5%)
Virginia	64	43	0	107 (40.8%)
Missing Cases	1	1	0	2 (0.8%)
Totals	156	104	1	261
Percent	59.5%	39.7%	0.4%	100%

(Respondents Employing African Americans)

Table 11.13
Korean-American Merchants:
Respondents' Self-Ratings of Sensitivity to African-American Culture

Choices	Number of Merchants	Percent
Not Sensitive (No)	30	11.3
A Little (Somewhat)	115	43.4
Sensitive (Adequately)	68	25.7
Very Sensitive	33	12.5
No Response	19	7.2
Totals	265	100

Table 11.14
Korean-American Merchants' Ratings of Customer Contacts by Race of Customer

Customer Race	Respondents' Ratings of Customer Contacts					
	Very Negative	Negative	Moderate	Positive	Very Positive	Total
White	0	3	37	13	11	63
Percent		(3.0%)	(58.0%)	(20.0%)	(11.0%)	(23.2%)
Black	3	9	85	66	22	185
Percent	(1.6%)	(5.0%)	(46.0%)	(36.0%)	(12.0%)	(74.0%)
Other	0	0	1	0	0	1
Percent			(0.4%)			(0.4%)
Totals	3	11	123	79	33	249
Percent	(1.2%)	(4.4%)	(49.6%)	(31.6%)	(13.2%)	(100%)

about their contacts with white customers, versus 48 percent positive ratings for their African-American customers. Whites received moderate ratings by 58 percent of the merchant respondents while African-American customers received 46 percent. Although small in number, African-American customers received four times the negative ratings of those received by whites, that is, 12 versus 2 such ratings. However, this table also indicates that over 94 percent of the merchants' ratings of *all* their customers ranged from moderate to very positive.

Table 11.15 presents data on the ethnicity of customer patronage and the ethnicity of the surrounding neighborhood. Clearly, the businesses are *location-specific* in that in neighborhoods of large African-American concentrations the Asian business *depends* upon African-American customers. Conversely, whites are the predominant customers in areas of high white concentrations. This pattern conforms to traditional practice in neighborhoods where the corner store is frequented by the local residents (neighbors), taking the form of "walk-ins" and purchases essentially influenced by the convenience of the stores.

As indicated above, business proprietors made ratings of their customers. These respondents were asked to rate their contacts with their customers on a *Likert-scale* of "very negative" to "very positive." Interestingly, female respondents' ratings were significantly more positive than male respondents' ratings, yet their negative ratings of customers were nearly identically small in number. Female ratings ranging from "positive" to "very positive," versus the male counterparts' ratings of 40.5 percent for "positive" choices. Females' ratings of "very negative" to "negative" were 6 percent versus 5 percent for males. However, male respondents were less extreme than the females in their views of customers—moderate interactions (not positive or negative). This latter rating difference was 53.5 percent for males versus 33.5 percent for females.

Korean-American Marketing in the African-American Community

Table 11.15
Korean-American Merchants:
Race of Customers by Ethnicity of Business Neighborhood

Customer Race	Race of Customers by Ethnicity of Business Neighborhood						Total
	Whites		Blacks		Other		
	N	%	N	%	N	%	
White	60	99.4%	1	0.4%	0	—	61 (24.6%)
Black	1	0.4%	184	99.5%	0	—	185 (74.0%)
Other	0	—	0	—	1	0.4%	1 (0.4%)
Totals	61	24.6%	185	75.0%	1	0.4%	247 (100%)

Table 11.16
Korean-Americans Merchants:
Sex of Merchants by Their Ratings of Customers

Sex of Merchant	Respondents' Ratings of Customer Contacts					Total
	Very Negative	Negative	Moderate	Positive	Very Positve	
Male	1	10	102	56	22	191
Percent			(53.5%)	(40.5%)	(40.5%)	(77.0%)
Female	2	1	19	23	11	56
Percent			(33.5%)	(61.5%)	(61.5%)	(22.6%)
No Response	—	—	—	—	—	1
Percent						(0.4%)
Totals	3	11	121	79	33	248
Percent	(1.2%)	(4.4%)	(49.6%)	(31.6%)	(13.2%)	(100%)

Offenses Experienced and Perceived Protection Needs

As a follow-up to the survey inquiry about offenses experienced by the Korean businesses, a key "true versus false" statement raised was, "The Korean businesses need *special* police protection in the neighborhoods where we operate." Table 11.17 shows over one-third (99, or 37.4 percent) of the respondents declaring this to be false while a close but greater number, 106 (40 percent), disagreed and said it was true. Significantly, 60 (nearly 23 percnt) declined to respond to the statement.

A key, open-ended question in this survey concerned the respondents percep- tions of why they experienced problems or crimes in their business operations. Although small in number(16 out of 66 responses), the most frequent categorical reason identified was "trouble with Blacks" which implies an issue of cultural or ethnic conflict. Table 11.18 shows an even smaller number who perceived a high crime profile of the neighborhoods as a reason for their victimization (11 out of 66 responses). More significant, however, is the respondents' perceptions that the city's police system is negligent in terms of indifference to their needs or providing sufficient police patrols (23 out of 66 responses). Seventy-five percent (199) of the 265 business respondents gave no responses to this inquiry concerning reasons for perceived need for *special* police protection. One quarter of the responding Korean merchants, however, claimed a need for *special* police services.

Significantly, the reasons given by the respondents claiming the need for special police protection were choices voluntarily articulated by the merchants themselves as solicited by the open-ended structure of the question.

Table 11.17
Korean-American Merchants Respondents' Perception of Special Police Protection Needs

Choice Responses	Number of Merchants	Percent
False	99	37.4
True	106	40.0
No Response	60	22.6
Totals	265	100

Table 11.18
Korean-American Merchants: Categorical Reasons Merchants Perceive for Police Services

Reasons Police Protection Needed	Number of Responses	Percent
Trouble with Black	16	6.0
High Crime Area	11	4.2
Police Indifference	14	5.3
Racism	6	2.3
Language Problems	5	1.9
No Police Patrol	9	3.4
Drug Traffic	4	1.5
Property and Life Protection	1	0.4
No Response	199	—
Total Responses	66	25

A large majority of the respondents (232 out of 265) agreed that "the longer we operate our businesses in the neighborhood, the fewer problems we experience" (See Table 11.19). Thus, a substantial number of the respondents indicated a strong relationship between the length of time they had operated their business in a particular neighborhood and the problems they experienced in that community. Therefore, nearly 88 percent express optimism in the adage, "time is a cure," at least of sorts. Relationally, Table 11.1 points out that 73 percent of the respondents in this study have operated at their business locations at least two years, and nearly 48 percent for over five years.

Table 11.19
Korean-American Merchants:
Perception of Respondents' Longevity in the Neighborhood by the Number of Problems They Experience

True or False Question: The Longer we operate our business in the neighgborhood, the fewer problems we experience.

Choice Responses	Number of Merchants	Percent
False	7	2.6
True	232	87.5
No Response	26	9.8
Totals	265	100

Respondents reported being victims of a large number of the eight offenses listed on the questionnaire (See Table 11.20). Thefts and shoplifting headed the list,

Table 11.20
Korean-American Merchants:
Types of Offenses Identified by Respondents

Offense Type	Applicable Number	%	Not Applicable* Number	%	No Response Percentage**	Total Responses
Abusive Language	79	29.8	144	54.3	41%	223
Physical Threats	40	15.1	183	69.1	42%	223
Threats	114	43.0	109	41.1	40%	223
Robbery	63	23.8	159	60.0	42%	222
Arson	6	2.3	216	81.5	42%	222
Boycotts	6	2.3	216	81.5	42%	222
Shoplifting	179	67.5	45	17.0	41%	224
Other	0	0	0	0	0%	0
Totals	487	%=***				

*NA = Number of merchants where offense did not apply.
**No Response = Respondents left choice blank.
***Total exceeds 100% due to overlap of categories.

with apparent overlaps—the questionnaire did not define the offenses. However, shoplifting was identified 179 times, amounting to over 67 percent of the responses, while thefts were noted 114 times by 43 percent of the Korean business persons. Relationally, 63 robberies of nearly 24 percent of the businesses were identified, which is indicative of the high crime areas in which most small Korean businesses are located in Washington, D. C., as they are likely to be similarly located in New York, Los Angeles, and so on. Nearly 30 percent reported being verbally abused, 79 responses, and hostility in the form of physical threats was reported 40 times by 15 percent of the business persons. Boycotts and arson were equally reported—2.3 percent for each offense, six times respectively. Significantly, 18.5 percent (approximately 41) of the respondents apparently identified no offenses.

Two-thirds of the District's Korean business persons who participated in the survey experienced one to three offenses, as shown in Table 11.21. Seventy-seven businesses reported one offense, 57 reported two offenses, and 40 reported three offenses. Less than five percent reported no offenses, and nearly 30 percent of the business persons declined to respond to this inquiry.

Table 11.21
Korean-American Merchants:
Volume of Offenses Respondents Identified

Number of Offenses	Frequency	Percent
None	12	4.5
One	77	29.1
Two	57	21.5
Three	40	15.1
No Response	79	29.8
Totals	265	100

A two-part question was asked to elicit an understanding of and the motivation for the pattern of Korean merchants' establishing their businesses primarily in African-American communities (See Table 11.22). The question posed was, "What determined your decision to open business and/or acquire property in the location of your business?" The first six listed reasons (closed-end choices) were responses related to: (1) a desire to be in close proximity to family and friends—economic, cultural, and psychological support reasons; (2) profitable investment in a relatively inexpensive environment in terms of business property costs; and (3) attraction to African-American communities, influenced particularly by knowledge or familiarity with the consumer behavior and buying habits of African-Americans. Nearly two-thirds (almost 65 percent) of the Korean business respondents confirmed these hypotheses by identifying their decisions on the location of their enterprises with the survey questionnaire choices. However, 20 percent of the respondents gave different reasons for their decisions, the most prominent of which were "economic necessity" and "personal experience and interests." These latter "other reasons" reinforced, as expected, that private enterprise overshadowed any interpersonal or sociometric considerations, that is, assimilation into the communities in which their businesses were located. In other words, less than three percent (2.3 percent) of the business persons surveyed indicated that the reasons for the location of their businesses were influenced by attraction to African Americans.

Business Types

Table 11.23 shows the scope and variety of types of businesses operated in Washington, D. C., by the Korean merchants who participated in this survey. A majority of 76 percent dealt in consumable products: 57 fast-food/carry-outs, or 21.5 percent; 98 neighborhood grocery stores, or 37 percent; 33 liquor stores, or 12.5 percent; 9 restaurants, or 3.4 percent; and 2 fish and ice cream stores (one each), or 0.8 percent. Strategically, the Korean business community in Washington, D. C., operates four wholesale grocery and merchandise outlets which provide built-in resources for supplying the shelves of their retail businesses as well as many local, small African-American businesses. The small number of these wholesale stores, combined with the variety of retail outlets, enables the Korean business community to clearly corner the market in the city's African-American neighborhoods—for convenience food buying in particular and small business facilities in general.

Table 11.22
Korean-American Merchants
Decision Basis for Location of Respondents' Businesses

Reason (Basis)	Number of Merchants	Percent
Family Business Already There	52	19.6
Business Friends There	47	17.7
Good Price of Property (Business)	36	13.6
Easy Purchase in African-American Neighborhood	14	5.3
Attraction to African Americans	6	2.3
Knowledge of African-American Buying Habits	16	6.0
Personal Experience and Interests	14	5.3
Good Business Opportunity	5	1.9
Economic Necessity	16	6.0
Envisioned Success	6	2.3
Incidental	6	2.3
Economic Independence	3	1.1
Geographical Convenience	3	1.1
No Response	41	15.5
Total	265	100

Challenges of a Changing America

The survey's primary objective was to examine some of the perceptual, cultural, and attitudinal variables existing in merchant-customer interactions. At the same time, the questionnaire was designed to provide data useful in distinguishing facts from misperceptions. In this regard a key inquiry was, "How were you able to start your business?" In African-American neighborhoods where so many Korean businesses—especially "carry-outs" and liquor stores—are located, it is a popular belief that they received special U. S. government funding. How else could this "invasion" of such massive business forces sweep through America's urban African-American communities with such potency of proprietorship and confidence and establish a virtual monopoly in these small business sectors in less than a decade?

Is the criticism by many African Americans legitimate? Is the U. S. government helping Indo-Chinese refugees obtain businesses?

Table 11.23
Korean-American Merchants Respondents' Types of Businesses

Business Types	Number of Merchants	Percent
Carry-Out	57	21.5
Grocery	98	37.0
Liquor Store	33	12.5
Dry Cleaning	27	10.2
Restaurant	9	3.4
Beauty Supplies	4	1.5
Car Wash	2	0.8
Newsstand	4	1.5
Sporting Goods	2	0.8
Print Shop	5	1.9
Used Merchandise	1	0.4
Grocery Wholesale	1	0.4
Surplus	1	0.4
Cookie Shop	1	0.4
Music Store	1	0.4
General Merchandise	1	0.4
Welding Shop	1	0.4
Gas Station	1	0.4
Icec Cream	1	0.4
Men's Clothes	1	0.4
Fish Market	1	0.4
Night Club	1	0.4
Gift Shop	1	0.4
Merchandise Wholesale	3	1.1
No Response	6	2.3
Missing Cases	2	0.8
Totals	265	100

In 1984, a high-level federal agency employee informed the researcher of selling his "moonlighting" liquor store to a Vietnamese refugee for $65,000 *cash*. "I didn't dicker over the price at all," said this former coworker and friend. Why? It was because this refugee entrepreneur reported that he had been aided by funds from a "*Relief Fund* sponsored by the *World Bank*." Such relief for Southeast Asians is not likely universal to all enterprising Vietnamese and certainly not to all Asian immigrants in general.

However, the data presented in Table 11.24 refutes the notion of special "seed" monies to Korean business development through U. S. government sponsorship or by special privileges from the World Bank. According to the respondents, the facts were as follows. Their own (independent) resources were the primary means—46.8 percent (124 respondents). Family assistance was the secondary means—41.5 percent (110 respondents), and partnerships were the third means—21.9 percent (58 respondents). Other external sources were the last means, that is, loans from the U. S. government *and* the World Bank—1.5 percent (4 respondents) and 2.6 percent (7 respondents) respectively, or only a total of 4.1 percent combined.

The question as to whether the government of Korea or financial institutions in Korea were accessible resources was not raised in the survey. Nonetheless, the success of immigrant entrepreneurs clearly benefits this population's country of origin, for example, in terms of returned or reinvested capital to the country of origin. Consequently, in this instance, the government of Korea has a stake in the success

Table 11.24
Korean-American Merchants Respondents' Means of Start-Up Support

Categories	Number of Merchants	Percent
Own Funds	124	46.8
Left Blank	114	43.0
No Response	27	10.2
Family Assistance	110	41.5
Left Blank	128	48.3
No Response	27	10.2
U. S. Government Aid	4	1.5
Left Blank	234	88.3
No Response	27	10.2
Partnership	58	21.9
Left Bkank	180	67.9
No Response	27	10.2
World Bank	7	2.6
Left Blank	231	87.2
No Response	27	10.2

of its migrating people as emphasized in the study by Light and Bonacich (1988) on Koreans in Los Angeles.

Significantly, the start-up funds were, as shown, obtained from more than one source by a large number of these entrepreneurs. Typically, personal funds were supplemented by family investments into the businesses. But even more revealing is the number of respondents who indicated that they had developed their businesses *without* personal (their own) or family assistance. This point is indicated by the "Blank" markings under the questionnaire's choices of *Own Funds* and *Family Assistance* which Table 11.24 shows as 124 (46.8 percent) and 110 (41.5 percent) respectively. Furthermore, 88 percent of these businesses reportedly did not receive aid from any other source identified in the questionnaire's choices, except partnerships—21.9 percent (58 merchants) which utilized this strategy. Also, the local Korean Federal Credit Union was another apparent source before it closed in the winter of 1991 (*Washington Post,* October 17, 1991). Indeed, the most apparent means through which a large number of these businesses could have been developed and funded was through the *Kye* or *Keh* system—a financial club network indigenous to the Korean community, described in the *Washington Post* by Garreau (1991). It is a creative, self-help club in which members contribute monthly into a "pot" and await their turn to be awarded the "pot." This strengthens their community bonding and has the added advantages of providing large sums of tax-free, interest-free capital with almost no paperwork necessary (November 3, 1991).

Reflections and Relevant Issues

Ethiopian scholars Metaferia and Shifferraw, who, earlier in this book, address the experiences of fellow exiles, refer to a resettlement strategy of a group-oriented, self-help association—the *iqub*. The *iqub,* they note, is a traditional practice in Ethiopia through which members contribute funds that are rotationally distributed to the members of the association to assist in their business developments. This method of acquiring "seed" capital for Ethiopian private enterprises, so comparable to the Korean *Keh* or *Kye* club strategy, has been the primary means by which a number of Ethiopian refugees have become *African-American* entrepreneurs following their immigration to the United States during the past two decades. Hence, we see the uniquely resourceful initiatives by many new Americans in establishing self-sufficient avenues for economic development rather than depending on governmental aid and the traditional labor market.

America's latest newcomers, handicapped by language barriers, color prejudice and ethnic bigotry—the legacy of European colonialism—are in large part compelled to engage in private enterprise, a challenge for self-sufficiency that many are complementing through in-group alliances rather than the Anglo-American tradition of so-called "rugged individualism." The benefits of their family and group-oriented economic strategies are ways to effectively negotiate within the American capitalistic environment. Employing themselves and their family members precludes the confrontation of applying for positions in a restrictive workplace requiring English fluency and U. S. citizenship. Avoiding the job market prevents them from competing directly with native U. S. citizens who might perceive of some loss of opportunity to "foreigners." Importantly, immigrants' host countries have historically been critical of the "perceived" welfare assistance increases and resettlement program costs incurred in the adjustment of new populations. Private enterprise has been an eloquent rebuttal to such criticisms, particularly by Asian entrepreneurs as well as others, including Ethiopians, Hispanics, and Caribbean populations.

In the District of Columbia alone, noted Spayd in the *Washington Post*, over half of all the city's small businesses were Korean-owned (October 17, 1991). A few weeks later, Garreau, also of the *Washington Post*, noted that "The 1990 Census found 44,000 Korean-Americans in the metropolitan area" and that "the Korean Association of Greater Washington claims the figure is closer to 70,000" (p. B1). This article further reported that Koreans "own over 4,000 businesses in the area," most of which are in the Maryland and Virginia areas. Yet, this number reportedly includes 54 percent of the dry cleaners in the District, and 16 percent of the city's liquor stores (November 3, 1991). An earlier report, by Wheeler of the *Washington Post*, noted Korean-American ownership of over half the District's 2,000 small convenience stores—food, liquor, and dry cleaning—while Chinese-Americans operated about 300 restaurants and carry-outs (May 17, 1987).

The actual figures from the 1990 U. S. Census (Table 5A, June 12, 1991) indicate that less than five percent of the nation's Asian population reside in the adjoining areas of the District of Columbia, Maryland and Virginia—309,695 of nearly 7 million (6,908,638). Of this total tri-state-area Asian population, Koreans make up less than 20 percent (61,298 of 309,695). The census count for the U. S. population versus total U. S. Asian population was 248,709,873 versus 6,908,638.

Metropolitan D.C. Tri-State Area Asian Totals Versus Korean Totals

Area	Asian Population	Korean Population
District of Columbia	10,923	814
Maryland	139,719	30,320
Virginia	159,053	30,164
Totals	309,695	61,298

Nearly three million, or *40 percent of all Asian Americans, are residents of California*, assumingly preferring California's proximity to Asian Pacific nations, weather conditions, and the multicultural atmosphere of the West Coast. According to a CBS television "special" (Jan. 8, 1991) on the Korean community's business developments in America, 44 percent of the 150,000 Korean families in Los Angeles maintain family businesses, largely in African-American neighborhoods, as is prevalent in large cities across the nation such as Seattle, New York, Chicago, Philadelphia, Baltimore, and Washington, D. C. As two-thirds of a million Asian immigrants resettled in key urban cities during the 1970s, followed by new waves in the 1980s, an historically remarkable transformation in African-American neighborhoods occurred *en masse—the* successive, systematic development of small businesses, mostly by Korean merchants operating convenient neighborhood grocery and liquor stores. At the same time, numerous Chinese fast food carry-outs emerged in these same areas. Thus, competition between Asian businesses is a reality, compounded by intercultural clashes with the surrounding African-American clientele. In many instances, these enterprising new Americans simply took advantage of the not so uncommon void in these communities—partly consisting of vacant or deteriorating buildings and, sometimes, insolvent African-American owned businesses not grounded in a family business tradition and unfortunately all too desperate for total *cash* sellouts beyond apparent known market values.

Economically, many of these areas were apparently rejuvenated through these restorations of dwindling, urban revenue bases which often coincided with municipal and political leadership priorities and interests. But the general African-American population has experienced a mixture of emotions and perceptions of this phenomenon. While the convenient corner stores and carry-outs are patronized, intercultural gaps of communication, impersonal demeanor and restrictive customer-proprietor dialogue have fueled recurrent misunderstandings. Even distinctive, non-verbal (body) language reinforces suspicions, and smiling faces are sometimes the only real *rare* commodity not found on either side of the counters. The few remaining African Americans in business in these communities resent this "invasion" of their territories of commerce by "distant" outsiders who often speak limited English and who frequently take fast food customer orders from behind bullet-proof, plexi-glass barricades. *Fences may make good neighbors,* but *walls* seem only to *convey distrust.* Structure and decor shape perceptions.

Implications of the Study

In the absence of any known empirical studies examining the psycho-social dimensions or interpersonal and intercultural dynamics between the African-American community and Korean merchants, this has been an exploratory research effort—a *maiden voyage.* This study was an attempt to initiate overdue research into a virginal arena, with implications for inter-group relations, community psychology, and consumer-market research. As an exploratory study, further research is needed to include a variety of ethnic and culturally diverse groups so that minority-minority inter-group relations, intercultural conflicts, and potential symbiosis or social alliances can be examined.

Korean-American Marketing in the African-American Community

As 60 percent (600) of the approximately 1,000 membership of the Metropolitan Washington Korean-American Chamber of Commerce (covering Washington, D. C., and suburban Maryland and Virginia) were contacted, resulting in 265 responses, this 44 percent response rate is highly representative of the profile and views of Korean-owned businesses inside Washington, D. C. Speculations about the applicability of the study's results in other cities must take into account that the respondent sample was not a nation-wide sample. However, implications of the data appear to apply beyond the borders of Washington in terms of Korean merchants' perceptions. In part, the results represent an exploratory analysis since the survey data was not subjected to a comprehensive statistical assessment. The preliminary findings of this study indicate that its exploratory purposes were achieved. Future research hypotheses are implied by the results of the survey's data.

As highlighted in this study, Korean-American merchants have experienced much success as entrepreneurs, generally depending upon African-American patronage. This success is often in spite of language difficulties, sometimes it is insensitivity to inter-group nuances and limited knowledge between the cultures that have been the foci of this study.

In addition, there are perceived threats of intimidation in these communities which are often burdened with high rates of drug traffic, assorted other crimes, and unemployment, particularly among African-American youths. However, a number of misperceptions which stereotype the Asian-American merchant were counterbalanced in the survey data. The non-Asian, native population of America has much to learn about Asians in America. Asians are not a monolithic group any more than are today's African Americans, as Yosef Ford discussed in his reflective article in this book, "Who Are the African-Americans?"

In Washington, Korean merchants and African Americans are increasingly demonstrating the capacity for cooperative relations. In late 1991, Korean merchants took a number of initiatives to promote positive customer and community relations in Washington, especially in the section of the city known as Anacostia where African-American and Korean business associations are jointly addressing community concerns. For example, during the Thanksgiving and Christmas holiday periods of 1991, the Korean Merchants Association reportedly fed over 1,000 homeless persons within their business sectors. This activity was recognized in a couple of local African-American news weeklies (*Washington Informer*, November 28, 1991; *Washington New Observer*, December 21-28, 1991). Reed's column in the *New Observer* also noted that the local Korean-American Grocers' Association made scholarship awards to some African-American youths in their service areas. Cardell Shelton, the African-American head of the Anacostia Professionals and Merchants Association, an organization in which some local Korean merchants have membership, joined hands with Korean merchants to jointly provide their *first* community-wide Christmas meal to 1,500 local residents (*Washington Times*, December 24, 1991). More significant, however, is the action taken by the National

Korean Grocers Association representing 17,000 businesses) which met in the Washington area in late 1991 and "vowed to improve relations between Korean merchants and Black communities by creating more jobs for Blacks and increasing contributions to Black charities" (*Washington Post*, December 2, 1991).

As one result of their associations with African Americans, some of these Korean business owners have tapped the skill and professional resources of some African Americans, who may find that the *key* to their own efforts for economic development lies in the Korean style mutual aid—*Keh* or *Kye*—fund-raising system. And, as mentioned earlier, the Ethiopian community's self-help method known as the *Iqub* is a similar alternative to private financial institutional loans. Yet, governmental assistance has and will continue to be another resource in the "world's greatest democracy."

Small business is the foundation of free (private) enterprise in the United States, and in 1953 the Small Business Administration (SBA) was established by Congress to cultivate this economic base. As an SBA (1990) brochure declares, "... small business is the backbone of the American economy. They create two of every three new jobs and produce 40 percent of the gross national product ..." (p. 60). Indeed, African-American communities have proven to be viable economic development sectors, evidenced in part by the small business development proliferation of Korean merchants in the past decade. At the same time, despite the intercultural clashes accompanying these experiences other cooperative business development alternatives are possible. New alliances can occur within and among minority groups seeking common goals. For example, the Asian-American business community has a more independent capital networking access base and family tradition of merchants than African Americans who: (1) are indigenous to many Asian merchants' business sites; (2) appear receptive to joint business ventures; (3) are the natural linkages for establishing expedient and positive rapport within the borders of the neighborhood convenience stores; (4) are increasingly interested, experienced and trained in small business activity as well as the larger corporate arena; and (5) are representative of established urban political power bases in many of the nation's largest cities. In the long run effective marketing plans in the African-American community will take these factors into consideration.

Further research on this vital topic of broad societal import may contribute more insight concerning issues of intercultural, commercial dynamics as well as human (inter-group) relations in our *rainbow society*.

Limitations of the Study

As an exploratory study, this survey of Korean merchants in the District of Columbia includes the following limitations:

1. The selected respondent sample was not randomized but based on the accessibility of the participants.

2. The response rate per questionnaire item varied, that is, although 265 respondents returned the survey forms from 600 mailings, all questions were not always fully answered.

3. The analyses of data are considered preliminary in view of: (a) the translations from Korean to English of the open-ended type questions in the survey were not communicated to the writer of this volume; and (b) computerized, cross tabulations of the data were not assessed.

Postscript

The following is an abstraction of data from a telephone survey conducted by Ivan Light and Edna Bonacich in 1977 in Los Angeles, as reported in their larger work, *Immigrant Entrepreneurs: Koreans in Los Angeles 1965-82*. This publication, however, is dated 1988.

The actual survey was conducted in 1977—by telephone. It included 138 interviews with both Korean merchants and non-Koreans. The study was sponsored financially by the University of California (Los Angeles) and the National Science Foundation. Telephone contacts (non-random) were made with 325 businesses, as listed in a 1975 Korean Business Directory, resulting in 138 completions (interviews) of a 90-item questionnaire. The authors observed, however, "Telephone surveys are notoriously unsuccessful in eliciting candid answers to sensitive questions" (pp. ix, 250, 437).

Findings by the Light and Bonacich study (1988), similar to the Myers study in Washington, D. C., are listed below:

1. They noted that in Los Angeles' Koreatown "the firms tended to service low income, *non-white neighborhoods* generally ignored and under-served by big corporations" (p. 6).

2. They noted that "Korean *Christians* were four times more likely than Korean non-Christians to operate small business enterprises in Los Angeles" (p. 293).

3. They noted that of the numerous types of businesses in Koreatown, the most popular in rank order were *grocery* stores (206), *eateries* and bars (169), and *liquor* stores (91); the percentages were 9.4, 1.8 and 5.5 respectively although Koreans were then less than one (1) percent of the Los Angeles County population (p. 228).

4. They noted that 56.8 percent of Los Angeles' Korean firms reported employing immediate or extended family members. Of the non-kin employees in these firms, 37.4 percent had only Koreans; 20.6 percent had "hired Americans"; 19.6 percent had "hired Mexicans"; and *22.4 percent employed other Asians, African Americans and various combinations*" (p.

179). Sixty-two percent of Koreans found employment in the Korean ethnic economy (p. 6).

5. They noted that the Korean proprietors reported their start-up capital from these sources: their own savings, 80; banks, 36; family and friends, 15; the SBA, 4; and Kye, 1 (p. 255). Light and Bonacich (1988) further cite the 1988 article of the *Korean Times* reporting on "at least 1,000" Kyes operating in Los Angeles (p. 252).

6. They note that the residential ethnic mix of Koreatown, a previously deteriorating area on the northern boundary of Los Angeles' African-American ghetto, was 22 percent Koreans; 39 percent African Americans, Hispanics and *other* Asians; and 39 percent whites.

7. Sixty-nine percent of the 1977 survey respondents indicated that they were graduates of four-year colleges (p. 288).

8. No data supported the notion of higher criminal victimization rates in Korean residential areas or business sites (p. 310).

References

Asian merchants find ghettos full of peril. (1986, November 24). *U. S. News and World Report.*
Enhancing community relations. (1991, November 28-December 4). Washington, DC: *Washington Informer.*
Fairchild, H. H. (1990, May 25). Look for remedies, not scapegoats. *Los Angeles Times*, p. B7.
Fairchild, H. H. (1991, March 24). A sad tale of persecuted minorities. *Los Angeles Times.*
Fairchild, H. H. (1991, May 5). World class tension: Ethnic rivalry heats up Southern California. *Los Angeles Times*, p. M2.
Gaither, V. (1990, November 15). Talks open in Mega Foods dispute. Washington, DC: *Capitol Spotlight*, p. 1.
Goodstein, L. (1990, May 8). Split between Blacks, Koreans widens in N. Y. court. *Washington Post,* p. A4.
Gupta, V. (1983, March). From other shores. *Black Enterprise*, pp. 51-53.
Keary, J. (1991, December 24). Koreans, Blacks unite to provide Anacostia lunch. Washington, DC: *Washington Times.*
Korean grocery store owner throws in towel. (1991, June 6). Washington, DC: *Capitol Spotlight,* p. 3.
Light, I., & Bonacich, E. (1988). *Immigrant entrepreneurs: Koreans in Los Angeles 1965-82.* Los Angeles, CA: University of California Press.
Reed, W. (1991, December 21-28). Business beat. Washington, DC: *The New Washington Observer.*
Sanchez, R. (1991, December 2). Korean grocers seek better ties with Blacks. *Washington Post,* p. C4.
Small Business Administration. *Small business: Building America's future.* (1990). Washington, DC: Small Business Administration.
Spayd, L. (1991, October 17). Korean credit union closes. *Washington Post*, p. D1.
Wheeler, L. (1987, May 7). Tragedy brings cooperation to Anacostia. *Washington Post,* p. D1.

Challenges of a Changing America

Part Six

Consumer Research and Intercultural Dialogue

Be not forgetful to entertain strangers, for thereby some have entertained angels unawares.
—Hebrews 13:2

Chapter Twelve

African-American Perceptions of Asian-American Merchants:
An Exploratory Study

Ernest R. Myers

There has been a hiatus of overtly expressed, intercultural confrontations since the 1992 riots in Los Angeles which exposed the recurrent hostile relationships between Korean merchants and African-American customers.

Korean merchants have increasingly monopolized small business operations in African-American communities during the past 20 years, or since the 1980s, including wholesale distribution facilities. However, they have often been criticized for neglecting to address community concerns of interest such as employment opportunities for African Americans, especially those who reside in the neighborhoods in which the businesses operate.

In 1991, I conducted a survey of African Americans in the Washington, D. C. area. The results suggest that at the turn of the century there may remain some unresolved communications gaps, resentment, and misperceptions which call for ongoing intercultural or intergroup relations development between these groups. Analysis of this survey's data had been put aside until I took leave from my university professorship to complete the task.

Significantly, while the language of the questionnaire referred to Asian Americans in general, the survey's respondents—African Americans—were informed that the specific concern of the study centered on their interactions with the perceptions of Korean merchants since they dominate the marketplace of convenience-store-type enterprises in predominantly Black-populated communities in a great part of urban America. For example, *Korean business owners* make up *two-thirds* of all such operations in *Washington, DC*.

Not surprisingly there was relevant correlation between the perceptions of African-American customers in this survey and the data analysis from my study of Korean merchants' perceptions presented in the previous chapter of this book.

The Survey Description

A description of the survey of African Americans' views of Korean merchants is presented below. Following this description is a list of key or major findings along with some key results of the earlier survey of a sample of merchants in the previous chapter. A full report of this study's data analysis follows this section.

Subjects: The Survey Sample

The subjects of this survey of African Americans totaled one hundred fifty (150) including the following: Federal agency employees, 29; Black small business owners, 19; graduate students of the University of the District of Columbia (UDC), 43; staff of UDC, 3; members of the D.C. chapter of the Association of Black Psychologists, 10; D.C. police, 26; and other African Americans (general public), 20. Just over eighty percent (80.7 percent) were surveyed in Washington, D.C., and nearly twenty percent (19.3 percent) in Maryland, 54 were actual residents of D.C. versus 46 from Maryland. Eight (5.4 percent) of the respondents were classified as "other" (two Whites, one Native American, and five unknown). There were 64 males (42.7 percent) versus 82 females (54.7 percent), and four (2.6 percent) whose gender was not identified. Eighty-eight percent (132) were between 18 and 50 years years of age, with nearly forty percent (38.6 percent) of these respondents between 30-40 years of age. Sixty-six percent had completed high school or beyond, and the majority of this same category had some college education, including one-half who had either a bachelor's, master's or doctoral degree.

At least 78 percent of the respondents were native born African Americans; twenty (13.3 percent) did not indicate their region of birth, and eleven (7.3 percent) were from African and Caribbean nations.

Survey Design

A six-page questionnaire, consisting of 26 major questions with six open-ended types, was designed to explore perceptions and attitudes of African Americans toward Asian-American merchants. This survey of 150 subjects was conducted in the summer of 1991 in the Washington, D.C., area. Significantly, the respondent sample was not randomized, but based on accessibility of the subjects.

A pre-testing of the survey questionnaire had earlier been conducted for content and analysis and to identify beliefs and concerns that some African Americans had about the merchants. For optimal and reliable data collection and analysis, this process determined how each categorical question was structured.

As an exploratory study of intergroup relations, the questions focused on customer contact and intergroup sensitivity, stereotypical perceptions about and relationships with Asians, and atittudes of African-American customers.

Results

Some of the key findings were as follows:

1. Over ninety percent (91.3 percent) of the subjects had patronized Asian-operated stores.

2. The majority of the customers (57.3 percent) were satisfied with services; 64 percent considered the merchants courteous.

3. Nearly sixty-five of the customers (64.7 percent) felt the merchants were respectful to them.

4. Nearly eighty percent (78.7 percent) of the customers thought the merchants understood their language.

5. Over sixty percent of the customers, however, perceived that the merchants were nonetheless discriminating and did not understand African-American culture.

6. Only 27 percent gave positive ratings to the merchants although 38 percent rated their contacts as "tolerable."

7. Forty-four percent of the customers did not consider the merchants to be concerned about the neighborhood surrounding their businesses while nearly 40 percent (39.3 percent) felt the merchants only wanted African-American patronage, not association or relationships.

8. Sixty-nine percent of the customers perceived that these merchants were opposed to employing Blacks and that they do not identify with Blacks.

9. Forty-seven percent of the customers *"welcomed"* Asian businesses in the Black community while 21 percent were opposed, and 27 percent were uncertain (ambivalent).

10. Thirty-three percent of the customers who welcomed these businesses agreed that these Asian merchants have the same right as any U. S. citizen to earn a living while another 20 percent observed that the merchants' businesses were convenient and had good prices, and that they worked hard which, in all, improved the city's revenue bases.

11. Nearly fifty percent (48 percent) of the customers believed Asians received special U. S. government business development aid.

An interesting exercise for the reader is to compare the data and perceptions that these groups have of each other. Some of these comparisons are listed from the two surveys as numbered under "results" below. The following selective findings are from my exclusive survey of Korean American merchants. See the previous chapter entitled "Korean- American Marketing in the Africa-American Community: An Exploratory Study in the Nation's Capital City."

Previous Study Results

The survey data revealed facts and perceptions of the 265 Korean merchants surveyed relative to their customer relations, intercultural sensitivity and awareness, hiring practices, merchant demographic profiles, and source of seed capital to start their operations.

1. Nearly half of these businesses had only operated for less than five years.

2. Most of the Korean merchants had yet to acquire U. S. citizenship (58 percent).

3. Less than 10 percent of the 265 merchants operating in D.C. resided in D.C.

4. Three-fourths of the merchants had resided in the Greater Metropolitan area for over five years.

5. Over 90 percent of the merchants completed high school, and over half of them completed four years of college.

6. Three-fourths of the merchants identified themselves as Protestants.

7. Nearly 60 percent of the merchants experienced language problems with their customers.

8. The more educated merchants had some associations with African Americans beyond business transactions.

9. Most of the merchants expressed ambivalence toward hiring Blacks, but 25 percnt were affirmative for future considerations, and over half would do so *depending on the situation.*

10. Over half of the merchants felt less than adequately sensitive to African-American culture, yet they rated their Black customers above their White customers (48 percent positive ratings versus 38 percnt positive ratings).

11. Two-thirds of the merchants reported experiencing criminal offenses, and one-third expressed a need for "Special" police protection.

12. The businesses were essentially located in Black areas because of affordability and closeness to other Korean family businesses. Only two percent claimed any governmental assistance for start-up capital.

The study suggests a rich area for further research: minority/minority conflicts in urban America, and inter-ethnic relations. The small business arena is an ideal focus wherein such dynamics are magnified in the controversy over cultural diversity in the nation. Intercultural alliances of "minorities" is one conflict resolution strategy that has potential, as this study's data indicated. However, the surveys highlight many areas of conflict such as distrust and misperceptions between Korean merchants and their African- American customers.

Highlights of Findings

The demographic profiles of the 150 African Americans surveyed consisted of 42.7 percent males versus 54.7 percent females. Blank responses (where no gender was indicated) were 2.6 percent. Sixty-three percent were a mature grouping between 30-50 years of age while 29 percent were under 30 years of age. Eight percent were over 50, and inquiries about age that were unanswered were four percent. A remarkable coincidence is that, like my earlier survey on Korean merchants, the African-Americans' academic achievement levels in this survey were almost identical in college-level educational experiences—66 percent for both groups.

Sixty-seven percent of the African-American customers were of Protestant religious affiliation, again reflective of the merchants' religious affiliation, and 18 percent were Catholics.

Fifty-four percent of the African-American repondents resided in the city of Washington, D.C., while 46 percent lived in nearby Maryland. Nearly 13 percent were themselves small business owners.

Seventy-eight percent of these respondents were native-born U. S. citizens, including 24.7 percent born in D.C., and 34 percent in southern states. Seven percent were immigrants from Africa and the Caribbean nations.

Customer Contact and Intergroup Sensitivity

Nearly 95 percent of the 150 Black Americans surveyed had contacts with Asian Americans. Ninety-one percent had experience as customers, generally at Korean-operated stores. They were satisfied with services 57 percent of the time; 30 percent, sometimes; and never satisfied, 8.7 percent of the time. Sixty-nine percent felt the merchants either showed disrespect or discriminated in services to them sometimes.

Overall, negative views of the merchants were expressed at a 21 percent level, with 38 percent of contacts seen as "tolerable." Twenty-eight percent gave positive ratings in their contacts with the merchants.

The demeanor of store merchants or employees necessarily influences how customers perceive the services. In terms of the merchants' services, 28.7 percent of the African-American respondents (customers) felt that sometimes the store employees (merchants) were discourteous while 3.3 percent marked "never courteous." However, nearly 64 percent noted that they were courteously served. This is in some contradiction to their perception of disrespect by merchants. In my previous study on the merchants' views of their Black customers, the survey findings were quite similar to the general respect shown to the customers.

Is language a problem? Not according to this survey. Over three-fourths of the respondents experienced no language barrier even though Korean merchants have problems understanding customers at a "sometime" level (55 percent), and "often" at a four percent level—as noted in the previous study reported in this book.

Forty-nine percent of the respondents felt that the Asian merchants over-priced their products. Forty-five percent felt it true that the merchants showed disrespect for the elderly and children, and nearly 40 percent felt that the Asian merchants maintained unsanitary or poor conditions in their stores.

Only 27.9 percent of the respondents gave answers to what they believed were the bases for communication problems with the merchants. The merchants' English-speaking inadequacies or their accents were noted by 20.6 percent of those surveyed while 7.3 percent felt that the merchants pretended not to understand them, and disrespected the young customers.

Stereotypical Perceptions

A series of 11 statements were included in this section of the survey to discern any stereotypical views held by African-American respondents regarding Asian merchants. The major findings in the survey are listed below.

Nearly 53 percent of the surveyed population or sample felt it to be true that the merchants' choices of their business locations correlated with how the merchants or their employees treated their Black customers. One respondent, for example, said, "They wouldn't be so discourteous if they were doing business in a community of Whites." Over 40 percent of the sample perceived no difference in the connection between business location and treatment of customers. Relatedly, 44 percent indicated that it was true that the Asian merchants did not prefer any association with their neighboring Black businesses, and 39 percent felt that the merchants' *only* interest was the profits and support obtained from Black customers.

One area of cross-cultural antipathy relates to employment in the businesses. Nearly 70 percent of those surveyed felt it to be true that Asian businesses hire no Black employees while 50 percent marked "true" that the merchants typically are opposed to even offering jobs to Blacks.

Only eight percent of the respondents felt that the African-American culture was understood by the Asian merchants, while just over 30 percent were uncertain. Nearly 45 percent of the respondents felt that the merchants failed to understand their "Black" language.

Nearly 30 percent of the respondents perceived that the merchants were negatively influenced primarily by the mass media. Yet, another 21 percent felt that the merchants were just insensitive or ethnocentric. Significantly, over two-thirds of the respondents felt it to be true that the merchants did not understand their culture while 59 percent agreed to this point of cross-cultural dissonance in the "customer contact and intergroup sensitivity" section of the survey questionnaire.

Relationships

Eighty-six percent of the respondents had apparently only related to Asian merchants as customers, around 13 percent in business associations, 18 percent as friends, one percent as marital partners, and around 17 percent as residential neighbors close to the Asian merchants' stores. Many of these relationship categories overlapped. The frequency (226), therefore, of responses to the question of African-American relationships with the merchants did not correspond to the actual number (150) or respondents.

Attitudes of African-American Customers

The concluding questions raised in the survey centered on the issue of African Americans' tolerance of and receptivity to Asian small businesses. How did the respondents feel about Asian businesses operating in their communities or neighborhoods?

Forty-seven percent welcomed the businesses while 27 percent were uncertain or had mixed views. This is particularly significant in view of the dissatisfaction that these same customers felt about Asian merchants, as strongly indicated in data noted earlier in this summary analysis. Yet, clearly, African-American customers of Asian small businesses commendably embrace the American philosophy of the right to free enterprise. Those respondents *not* welcoming Asian businesses in their communities referred to their preferences to shop in stores under Black ownership, or opposition to any commerce in their residential areas, or that the Asian merchants did not contribute to the Black communities' interests where they operated.

Conclusions

The survey data conclude that typically while the Asian merchants tended not to trust or employ Blacks, or cultivate positive relationships with them, African Americans tend, nevertheless, to respect the rights of entrepreneurs. Nearly one-half, or 47 percent, expressed a positive attitude—welcoming the Asian businesses—although another 27 percent were ambivalent, that is, persuadable rather than prejudically opposed to what has been called the "Asian invasion" of urban America's Black neighborhoods.

It is interesting to note that 20 percent of the Blacks surveyed pointed out that the Asian merchants have "the same rights as any U. S. citizen" and they have "the right to earn a living." Yet, significantly, in the earlier survey in this book, of the 265 Korean merchants, only 112 (or 42 percent) had acquired U. S. citizenship while 143, or 58 percent, were still "green card" holders.

Overall, this survey documented a number of stereotypical views held by African Americans of Asian-American merchants. One view is that Asian merchants, collectively, are favored and given special support by the U. S. Government to engage in small businesses—at the expense of a decreasing number of small Black entrprises in Black neighborhoods. This is a misperception, based on data from this survey and my other research of Korean merchants. In addition, the survey substantiated a significant degree of resentment by African-American customers toward Asian convenience store merchants on the basis of perceptions, or realities, that these businesses provide no real employment opportunities or economic benefits for Blacks. This resentment is further exacerbated by the perception that often these business owners are seen as "business landlords" who economically exploit the urban Black community while residing themselves in Maryland and Virginia.

Optimistically, forty-three percent of this survey's Black respondents made numerous suggestions to improve communications and community relations regarding the above issues to promote intercultural understanding.

Considering that this survey occurred nine months before the 1992 Los Angeles riots, which included L.A.'s Koreatown's massive destruction, both the findings of this study of 1991 and the respondents' recommendations for improving intergroup relations were prophetic and remain relevant. This is particularly pertinent as we enter the 21st Century with ever-growing, unresolved challenges in this and other multicultural American arenas.

In the riots in Los Angeles in 1992 numerous stores in the nearby Koreatown area were devastated. One explanation for this unexpected attack, as this survey verified, was the smoldering resentment that many other minority groups in the area manifested toward the Korean merchants. For example, one of the African Americans surveyed referred to the proliferation of Asian convenience stores, fast-food carryouts, and liquor stores as *"the Asian invasion"* of Black communities. This notion of invaders or intruders further explains some of the negative or often ambivalent feelings toward and perceptions of the merchants who are typically Korean, or less often Chinese, whose employees immigrated to the U. S. during the 1980s or 1990s. In many respects the resulting *intercultural conflicts* appear to emerge within a *human ecological context*, that is, a focus on the survival of a community's inhabitants and their identity with the community's welfare engenders a sense of ownership of the turf or area by the native residents. Non-residents or outsiders with *singular* business enterprising intentions are consequently suspect or distrusted.

The question might be raised: Why are the Chinatowns of America not viewed in the same context as are so many Korean small businesses in the U. S.? It appears that the answer is in what I would call the *ecological business sector of preference* that differentiates these cultural groups. *Chinatowns* are traditionally *exclusive* communities offering a cuisine-oriented *cultural experience* in *restaurant fashion,* while Korean businesses often directly compete with diverse small business interests of other minority cultures inside the neighborhoods of these other groups and distanced from customers by shields of plexiglass. Intergroup communications are therefore discouraged or minimized. The architectural adage that form (business structure) follows function (purpose) has particular relevance in these observations.

Finally, as noted earlier, 40 percent of the African Americans surveyed offered suggestions to improve intergroup relationships as opposed to mere marketplace transactions with Asian merchants. Among the numerous recommendations, *instituting initiatives* was expressed as primary. In this regard, *multicultural community workshops* led the type of programmatic actions. The *employment* of African Americans by the merchants was the next highest or cited suggestion. Intercultural or *intergroup exchange visitations* in churches or at social events followed the employment suggestion. The last, but not the least, suggestion was that Asian merchants take initiatives to *learn of African-American history and culture.* Undoubtedly, all of these recommendations, if carried out, would substantially contribute to symbiotically sensitive relations.

In the spring of 1996, I initiated a day-long community, multicultural seminar to: (1) promote understanding and confront misperceptions between African Amricans and Korean merchants, (2) develop respect for cultural differences and achievements, and (3) explore potential joint sponsorship of community projects or programs. A full description of this effort is detailed in the following chapter.

Chapter Thirteen

Multicultural Sensitivity in the Marketplace:
A Seminar-Workshop

Ernest R. Myers

As the nation's singular, urban land grant university, the University of the District of Columbia (UDC) is under a mandate to initiate community services and to engage in urban problem solving as part of its higher education mission.

In this context this project was a follow-up effort to my 1991 exploratory study of "Korean American Marketing in the African-American Community" described here in chapter 11 as well as in an earlier edition of this book. The basic agenda for this pertinent data was to share it, along with the published book, with Korean and African Americans at business association meetings or an assemblage of these groups. The format with which I chose to carry out this agenda was a planned, multicultural, community seminar-workshop which I conducted at UDC, with support from the Consortium of Universities of the Washington Metropolitan Area on April 27, 1996.

Background

In relationship to the seminar this book includes two chapters on the controversy of inter-cultural conflicts of Korean merchants' operations in urban America's predominantly African-American communities.

The study, "Korean American Marketing in the African-American Community," was based on an exploratory investigation of the friction between Korean small businesses and their African-American clientele in the nation's capital city. As the curtain opens on the stage of the 21st Century, there remains the need for dialogue between so-called minority groups such as African Americans and Koreans to not only narrow the communications gaps, but to contribute to the improvement of community relations and the symbiotic dynamics in relationships such as those of Korean small businesses and African-American customers. This relationship—characterized by ambivalence, interdependence, resentment and tension—in great part was corroborated in the counterpart study conducted in a survey of 150 African Americans, a survey which was administered through a questionnaire in the spring of 1991. A substantial number of the questions raised in this research were similar to and in some instances identical to those applied in my research of Korean merchants. Again, the focus was on inter-cultural awareness and misperceptions, attitudes, stereotypical beliefs, and inter-group sensitivity.

Much of the data analyses from both of the above-noted surveys were presented in summarized form at the community seminar-workshop on April 27, 1996. The survey data were particularly used to help to set the tone for this day-long event, and were shared after presentations by a multicultural panel of business representatives. Just before the seminar, participants (audience) were given instructions to engage in dialogues in the workshop phase of the program. The data analyses from the African-American community survey were included along with the project report.

Originally, it was envisioned that the survey data would be shared before the seminar-workshop at distinctive meetings of the Korean-American Chamber of Commerce (KACC) of the Metropolitan Washington Area and the African-American Business Association. However, neither organization accepted the offer, and neither participated in the seminar-workshop even though they cooperated in dialogues to plan the seminar-workshop. This irony of distant involvement is the characteristic ambivalence which I noted earlier. The *idea* of closing the communications gap is embraced, but there is stark reluctance by many small business entrepreneurs to actually engage in face-to-face exchanges.

Indeed, this is one of the "challenges of a changing America." Eventually the interdependent reality of these businesses and their clientele and the recurrent minority group versus minority group conflicts suggest the call for potential social alliances similar to the mission of Reverend Jesse Jackson's National Rainbow Coalition and the new multicultural objectives voiced by the leadership of the NAACP in recent years.

A Workshop

The concluding activity of the project, the "Multicultural Sensitivity in the Marketplace: A Workshop," was held on the main campus of UDC on April 27, 1996, after nearly six months of planning. As an historical, first-time occurrence in the Washington, D. C., area, a day-long program of its type was a difficult undertaking involving countless letters, meetings, and telephone conversations with potential participants, particularly the invited panelists representative of Korean and African-American business organizations. Initially, four African-American and 12 Korean business associations were contacted in the planning phase. Ultimately, five of the 10 *invited* panelists participated. Three of the five absentees gave short advance notices of other extenuating priorities.

Participating organizations and institutions included: Howard University, the University of the District of Columbia, the U. S. Small Business Administration, the National Coalition Building Institute, the Capital Martial Arts and Fitness Center, the Anacostia Professional and Merchants Association, the Washington Constructors' Guild, Diversity Solutions, and the Howard University Small Business Development Center. Some of the organizations and institutions represented by the participating audience included: the Prince George's County Foundation School, the D. C. Public Schools, the D. C. Metropolitan Police Department, George Washington University, American University, the D. C. Commission on Mental Health, El Shaddai Ministries, the Beltsville Presbyterian Church, and the *Asia Fortune* newspaper. A total of 18 organizations were represented.

Demographics of the Participants

There were 31 participants including 11 Asian Americans (35 percent), 18 African Americans (58 percent), one Hispanic, and one White American. Nine of the Asians, or 30 percent of the participants, were Koreans who represented 80 percent of the Asian Americans attending. Forty-five percent of the participants were educators including seven from UDC. There were 13 participants representing businesses (some self-employed), amounting to 40 percent of all participants. Three ministers of churches participated, as noted earlier. Significantly, there were no typical, convenience-store small businesses represented—a category which in many respects has the greatest need for multicultural sensitivity in the marketplace.

The Publicity

Publicity for the community seminar was covered by the Consortium of Universities, the UDC Public Affairs Office, the *Washington Afro-American* newspaper, *The Washington Sun* newspaper, flyers, and word-of-mouth by the seminar planning participants and seminar panelists. Like most of the organizations which were solicited to participate, obviously many potential, individual participants were unwilling to commit themselves to an all-day program on a weekend day, Saturday, which is normally free time or a popular day for business operations. Some participants, in fact nearly half, departed following the discussion period after the panel presentations. A number of them indicated, apologetically, that they needed to attend to business.

Afternoon Workshop Participation

There were 15 participants in the afternoon workshop—three (20 percent) were Asians, and 12 (80 percent) were African Americans. Of these total participants, 13 (80 percent) were entrepreneurs. Their businesses were located in the following jurisdictions: D. C., 12 (80 percent), Maryland, 2 (over 10 percent), Virginia, 1 (less than 10 percent).

The dialogues of the workshops were led by assigned group facilitators over a period of approximately one and a half hours. These exchanges of views and perceptions were a rewarding experience according to 14 of the 15 workshop participants, and 18 (85 percent) of the 31 seminar participants agreed that the seminar group discussions were beneficial. It should be noted that while 16 of the 31 participants departed before the workshop, 21 (70 percent) of the attendees completed the seminar evaluation forms—seven by mail.

In addition to the above assessment data, evaluation forms completed by those 21 participants who responded showed that 20 (90 percent) considered the event worthwhile as an effort to improve cross-cultural relations. Nineteen agreed that the panel speakers provided useful information concerning the small business market. Twenty (95 percent) agreed that this kind of community seminar should occur more often, and 18 (85 percent) were interested in receiving a summary report on the workshop. Master summary sheet evaluations were later shared with all participants.

Workshop Facilitators' Summary

In brief, the views and recommendations of participants were insightful. Participants all agreed that the mass media is inclined to perpetuate stereotypical notions about the African-American community which fosters misperceptions in the minds of Koreans. Thus, there are *mis*-communications between these cultural groups.

Some African Americans felt that the playing field is not level in that often middle-class Koreans compete with low-income-class Blacks in small business developments. Proportionally it appears that middle-class Blacks gravitate to non-business professions while many middle-class Koreans enter the small business market. Another area of some concern was that Koreans prefer to operate businesses in the inner city, yet reside in the suburbs. My study of 1991, in fact, revealed that less than 10 percent of the Korean merchants in the District of Columbia resided in the city proper.

A major concern centered on how these groups can move from discourse to undertaking practical applications to diffuse intercultural conflicts and potential hostilities. All participants agreed that all merchants should contribute to community betterment along with business success in areas where they operate. An excellent example is the Capital Martial Arts and Fitness Center founded by the Joon Park family in 1993 in Northwest Washington, D. C. This center is adjacent to a second-hand merchandise and clothing store which the family has operated for 12 years. Mr. Park compassionately uses the profits from the merchandise and clothing store to finance the Center's expenses. The Center is a place where youngsters in this predominantly Black community learn to be disciplined and physically fit. (Joon Park and his son, Steve, enthusiastically participated in this seminar-workshop.)

Key ideas and recommendations from the workshop were:

1. More workshops are needed periodically to promote awareness of the history and culture of both groups.

2. Initiatives must be value-based and spiritually rooted to achieve peaceful, inter-group relations.

3. Multiculturalism (cultural pluralism) and cross-cultural understanding require transformations based on an introspective acknowledgment of our individual responsibility to be tolerant of ethnic group differences, to be community oriented, and to be committed to conflict resolution.

4. The news media must be more responsible and assume a key role in promoting cultural diversity appreciation.

5. These cultural groups could exchange newsletters concerning educational and community activity information in which intergroup relations, intercultural sensitivity, and harmony can be advanced.

Perhaps the essence of this community seminar is best articulated in a note by one of the Korean-American participants, a note which he attached to the Seminar Evaluation Form: "Thank you for giving me a chance to express my thoughts at this worthwhile event."

Overall, this event was an opportunity for constructive ventilation of views where misconceptions were examined. It was a modest attempt to plant seeds to cultivate multicultural understanding and, therefore, conflict resolution.

Appendix I
Seminar Evaluation Form and Summary Results

Please take a few minutes to complete this form and leave it with Dr. Myers or Dr. Adair. Your identity is not required.

Questions and Results

1. This was a worthwhile experience toward improving inter-group or cross-cultural relations. (11 strongly agree; 9 agree; 1 somewhat agree; 0 disagree).

2. The seminar met my expectations. (2 strongly agree; 12 agree; 7 somewhat agree; 0 disagree).

3. The seminar's small group discussions were beneficial to advance understanding

between Korean Americans and African Americans. (10 strongly agree; 8 agree; 1 somewhat agree; 0 disagree; 2 no response).

4. The panelists (speakers) provided useful information about the small business market. (2 strongly agree; 17 agree; 2 somewhat agree; 0 disagree).

5. This kind of community seminar should occur more often. (10 strongly agree; 10 agree; 1 somewhat agree; 0 disagree).

6. I am interested in receiving a *summary* report of the discussion groups' reports. (6 strongly agree; 12 agree; 3 somewhat agree; 0 disagree).

Comments: 21 (or 70 percent) of the 31 participants responded. Ten participants departed before distribution of evaluation forms just prior to the workshop adjournment. See Participants' Evaluation Comments in Appendix II.

Appendix II:
Participants' Evaluation Comments

"Well organized and useful hand-outs."

"More people could benefit in (sic) this kind of involvement."

"Great enthusiasm was shared among moderator, speakers, and audience which shows the importance and timeliness of the subject matter. Please, make this a yearly program!"

"Good program. Congratulations."

"I thoroughly enjoyed participation and would invite additional opportunities to assist in this kind of forum in the future."

"The group discussions were very lively and informative."

"Dr. Myers, your research disproved commonly held beliefs about government financing of Korean businesses. I would personally have enjoyed hearing more from Korean panelists about their business financing strategies."

"This should be an annual event and well publicized."

"As an Asian-American, this was a first-time experience I really enjoyed. Thank you for your concern."

"Dr. Myers, I first read about your research in the *Korean Weekly* about two years ago. It is the topic (Korean Merchants and African American relations) of my dissertation I'm working on. It will be much appreciated if I can call on you for help."

Note: Comments solicited on the Evaluation Forms were optional. Although the above comments were the only ones received, there were no negative comments.

Part Seven
Epilogue

The earth is the LORD's and the fullness thereof; the world and they that dwell therein.
—Psalms 24:1

Multiculturalism and cultural diversity challenge the heart of what it means to be American.
—James M. Jones
Prejudice and Racism
(New York: McGraw-Hill, 1997)

Diversity and even a certain chaos is better than unity under a wrong idea.
—W. E. B. Dubois (1917)

Epilogue

Can We Get Along?

Ernest R. Myers

In 1992, several events that captured national and global attention—the civil disorder and chaos in Los Angeles following the jury's acquittal of the police who brutally attacked Rodney King, and the "Earth Summit" in Rio de Janeiro (the United Nation's Conference on Environment and Development)—reinforce the relevance of the articles contained in this volume.

The first event, the Los Angeles "riots," was partly an eruptive manifestation of the pervasive economic strain experienced in the lives of the broad range of minority groups that reside in urban America. The fact that grocery stores and eating establishments were key targets of the looting indicated a greater preoccupation concerning nourishment than other material gain. While this rebellious event also included white participants, it was largely composed of populations from the underclass of Hispanics and African Americans, as well as Hispanic immigrants. Importantly, the environmental conditions surrounding this disorder are but a microcosm of urban America in general and the African-American ghettos in particular.

For many years, unemployment and school dropout rates have averaged about 40 percent for both young Hispanics and African Americans in the nation's largest cities. Few of these young adults have skills that are recognized as marketable in today's workplace. Language barriers add to the difficulties, while many socioeconomic and cultural adjustment problems are compounded by the deteriorating infrastructures in American cities. The past decade of nationwide, urban renewal stagnation has nurtured this decline simultaneously with the acceleration of increasing cultural diversity in these urban areas. Thus, these urban communities are burdened with increasingly diverse, low-income minority groups while in desperate need of renewal, culturally-sensitive economic infrastructures, and community development subsidies, plus also facing bankrupt revenue bases.

Increasing business opportunities for African Americans and other minorities will foreseeably contribute to greater balance and sustained economic development of inner-city infrastructures. And though African-American businesses were also destroyed in the Los Angeles "riots" (Black owners of six Burger Kings, for example, lost two of their franchises in the burnings.), Korean-American merchants experienced proportionately the greatest hostility and losses commensurate with their ownership of the vast majority of businesses in the ghetto community of the area. Obviously, much of the pent-up rage and resentment that erupted was against Koreatown proprietors' dominance of business holdings in the area. It was a pivotal influence in the attacks by competing minority groups, especially struggling African-American and Hispanic-American groups.

In the wake of this community devastation numerous "urban aid" proposals were recommended by leaders in the public and private sectors. However, investment in America's inner cities has long been viewed to be in competition with foreign aid. The so-called "unconditionally" declared "War Against Poverty" in the 1960s was aborted by the costs of the Vietnam War. Today, the democratization movements in Eastern Europe, particularly *former* Soviet Union countries, will foreseeably receive U. S. foreign aid preference over domestic investments, resulting in further subordination of comprehensive programs for urban America.

Since the 1960s, two solutions relevant to these current conditions have been proposed: the Community Development Corporation (CDC) and the "Enterprise Zone" concepts. The CDC, experimentally implemented by the "War on Poverty" agency (the Office of Economic Opportunity) in the mid-1960s, is a cooperative, community-based and owned organization designed to create capital formation, jobs for local residents, and build economic and political bargaining power in inner cities and impoverished rural areas. The CDC eventually becomes self-sustaining through business solvency and payment of dues by its members. Twenty-six CDCs were still in operation in the late 1970s (Cross, 1986, p. 815).

The urban enterprise zones, in contrast to the CDCs self-help approach, depend on outside business aid. In the case of the proposed enterprise zones, "... federal tax incentives that provide jobs and credit ... would be offered to businesses. Firms operating in the enterprise zones would receive generous benefits such as elimination of capital gains taxes on investments, partial tax exemptions on income, and tax credits for the employment of workers formerly on welfare rolls" (Cross, 1986). Ironically, this enterprise zone concept resurfaced in mid-1992 as a much-lauded urban aid recommendation for the devastated Los Angeles area. However, Cross observed that the CDC offers genuine community empowerment for "... it cuts through superficial reforms such as urban enterprise zones which save privileges for whites while protecting the public order against Black civil disturbance" (p. 817).

The world population factor is another important focus of concern. It is tangentially related to the United Nations' Earth Summit which attracted representatives from 178 nations who gathered to negotiate a unified, global attack on environmental and developmental problems which threaten *all* life on the planet (*Washington Post*, June 15, 1992). Significantly, we are warned that the world's current population is increasing by a billion people every decade, and "... more than 90 percent of this population growth is in the developing Third World" (Robinson, 1992, p. A 14). This observation, however, must be contextually balanced with the fact of global demography—three-fourths of the world's population *resides* in Third World nations. A subordinate agenda item of the Earth Summit included a call for "appropriate demographic policies" relative to the "world population boom" that forms an integral part of international ecological concerns for the preservation of bio-diversity. Ironically, the Summit participants' agreement to rescue tropical rain forests in Brazil will ultimately support survival efforts of the native humanity residing in the forests—a key element in the cultural dimension of bio-diversity of that region as championed by the indigenous tribes of the Amazon.

Much of the Third World nations' pollution problems threatening their ecosystems are produced by the "superpower" nations' industrial operations which are located in underdeveloped countries. The United States, for example, produces over 50 percent of the world's garbage but has only 5 percent of the world's population (Public Interest Research Group, 1992). Ecological realities of the environment and its inhabitants are not mutually exclusive concerns, as the Summit recognized. Consequently, world population demographics are necessarily an issue for all nations. Pollution is disruptive to agricultural potential which affects a nation's capacity to feed its people, especially as this challenge is compounded by periodic droughts and civil strife. In the face of any of these obstacles, and just as European immigrants ventured *en masse* to greener pastures for survival in past generations, so populations of underdeveloped or Third World countries seek relocation as a survival option—as typical immigrants or as refugees.

It has been immigration policies, not habitable or inhabitable lands, that have precluded a greater balance in the distribution of the earth's populations. On the other hand, international law recognizes as a sovereign right a nation's freedom to determine how many immigrants may enter its borders. Yet, these laws were strategically instituted *after* European nations systematically colonized most of the Third World in centuries past. United States' immigration policy reforms have permitted the admission of a greater number of Third World people during the past generation than at any other period in America's history. At the same time, the European emigre population declined and may continue to do so in view of the revolutionary, democratization developments in governmental systems in Eastern Europe during this decade. For example, the disuniting of the Soviet Union and the evolving democratization and popularizing of private enterprise throughout much of Europe are developments that may greatly decrease the demand of Europeans to immigrate to long-standing capitalist nations. The evolving emergence of a singular European Common Market may also strengthen a holding influence on their populations.

Ultimately, a key issue is whether the most spacious lands will maintain their restrictive immigration policies while many of the earth's populations struggle for "standing room" and hygienic air in underdeveloped, ecologically imbalanced, and polluted regions.

Yet, while U. S. foreign priorities and International Monetary Fund commitments continue to Russia, Poland, and other emerging Eastern European "democracies," efforts to develop new Third World democracies, such as governments in Africa, are losing even their former allocations of Peace Corps assistance, much less serious foreign aid funding. Under President Clinton's leadership, however, some aspects of Africa's international trading capacity were being mainstreamed. The U. S. Congressional Black Caucus has played key roles in legislating this global policy.

Meanwhile, America's inner cities and Third World populations, like Third World nations, are not priority targets of America's investment portfolios. Perhaps this is the nation's greatest challenge for a "Changing America." Just as a diversified financial investment portfolio is the counsel of economic experts, we must recognize America's cultural diversity as an inheritance of democracy's magnetism. Consequently, America as heir to an incalculable fortune of human resources must also pay a cultural inheritance tax. For without a substantive, long-range, and comprehensive plan for community development in our cities, the cultural diversity which characterizes them will increasingly be a liability, fostering further welfare dependence, unemployment, drug trafficking, juvenile delinquency, inter-ethnic and racial conflicts, and recurrent civil turmoil.

Then President-elect Bill Clinton met the most fundamental challenge of today's America by involving an impressive number of minority group representatives in a two-day "Economic Summit" held in Little Rock, Arkansas, in mid-December, 1992. This historical event, equivalent to a "White House" conference, was particularly unique as an expedient problem-solving forum geared toward identifying governmental reform alternatives and strategies for reducing the national debt while investing in the revitalization of the nation's infrastructure, the work-force, and the general economy. Despite the fact that a master treatment plan was not the output of the Little Rock conference, the diagnostic inputs provided by a largely multicultural, interdisciplinary body representative of America's kaleidoscopic leadership made a hopeful prognosis for the nation's socio-economic health. The hope of any nation is in its people.

We have since witnessed President Clinton's bold follow-through in forming his presidential cabinet with more minority group representatives than the combined totals of all other U. S. presidents' cabinets in our nation's history. On the other hand, flames of despair still characterize urban America—inner city unemployment, drug trafficking, violence, and deteriorating infrastructures continue. Clinton's braintrust (cabinet) had, for the first time, however, a multicultural composition sensitive to these the turbulent conditions.

There is also a festering societal problem which threatens America and relates also to issues of multiculturalism. This formidable challenge is the proliferation of racist hate groups. According to the Southern Poverty Law Center reports and television commentator Roger Mudd, there are currently over 500 white, militia-type hate groups in 25 states in the U. S. Selectively, some of these "cesspools of vigilantes" were highlighted in the television special, "Nazi America: A Secret History" (January 17, 2000), narrated by Mudd.

Multiculturalism is necessarily a belief in the tolerance of cultural diversity and the affirmation of pluralism. Since, however, the U. S. minority populations are expected to reverse the majority profile in the U. S. within a few generations, the media's frequent forecasting of these demographic changes acts as fuel to the already inflamed, delusional fears of the "Nazi America" subculture whose members are obsessed with preparations for a so-called "holy race war" to allegedly "preserve the white race" and secure its *privileged* status. As such, these groups are but an updated, camouflage khaki-attired version of the hooded KKK. They have also contaminated the global Internet.

Yet, the contemporary socioeconomic status and privileges of whites has deep roots in America's institution of black African slave labor throughout a three-century period. This slave industry *established* the sustaining wealth enjoyed by this nation as well as Western Europe. Consequently, the African Americans' drive for restitution or reparations for these racist-based, unjust enrichments has grown and evolved into a national movement since the 1980s. This movement deserves timely recognition and action as we phase into the 21st Century.

In this new century, the embracing of multiculturalism has the potential to diffuse the "future shock" in the stormy emergence of our rainbow society. The many cultural identities that make up America are like links in a chain. The popular adage that a "chain can be no stronger than its weakest link" carries a message beyond rhetoric or conventional wisdom. Cultural diversity is not only descriptive of the nation's profile, it defines America and its greatest challenge.

References

Cross, T. (1986). *The Black Power Imperative.* New York: Faulkner Books, pp. 811-817.
Public Interest Research Group. (1992). [Newsflyer]. Washington, DC.
Robinson, E. (1992, June 1). At earth summit, South aims to send bill North. *Washington Post*, pp. Al-A14.
Weisskopf, M., & Preston, J. (1992, June 15). Rio organizer says summit fell short. *Washington Post*, p. A13.

Appendix

African-American Perceptions of Asian-American Merchants

Ernest R. Myers

Exploratory Study Data

Respondent Categories of Korean Merchants' Customers	Frequency	Percent
UDC Graduate Students	43	28.7
Federal Agency Employees	29	19.3
Black Small Businesses (Merchants)	19	12.7
Association of Black Psychologists	10	6.7
Metropolitan DC Police (Public Officials)	26	17.2
Black Youth (A Conference of Youth in DC)	10	6.7
General Public (Black Community, No Known Group Affiliation)	10	6.7
University Staff (UDC)	3	2.0
Total Survey Sample	150	100

Survey Sites:
 121 or 80.7% of respondents surveyed in D. C.
 29 or 19.3% of respondents surveyed in Maryland

Respondents Profile Data

Respondent Residence	Location	Frequency	Percent
54% in DC	NW	36	24.0
	NE	28	18.7
	SW	2	1.3
	SE	15	10.0
46% in MD	MD	69	46.0

(DC)N=81; (MD)N=69; Total=150

Length at Residence	Frequency	Percent
At least 2 years	29	19.3
2-5 years	44	29.3
Over 5 years	72	48.0
No response (Blank)	5	3.4

Challenges of a Changing America

Sex	Frequency	Percent	
Male	64	42.7	
Female	82	54.7	
No Response (Blank)	4	2.6	

Age	Frequency	Percent	
18-29	37	24.7	
30-40	58	38.6	
41-50	37	24.7	
(18 through 50)			63.3%
51-60	9	6.0	
Over 60	3	2.0	
(over 51)			8.0%
No Response (Blank)	6	4.0	

Educational Achievement	Frequency	Percent	
Grade School	3	2.0	
High School Completion	9	6.0	
Some College or Tech School	47	31.3	
BA, BS, or Tech Certificate	18	12.0	
Grad. Degree (Master's or Doctorate)	25	16.7	
No Response	47	31.3	
(High school plus)			66%

Race	Frequency	Percent
African American (Black)	140	93.3
Black Hispanic	2	1.3
Other (2 Whites, 1 Native American)	8	5.4

Employment Status	Frequency	Percent
Self Business Owner	19	12.7
Employed	116	77.3
Unemployed	5	3.3
Student Only (Full Time)	8	5.3
No Response/Other	2	1.4

Place of Birth	Frequency	Percent	
North	14	9.3	
South	51	34.0	
Midwest	11	7.3	
West	4	2.7	
DC	37	24.7	
USA (Region Not Indicated)	20	13.3	
Foreign Country (Africa, Caribbean)	11	7.3	
No Response (Blank)	2	1.4	
(Total percentage from known USA regions)			78%

Appendix

Religion	Frequency	Percent
Protestant	101	67.3
Catholic	27	18.0
Islamic	1	0.7
Buddhist	1	0.7
Other (Not Identified)	5	3.3
No Response	15	10.0

Customer Contact and Intergroup Sensitivity

Contact with Asians	Frequency	Percent
No	6	4.0
Yes	142	94.7
No Response	2	1.3

Customer Experience at Asian Stores	Frequency	Percent
No	7	4.7
Yes	137	91.3
Unknown	5	3.3
No Response	1	0.7

Ever Patronize an Asian Store?	Frequency	Percent
No	15	10.0
Yes	130	86.7
Uncertain	3	2.0
No Response	2	1.3

If Not, Would You Consider It?	Frequency	Percent
No	10	6.7
Yes	10	6.7
Uncertain	0	0
Not Applicable	130	86.7

Satisfied with Services	Frequency	Percent	
Never	13	8.7	
Sometimes	45	30.0	
(Combination of Never and Sometimes)			38.7%
Often	14	9.3	
Generally	59	39.3	
Always	13	8.7	
(Combination of Often, Generally, and Always)			57.3%
No Response	6	4.0	

Courteous Service	Frequency	Percent	
Never	5	3.3	
Sometimes	43	28.7	
(combination of Never and Sometimes)			32%
Often	18	12.0	
Generally	58	38.7	
Always	20	13.3	
(Combination of Often, Generally, and Always)			64%
No Response	6	4.0	

Shown Respect	Frequency	Percent	
Never	6	4.0	
Sometimes	41	27.3	
(Combination of Never and Sometimes)			31.3%
Often	25	16.7	
Generally	54	36.0	
Always	18	12.0	
(Combination of Often, Generally, and Always)			64.7%
No Response	6	4.0	

Language Understood by Merchant	Frequency	Percent	
Never	6	4.0	
Sometimes	19	12.7	
(Combination of Never and Sometimes)			18.7%
Often	25	16.7	
Generally	69	46.0	
Always	23	15.3	
(Combination of Often, Generally, and Always)			78%
No Response	5	3.3	

Actually Experienced Programs (When Not Understood)	Frequency	Percent
Due to Customer's Speech	4	2.7
Due to Merchant's Speech	20	13.3
Due to Merchant's Attitude	9	6.0
Unspecified	1	0.7
No Response	116	77.3

Discrimination Perceived (By Black Customers)	Frequency	Percent
Never	23	15.3
Sometimes	40	26.7
Often	29	19.3
Generally	25	16.7
Always	10	6.7
No Response	23	15.3

Appendix

Do Asians Understand Black Culture?	Frequency	Percent
No	89	59.3
Yes	12	8.0
Uncertain	46	30.7
No Response	3	2.0

Reasons For/Against Understanding	Frequency	Percent
For: Store's Priducts Evidence	4	2.7
Against: Don't Understand Black Language	67	44.6
Ethnocentricity	5	3.3
Influenced by Negative Media Hype	27	18.0
Insensitivity	12	8.0
Recent Arrivals to U.S.	18	12.0
Only Respect Money	15	10.0
Uncertain: But Provide Convenientn Services	2	1.3

Rate Contacts with Asian Merchants	Frequency	Percent	
Very Bad	4	2.7	
Negative	27	18.0	
(Combination of Very Bad and Negative)			20.7%
Tolerable	57	38.0	
Positive	35	23.3	
Very Positive	5	3.3	
No Response	22	14.7	

Stereotypical Perceptions

No Difference in Their Decision To Locate Business or Treatment of Customers	Frequency	Percent
True	61	40.7
False	79	52.7
No Response	10	6.7

They Only Seek Blacks' Money, Not Association	Frequency	Percent
True	59	39.3
False	29	19.3
No Response	62	41.4

Prefer No Association with Neighboring Black Businesses	Frequency	Percent
True	66	44.0
False	57	38.0
No Response	27	18.0

They Employ No Blacks (Only Family)	Frequency	Percent
True	104	69.3
False	37	24.7
No Response	9	6.0

Challenges of a Changing America

No Job Offers to Blacks	Frequency	Percent
True	75	50.0
False	50	33.3
No Response	25	16.7

Treat All Customers the Same	Frequency	Percent
True	45	30.0
False	89	59.3
No Response	16	10.7

Don't Understand Black Culture	Frequency	Percent
True	103	68.7
False	27	18.0
No Response	20	13.3

Identify with Blacks (Empathy)	Frequency	Percent
True	22	14.7
False	112	74.7
No Response	16	10.7

Prices Too High	Frequency	Percent
True	74	49.3
False	62	41.3
No Response	14	9.3

Poor Maintenance of Facility	Frequency	Percent
True	58	38.7
False	77	51.3
No Response	15	10.0

No Respect for Black Elderly and Children	Frequency	Percent
True	68	45.3
False	62	41.3
No Response	20	13.3

Black Perceptions of Merchants	Frequency	Percent
Disrespect Black Youth	4	2.7
Depends on Their Personality	7	4.7
Respect Only Money	3	2.0
Disrespect Customer Complaints	6	4.0
No Response	130	86.7

Merchants' Problems Communicating	Frequency	Percent
Yes	54	36.0
No	90	60.4
No Response	6	4.0

Appendix

Nature of Communication Problems	Frequency	Percent	
Their Speech/Accent	5	3.3	
Their English Inadequacy	26	17.3	
They Pretend Not to Understand	8	5.3	
They Disrespect Youth	3	2.0	
(Combination of Above Four Responses)			27.9%
No Response or Not Applicable	103	72.0	

Believe Asians Get U. S. Government Aid	Frequency	Percent	
Yes	72	48.0	
No	24	16.0	
Uncertain	49	32.7	
(Combination of No and Uncertain)			48.7%
No Response	5	3.3	

Relationships with Asians

Nature of Relationship	Frequency*	Percent
As Customer	129	86.0
As Business Associate	19	12.7
As Friend	27	18.0
As Marital Partner (Mate)	2	1.3
As Neighbor (Residential Proximity to Asian Business)	25	16.7
Other	24	16.0

*Many Overlaps of Multiple Responses, Thus N=226

Knowledge of Recent Problems	Frequency	Percent
Yes	26	17.3
No	96	64.0
Uncertain	23	15.3
No Response	5	3.3

Reasons for Recent Problems	Frequency	Percent
Black Youths' (Abusive) Language	3	3.3
Opposition to Asians	6	4.0
Opposition to Asian Ownership	7	4.7
Hostility Toward Asians	4	2.7
Not Applicable	128	84.0
No Response	2	1.3

Attitudes

Feelings about Asians Business in Black Community	Frequency	Percent
Welcome	71	47.3
Not Welcome	31	20.7
Uncertain (Ambivalent)	41	27.3
No Response	7	4.7

Why Welcomed?	Frequency	Percent
They Provide Needed Services	7	4.7
They Have Same Rights as Any U. S. Citizens	30	20.0
They Have Good Prices	1	0.7
They Have Good Locations & Hours	4	2.7
They Work Hard	3	2.0
Their Business Improves Community Tax Base	11	7.3
Yes, If They're Citizens	2	1.3
They Do Great Laundry	1	0.7
They Have a Right to Earn a Living	19	12.7
No Response	72	47.9

Why Not Welcomed	Frequency	Percent
Oppose Commerce in Residential Area	3	2.0
They Don't Contribute to Community	9	6.0
They Are Just Slum Landlords (Capitalistic)	3	2.0
Prefer Buying from Blacks	12	8.0
They Don't Hire Blacks	1	0.7
The Don't Trust Blacks	4	2.7
Unsanitary Food Services	1	0.7
No Response or Not Applicable	117	78.0

Suggestions for Improving Relations	Frequency	Percent
None	76	50.7
Yes	65	43.3
No Response	9	6.0

Specific Suggestions	Frequency	Percent
Community Newsletters	1	0.7
Make Efforts to Understand Each Other	23	15.4
Community Workshops (Multicultural Relations & Networking)	11	7.3
Exchange Visitations (Churches, Socials)	9	6.0
Hire Blacks	10	6.7
Lower Prices	3	2.0
Learn African American History	7	4.7
We Need Classes on Each Other's Cultures	3	2.0
We Need Human Relations Workshops	4	2.7
They Should Be Charitable (Especially to Youth Programs)	2	1.3
They Should Practice the Golden Rule	3	2.0
Unspecified	1	0.7
Yes, But No Comments	4	2.7
No, But No Comments	69	46.0

About the Editor and Contributors

Editor

Ernest R. Myers, Ph.D., LICSW, LPC, is a community psychology pioneer, Fellow of the American Psychological Association (APA), and Professor of Psychology and Counseling at the University of the District of Columbia (UDC) where he has formerly chaired two academic departments and directed a college-community relations unit. Prior to his academic career, he served as an Expert Consultant (full time) at the U. S. Department of Health, Education and Welfare (Bureau of Higher Education). In 1971 at the U. S. Department of Health, Education and Welfare, he designed and administered the Servicemen's Early Educational Counseling Program (SEEC), the first federal interagency services program of international scope in the history of the U. S. Office of Education. It provided outreach counseling services to active military troops in Vietnam, Europe, and the Far East. Earlier, he was Assistant Director of the National Urban League's Washington Bureau, Manager of Development for the Westinghouse Learning Corporation, and the Regional Evaluation Officer (Western states) for the U. S. Office of Economic Opportunity's VISTA agency. He also was a consulting member of the President's Task Force on the War Against Poverty in the 1960s before serving as the Midwestern States Regional Neighborhood Services Program Officer at the U.S. Department of Housing and Urban Development. For over twenty years he has been a consultant and trainer in staff, organizational, community, management, and human relations development for numerous public and private agencies, schools, universities, and corporations.

His publications and presentations include over 100 authored articles, book reviews, and commentary in a wide scope of professional journals, magazines,

Ernest R. Myers

newspapers, and four distinctive books. He has served on the Brain Trust of the U. S. Congressional Black Caucus in areas of mental health and veterans affairs. His city council legislative testimony in the nation's capital, jointly-sponsored in representation of the American Psychological Association (APA) and four other national, professional psychology associations, influenced the historical achievement of hospital rights for psychologists in Washington, D. C., in 1983. His book credits include *The Community Psychology Concept*, for which he received the 1981 annual award for distinctive scholarship from the National Association of Black Psychologists, and *Race and Culture in the Mental Health Service Delivery System, A Primer* (editor). At the 22nd Inter-American Psychology Congress held in Buenos Aires, Argentina, in 1989, he presented a paper on "The Refugee Crisis in the United States." He gave the closing keynote address at the National Cross-Cultural Mental Health Conference in Myrtle Beach, South Carolina in 1995, and chaired the International Cultural Conference on Africa and the African Diaspora at the University of the District of Columbia in 1999. His foreign travels include having been to Central and South America, Africa, Caribbean nations, and extensively in Europe.

Contributors

Michealanthony Brown-Cheatham (deceased) was a lecturer in the Department of Counseling and School Psychology at San Diego State University.

Constance M. Ellison, Ed.D., is an assistant professor in the School of Education at Howard University. Her areas of specialization are in the domains of cognition and learning.

Denise Fairchild, Ph.D., an urban planner, is Director of the Los Angeles Office of the Local Initiatives Support Corporation.

Halford H. Fairchild, Ph.D., is the former national president of the Association of Black Psychologists, and current editor of the Association's *Psych Discourse*. He has authored numerous articles that have been published in professional journals such as the *American Psychologist, The Journal of Black Psychology,* and others, and a column in the *Los Angeles Times*. He is also a distinguished contributor in the *Encyclopedia of Psychology*, a new, landmark publication of the American Psychological Association (APA) and the Oxford University Press.

Yosef Ford, M.A., an anthropologist, has been an adjunct professor at the University of Maryland. He is a former member of the board of directors of the D.C. Mental Health Association, and the senior counselor of the Ethiopian Community Center in Washington, D.C. where he was case manager and cross-cultural consultant. He has served on the Center's board of directors, and authored articles in international news publications. He has taught in areas of race and ethnic relations.

Leland K. Hall, Sr., Ph.D., is a professor at the Union Institute, Cincinnati,

Contributors

Ohio. His extensive mental health leadership experiences include Chief of Community Mental Health Centers in New Jersey and Washington, D.C., Deputy Director of the D.C. Mental Health Administration, and Chief of D.C. Health Planning Development. He directed mental health services for the largest Hispanic population in the Nation's Capital.

Courtland C. Lee, Ph.D., is a professor and director of the Counselor Education Program at the University of Virginia. He has published numerous articles, book chapters, several books on adolescent development and cross-cultural counseling. He has also served as editor of the *Journal of Multicultural Counseling and Development*, the *Journal of African American Male Studies*, and *Counseling for Diversity* (a guide book for school counselors and related professionals).

Getachew Metaferia, Ph.D., is an Assistant Professor of Political Science, University of Maryland, Eastern Shore campus. He has authored articles and several book chapters in public administration and civil service training. He co-authored the book *The Ethiopian Revolution of 1974 and the Exodus of Ethiopia's Trained Human Resources*.

Maigenet Shifferraw, Ph.D., is a Peace Leader of the Institute for Multi-Track Diplomacy, a non-profit, membership organization which conducts conflict resolution seminars, internationally, to promote world peace. She has taught graduate courses in adult education at the University of the District of Columbia and Virginia Polytechnic University. She has published on topics of women's education in Africa, and co-authored the book, *The Ethiopian Revolution of 1974 and the Exodus of Ethiopia's Trained Human Resources*. She has also worked for the World Bank.

Robert Staples, Ph.D., is an Associate Professor of Sociology at the University of California Medical Center at San Francisco. His publications include more than 100 articles in professional and popular periodicals, and seven books. He has served as a Visiting Fellow (Professor) in the Institute of Family Studies in Canberra, Australia, and has traveled widely throughout the South Pacific.

Aaron B. Stills, Ed.D., is Professor and Chair, Department of Human Development and Psychoeducational Studies, Howard University, in Counseling Psychology. He is a consultant in multicultural education, and is President of the Center for Multicultural Counseling and Training. He has also served as a training consultant to universities and public schools. He was the first president of the Association for Multicultural Counseling and Development, and is completing a book on multicultural counseling.

Tran Minh Tung, M. D., a native of South Vietnam, is a psychiatrist who taught on the Faculties of Medicine of Hue, Saigon and Minh Duc. He was the Minister of Health of the Republic of Vietnam (1969-1974). He has lectured and written extensively on the subject of the refugees' adjustment and mental health problems.

His most recent work is *Indochinese Patients*, a book on the cultural aspects of medical and psychiatric care for the Indochinese.

Roberto J. Velasquez, Ph.D., currently a professor in the Department of Counseling and School Psychology at San Diego State University, was a mental health counselor at Fort Chaffee's Cuban Refugee Readjustment Center in Arkansas in 1980-81. He also served as a clinical psychologist for the U. S. State Department's Cuban-Haitian Task Force. He has published on the cultural relevance of psychiatric diagnostics and other topics in professional journals.

Indexes

Author Index

Adams, J., 10, 27
America, R. F., 8, 27
American Council on Education, 50
American Psychiatric Association, 71, 88
Anders, A., 73-80
Ascher, C., 92
Australian Council of Churches, 38
Australian Encyclopedia, 6, 14
Azicri, M., 84

Bach, J. B., 83, 92
Bach, R. L., 83, 82
Banks, C. A., 123
Banks, J. A., 121
Baptiste, H . P., 123
Baptiste, M. L., 123
Bartholdi, F. A., 11
Bennett, C. I., 121, 123
Bennett, L., Jr., 10
Bernal, G., 83, 87, 93
Berry, J. W., 83
Billingsley, A., 49
Blackwell, J. E., 48
Blustein, P., 3
Bonacich, E., 162, 167
Bontemps, A., 24
Boorstin, D. J., 3, 4, 8
Boswell, T. D., 83, 84
Boxer, P. A., 93
Boykin, A. W., 119, 121, 122
Briquets, S. D., 84, 93

Brisk, M., 123
Brown, B., 45
Brown M., 9, 11, 13,
Brown-Cheatham, M., viii, 81
Brumby, J., 38
Burstein, D., 30

Capitol Spotlight, 168
Caplan, N., 70
Carlin, J., 68
Chalmers, D., 12, 28
Children's Defense Fund, 45, 46
Choy, M., 69
Chaiborn, C. D., 48
Clifford, P. R., 46
Cohen, P., 82
Cohen, R., 86, 93
Comer, J. P., 46
Cordes, C., 45, 46
Cross, A., 47
Cross, T., 193
Cross, W. E., 51
Cruces, M., 21, 28
Curtis, E., 34, 38
Curtis, J. R., 83

Daniels, R., 8, 9
Davidson, B., 123
Davis, D. K., xiii,
Davis, J. J., 28
Davis, J. P., 28
Department of Aboriginal Affairs, 33
Dillard, 48

Indexes

Diop, Cheikh Anta, 28
Dixon, H., 83, 87, 93
Dorias, L. J., 65
Dudley, W., 12, 28

Ellison, C. M., viii, 119
Ellison, R., 8
Encyclopedia Americana, 3, 4
Espino, C., 80
Ethiopian Community Center, 97
Ethiopian Community Development Council, Inc., 28, 116

Fairchild, D. G., viii, 137
Fairchild, H. H., viii, 137, 142, 143, 168
Fallows, J., 23, 28
Faulkner, H. U., 9, 10, 28
Fernandez, G. A., 84, 87, 93
Ford, D., 59, 69
Ford, Y., vii, 41

Galbis, R., 72
Gaither, V., 168
Gamarra, E. A., 83
Garcia, R., 123
Garreau, J., 163
Gary, L. E., 46
Gates, D., 4
Gay, G., 123, 126, 127
Giago, T., 28
Gibson, M., 123, 125
Gil, R. C., 93
Ginsburg, H. P., 122
Giroux, H., 121
Goodstein, L., 168
Gordon, M. M., 105
Gordon, T. A., 49
Grant, C. A., 126
Gupta, V., 143
Guthrie, R. V., 47
Gutierrez, 83

Hale, J. E., 120
Hall, L. K., Sr., xvii, 71
Handlin, O., 28
Helms, J. E., 48

Hernandez, R. E., 82, 84, 95
Hill, R., 49
Hoffman, F., 93
Hudson Institute, xvi
Hughes, L., 24
Huy, N., 70

Jackson, J. L., 21
Jennings, F., 38
Jet, 21, 28
Jones, D. J., 46, 49
Jordan, T., 24

Kamen, A., 28
Keary, J., 168
Keller, J. L., 88
Kennedy, J. F., 28
Kim, U., 93
King, L. M., 46
Klarreich, K., 20, 28
Kramer, B., 46
Kunz, E. F., 88, 94

LaFromboise, T. D., 48
Larzalere, A., 81, 94
Lee, C., xvii
Leibowitz, A. H., 17
Lega, L. I., 94
Light, I., 167, 168
Lin, K. M., 94
Liu, W. T., 67
Llanes, J., 94
Los Angeles Times, 142
Lurie, 12

Manuel, G., 36, 37
Marable, M., 24
Marina, D. R., 94
Masanz, 20
Mazrui, A. A., 28
McCoy, C. B., 83
McFerson, H. M., 38
McLaren, P., 167, 121
Melnick, S. L., 132
Metaferia, G., xviii
Minde, T., 83

Miranda, M. R., 73
Mitchell, L. K., 31
Mok, D., 83
Montero, D., 64
Mozo, R., 84
Myers, E. R., xiii, 3, 29, 30, 46, 143, 171, 181, 189, 195, 203

Narvaez, L., 84
Negash, G., 104
Nobles, W., 47, 49
North, D., 50, 70

Ogbu, J. U., 121

Parham, T. A., 48, 51
Passel, J. S., 17, 29
Pasteur, A. B., 47
Pedraza-Bailey, S., 84
Perez, R., 82, 86, 87
Peterson, M. F., 94
Phinney, J. S., 123
Pierce, W. D., 48, 51
Pilo-Le, L., 70
Pomales, J., 48, 51
Portes, A., 94
Preston, J., 29
Public Interest Research Group, 191

Queralt, M., 87

Reed, W., 165
Rene, A. A., 50
Rensberger, B., 44
Rivera, M. A., 84
Robbins, R., 6, 8, 29
Robinson, E., 193
Robinson, R., 6, 8
Robinson, L., 9, 22
Rotheram, M. J., 123
Rumbaut, R., 94
Rumbaut, R. D., 94
Rowntree, L., 24

Sanchez, R., 168
Schemick, N., 75

Schleisinger, A., xv
Shelton, C., 165
Shifferraw, M., xvii, 97
Simon, J., 23
Sleeter, C. E., 123, 126
Small Business Administration, 166
Smith, R., 9, 10, 11, 12, 29
Sokoloff, B., 68
Spayd, L., 168
Spencer, F., 94
Spolar, C., 97
Staples, R., xvii, 23, 29, 31
Stein, B. N., 88
Steiner, S., 8
Stent, M. D., 120
Stepik, A., 84
Stevens, F., 36
Stills, A. B., xviii, 123
Sue, D. W., 121
Swinton, D. H., 9, 29
Sykes, B., 32
Szapocznik, J., 86, 87, 95

Taft, D. R., 3, 6, 7, 8, 29
Taft, J., 70
Thomas, C. S., 51
Time Magazine, xvi
Toffler, A., 29
Toldson, I. L., 47
Triplett, T., 84, 86
Troike, R. C., 123
Tung, T. M., xvii, 55, 61, 62, 70
Twain, M., xvi

U. S. Bureau of the Census, 13, 19, 29, 45, 51
U. S. Central Intelligence Agency, 29
U. S. Congress Committees on Judiciary and U. S. Senate, 29
U. S. Department of Commerce, 80
U. S. Department of Health and Human Services, 58
U. S. Department of Justice, 14-17, 29
U. S. Department of Labor, 45, 51
U. S. General Accounting Office 55, 70
U. S. News and World Report, 143

Indexes

Vargas, G. E., 73, 75
Vega, W. A., 74, 78
Velàsquez, R., xvii, 81, 86, 87, 95
Vialet, J., 10, 29
Walsh, A. C., 33
Washington Post, 16, 20, 22, 29, 107, 162, 166
Washington Times, 165
Watts, T. D., 46
Weisskopf, M., 193
Westermeyer, J., 81, 95
Wheeler, L., 168
Whitaker, B., 37
White, J. L., 51
Williams, C. L., 94
Willie, C., 46
Wood, G. A., 38
Woodson, C. G., 44
World Almanac and Book of Facts, 7
World Book Encyclopedia 2000, 18, 22
World Council of Churches, 35

Yu, E., 67

Zinn, H., 8, 9, 30
Zucker, N. F., 9, 20, 30

Subject Index

Aboriginals. *See* Australia.
"affirmative action", xviii
Afghanistan, 7
Africa, 3, 4, 5, 13-17, 22, 24, 41, 44
African immigrants (voluntary), 7-10
African Americans (Black Americans), xiii, xvii, 8-10, 21, 31, 41, 45, 137, 143, 171, 195
African-American Psychology, 45-50
African Diaspora, 32, 44
Afro-Cubans, 84
America, viii, xvi, 10, 23, 193
American Dream, 10
American Revolution (U. S.), 3, 12
Anacostia (Washington, D. C.), 165
    Anacostia Professional and Merchants Association, 165, 183
Anglo-Americans, 18
Anglo-Saxons, 3, 35
Antarctica, 13
"Anti-polyglotism", 12
Argentina, 23
Asia, 3, 11, 13, 14, 15, 17
Asia Fortune Newspaper, 183
Asian Americans, 55-69
Asian entrepreneurs, 143-168. *See also* Korean Merchants.
Asian immigrants, 7, 55, 137, 164
Asian Pacific Legal Center, 141
Asiatic Barred Zone, 7
Association of Black Psychologists, 172
Atlanta Federal Prison, 21, 67
Attucks, Crispus, 12
Australia, 3, 5-7, 13-14, 15, 32, 43

Balkanization, xv
Baltimore (Maryland), 164
Bedford-Stuyvesant (Brooklyn, NY), 143
Belgium, 3
Belize (Central America), 22
Black Church, 49
Black Cubans. *See* Afro-Cubans, 84
Black History Month, 20, 44
Black/Korean Alliance (Los Angeles), 139, 141
Black Minutemen, 12
Black Power, 43
Black Sailors, 31, 84
Black Soldiers, 32
Boston, 13
Bracero Program, 26
"Brain drain", xvii
Brazil, 7, 191
British Honduras, 22
Bubonic plague (Black death), 4
Burma, 7
Bush Administration, 124

California, 137, 158, 167. *See also* Los Angeles.
Cambodians, 55, 57
Cameroon, 22
Canada, 22

Capital Martial Arts and Fitness Center, 184
Caribbean, 5, 9
Central Americans, xvii, 15, 17, 20, 21, 29, 77
Chicago, 164
Child abuse, 75
China, 3, 7, 14, 15, 17
Chinese, 7, 18
Chinese Americans, 143, 178, 179
Chinese Exclusion Act, 25
Christianity, 4. *See also* Papal Bull.
Chronology of U. S. Immigration Policy, 24-27
Illegal Immigration Reform and Responsibility Act - 1996, 27
Clinton, Bill (President-elect), 192
Colonialism Movement, 4
Columbus, Christopher, 4, 5
Community Development Corporation (CDC), 190
Cuba, 20, 81-85
Cuban refugees, xvi, 21, 81-86
    acculturation, 82, 83
    assimilation, 86
    boatlift of Marielitos, 81-85
    discrimination, 84
    employment, 84
    identity, 84
    mental health, 82-92
    migration experience, 83-85
    refugees: 1960s vs. 1980s, 84
Cultural diversity, 119
Cultural ecology, 24
Cultural geography, 24
Cultural homogeneity, 7
Cultural shock, 83
Declaration of Human Rights (United Nations), 19
Diagnostic and Statistical Manual of Mental Disorders (DSM-III), 88, 89
Displaced Persons Act, 26
District of Columbia (Washington, D.C.), 165, 171
Dominican Republic, 4
DuBois, W. E. B., 44
Dutch, 5

Duvalier, Jean-Claude, 20

"Earth Summit", 189, 192
East Indies, 7
Eglin Air Force Base (Florida), 86
El Salvador, 71-74
Ellis Island, 25
Emergency Quota Act of 1921, 12
England, 3
English Puritans, 6
"Enterprise Zones", 190
"equibs", 109. *See* also Ethiopians' mutual aid, and Iqub
Ethiopia, 97, 98, 102, 105
Ethiopian Community Development Council (ECDC), 18
Ethiopian refugees (exiles), x, 10, 97-116
    acculturation, 98, 109, 112
    assimilation, 105-106, 109
    business ownership, 108
    culture and values, 104, 111
    discrimination, 108
    education, 102, 103
    employment, 102, 106, 107
    family relations, 112, 113
    food preference, 112, 113
    identity, 104, 111
    inter-group relations, 109, 110
    migration experience, 97
    mutual aid and self-help, 109, 162
    religion, 109, 111
    skills and occupations, 101, 107
    stress and mental health, 105, 114
Ethnocentrism, 3, 13, 26
Eurocentric curricula, 126-128
Europe, 3-16
European Common Market, 191
Europeans, 3-15, 18, 22
Executive Order 12324, xvi, 20. *See* Reagan Administration.

Fiji Islands, 32
Fort Chaffee Readjustment Center (Arkansas), 21, 85, 86
Fort Indiantown Gap (Pennsylvania), 86
Fort McCoy (Wisconsin), 86

Fourth World View, vxii, 36-37
France 3
"Freedom Flotilla", 83

Genocide, 4, 6, 23
Georgia, 10
Germans, 5
Germany, 3
Global Exchange, 20
Greece, 3
Guantanamo (Cuba), 20

Haiti, 4, 10
Haitians, xvi, 19, 20
    refugees, 18-19
Harlem (New York), 143
Harlins, Natasha, 138
Hawaii and Hawaiians, 35
Hispanic Diaspora, 17. *See* Cuban refugees *and* Central Americans.
Hispaniola (Dominican Republic and Haiti), 4
H'Mong. *See* Indo-Chinese.
Homogenous nation-building, 14, 15
Howard University, 183
Hudson Institute, xvi
Human ecology, 21-22, 178, 191
Hungarian Refuge Act of 1958, 36

Illinois, 56
Immigrant Entrepreneurs: Koreans in Los Angeles, 162, 167
Immigration: quotas, xvi, 6, 12-15
    waves, 13
    double standards, 9
    by continental areas, 14-17
Immigration Act of 1924, 23
Immigration and Nationality Act of 1952 (INA), xvii, 12, 13, 17
    INA amendments of 1964, 34
Immigration and Naturalization Service (INS). *See* U. S. Department of Justice.
Immigration Reform and Control Act of 1986 (IRCA), 17, 27
Imperialism, 3, 5, 10
India, 5, 7, 13, 14, 15

Indo-Chinese, 17, 55-59
    refugees, 55-57, 68
Institute of Family Studies (Australia), 31
Insurrections, 10, 11
Intercultural sensitivity, 119-130, 181-185
Interdiction program, 20. *See* Executive Order 12324.
    Haitians, xvi, 19, 20
Inter-ethnic scapegoating, 138
Intergovernmental Committee for, 22
International Migrations, 8
"invisible man", 8
Involuntary immigrants, xvi, 8, 9
Iqub, 109. *See* "equibs".
Iran, 14
Island nations, 3
Israel, 14
Italy, 3, 4

Jackson, Jesse L., iii, 21, 41, 43, 182
Japan, 3, 7, 13, 14-17, 22
Japanese, 3, 33
Johnson-Reed Act of 1924, 12

"King Cotton", 10
King, Martin Luther, Jr., 42, 142
King, Rodney, 189
Korea, 3
Korean-American Chamber of Commerce (of Greater Washington), xii, 145, 146
Korean Americans, 163
Korean Association of Greater Washington, 163
Korean Grocers' Association, 165
Korean Merchants, 143-168
    Los Angeles (South Central), 143-148, 167-168, 171
    New York, 137, 158

    Washington, DC Survey, 144-166
    African-American Perceptions, 171-183, 195-202
    association with African Americans, 151-155
    business funding means, 160
    business types, 160
    citizenship status, 149, 150

212

customer relations ratings by merchants, 154
decision basis for business locations, 159
education of merchants, 149, 151
employing African Americans, 151, 152
language barriers, 150
length of time in business, 147, 157
offenses experienced at business site, 157, 158
perception of longevity at business site, 147
perception of need for special police protection, 156
potential hiring of African Americans, 151, 152
religion, 149
sensitivity to African-America culture, 153
sex and marital status, 148

Korean Merchants Association, 165
Korean Times, 168
"Koreatown", 146, 147, 178
Krome Detention Center, 20, 21. *See* Haitians.
Ku Klux Klan (KKK), 12, 193
Kye (or Keh), 162, 166

Laotians, 55
Latin America, 5, 11-17
Latinos. *See* Central Americans, Cuban refugees.
Let America Be America Again, 24
Los Angeles, 137-141, 158, 167, 189
Los Angeles Times, 142, 143
Louisiana, 56
L'Ouverture, Toussaint, 10
Luxembourg, 3

Malay States, 7
Maoris, 33-38
"Mariel Boatlift", 81
Marielitos, *See* Cuban refugees.
Maryland, 9, 146, 152, 153, 163
Massachusetts, 31

McCarran-Walter Act, 7
Melanesians, 31
"Melting Pot," 8, 141
Mexicans, 84
Mexico, 11, 14, 15, 17
Miami (Florida), 18, 83
Micronesians, 31
Minnesota, 56
Minorities, xvi, 23, 24, 32, 144, 192
Mis-education of the Negro, 44
Multicultural curriculum, 128-132
Multiculturalism, 119, 123
Multicultural sensitivity, 181-186
Mutual aid, 66, 149
Mutual Assistance Associations (MAA), 66
National Association for the Advancement of Colored People (NAACP), 35, 182
National Institute of Mental Health, 77
National Kourier, 13
National Origins Law (Quota System), 13, 33
National Science Foundation, 167
Native Americans, 6, 26
neo-Nazi youths, 24, 193
New Caledonia (South Pacific), 32
New World, 4, 5, 24
New World Order, 5
New York, 138, 143, 158
New Zealand, 32-38, 43
Newfoundland, 17
North America, 23
North Carolina, 11

Office of Economic Opportunity (OEO), 190

Pacific Islands, 11, 14, 15, 17, 31
Pan-Africanism, xvii
Papal bull (Intera Caetera of 1493), 43
Papua-New Guinea, 32
Park, Joon, 184
Peace Corps, 192
Pennsylvania, 56
Persia, 7
Peruvian Embassy, 102, 104
Philadelphia, 164
Philippine Islands, 3

Indexes

Pluralism (cultural), xxi, 52, 165
Poland, 192
Polynesians, 31-34
Port-au-Prince (Haiti), 20
Portuguese, 4
Population in the U. S., 19
Post-traumatic stress disorders (PTSDs), 75
Prince Henry, 4
Private enterprise, 150-152. *See also* Small Business Administration.
    Korean merchants, 143-168
Push-pull migration factor, 99, 104-106

Quota system, 10-27

Racism, 3-24, 32-38, 41-44, 64, 84, 108, 141, 193
Reagan Administration, 20, 35
Refugee Act of 1980, 17, 20
Refugee camps, 73
Refugee Escape Act of 1957, 26
Refugee Relief Act of 1953, 26
Renaissance, 4
Reparations, 8-9, 193
Revolutionary War (U. S.), 12
Rhode Island, 31
Richmond, Virginia, 10
Rio de Janeiro, 189
Romania, 3
Russia, 192

Salvadoran immigrants
    acculturation, 73-74
    assimilation, 73
    culture and values, 73
    education, 75
    employment, 74
    family resettlement and relations, 72, 73, 74
    language, 73
    mental health, 74-77
    migration experience, 71-73
    skills and income, 74
    Washington, D. C., 71-78
    work adjustments, 74
Samoa, 32

Seattle (Washington), 164
Selassie, Haile, 97
Select Commission on Immigration and Refugee Policy, 36
Self-help. *See* Mutual aid.
Siam, 7
Slavery, xvii, 4, 8-11, 193
Small Business Administration (SBA), 166
Solomons (South Pacific), 32
South Africa, 5, 42
South America, 11, 13, 14, 15, 17
South Carolina, 10
South Pacific, xix, 31-38
Southeast Asians
    acculturation, 60-67
    assimilation, 59, 64, 67, 69
    culture and values, 63
    discrimination, 63
    family relations, 68
    food preference, 57
    identity, 64, 67
    intergroup relations, 67
    language, 57, 58
    mental health, 67
    migration experience, 69
    mutual aid, 66
    refugee program management, 55, 61
    skills and occupations, 62-63
    sponsorship, 59-60
    work attitudes and adjustments, 62, 63
Southern Poverty Law Center, 193
Soviet Union, 3, 16
Spain, 4, 89
Statue of Liberty, 11, 14, 21
St. Elizabeth's Hospital, 77
Super power, 8

Tahiti, 32
Texas, 69, 79
Third World, xviii, 3, 18, 22, 37, 191
Turkey, 14-17
Twain, Mark, xvi

United Nations, 17, 19. *See* Declaration of Human Rights.
United Nations Earth Summit, 189

United States, 5, 8-27
University of California (Los Angeles), 139
University of the District of Columbia (UDC), xix, 172, 181-183
U. S. Catholic Conference, 86
U. S. Congress, 6
U. S. Congressional Black Caucus, 192
U. S. Department of Justice, 11, 15, 17, 29
U. S. Immigration Policy, 25, 26
U. S. Naturalization Act of 1906, 25
U. S. News and World Report, 143
U. S. Population, 19
U. S. Revolutionary War. *See* American Revolution.
USSR, 57, 192

Vietnamese, 17, 55, 81. *See also* Southeast Asians.

Virginia, 11, 146, 147, 165
Virginia Tidewater Region, 8-9

"War Against Poverty", 190
Washington, George (first U. S. President), 23, 32
WASP (White, Anglo-Saxon Protestant), 23
Wealth of Races, The, 8
West Indies, 17
"White Australia Policy," 6, 15, 23
White flight, 140
Wife battering, 75
Workforce 2000, xvi, 23
World Bank, 97, 161
World Population, 13, 18, 22
World War II, 32, 138

"yellow peril", xvi, 7, 25